Holding on to Humanity—
The Message of Holocaust Survivors

Professor Shamai Davidson, F.R.C. Psych., M.D., died on March 18, 1986, at the age of fifty-nine. He was Medical Director of the Shalvata Mental Health Center, Israel, Associate Professor of Psychiatry at Tel Aviv University School of Medicine, and held the Elie Wiesel Chair for the Study of the Psychosocial Trauma of the Holocaust at Bar Ilan University.

Holding on to Humanity— The Message of Holocaust Survivors: The Shamai Davidson Papers

Shamai Davidson

Edited by Israel W. Charny
with the editorial assistance of Daphna Fromer

Foreword by Robert Jay Lifton
Biographical Note by Micha Neumann

A Publication of the Institute on the Holocaust and Genocide, Jerusalem

NEW YORK UNIVERSITY PRESS
New York and London

NEW YORK UNIVERSITY PRESS
New York and London

Library of Congress Cataloging-in-Publication Data
Davidson, Shamai.
Holding on to humanity—the message of Holocaust survivors : the
Shamai Davidson papers / Shamai Davidson ; edited by Israel W.
Charny with the editorial assistance of Daphna Fromer ; foreword by
Robert Jay Lifton ; biographical note by Micha Neumann.
p. cm.
"A publication of the Institute on the Holocaust and Genocide,
Jerusalem."
Includes bibliographical references and index.
ISBN 0-8147-1481-1 (cl. : acid-free paper)
1. Holocaust survivors—Psychology. 2. Holocaust survivors—
Mental health. 3. Post-traumatic stress disorder—Case studies.
I. Charny, Israel W. II. Institute on the Holocaust and Genocide.
III. Title.
D804.3.D376   1992
940.53'18—dc20   92-15639
                          CIP

New York University Press books are printed on acid-free paper,
and their binding materials are chosen for strength and durability.

Manufactured in the United States of America

c 10 9 8 7 6 5 4 3 2 1

The Last Word from Shamai Davidson's Family in the Lodz Ghetto

. . . Our material situation is very critical and we have nothing to live on. . . . Help is very needed. Luba and Zenia and Natan send you hearty regards and we all send regards to Bunie and her children. They should live. Yours truly, M. Berman.

This book is dedicated to the memory of
Shamai Davidson's aunts,
Berta and Luba, and their eight children
murdered in the gas chambers of
Treblinka concentration camp, 1942–1943.

Contents

Editor's Preface

Shamai Davidson and I, together with Elie Wiesel, founded the Institute on the Holocaust and Genocide around 1980. I became executive director of the institute, and Shamai became co-director alongside me. Together, we undertook many projects and shared many memorable experiences in our mutual devotion to the special subject of the Holocaust and genocide. We shared the conception that the Holocaust is a reminder not only to the Jewish people to be strong, but also of the necessity of developing means of prevention of genocide for all peoples in the future. Shamai undertook specifically and devotedly the subject of the fates of Holocaust survivors, their families, and their post-traumatic adjustment, while I specialized in the study of the genocides of all people, and in developing concepts of early warnings of genocide.

Some nine months following his death, Shamai's wife called me and asked me to undertake completion of his "unfinished symphony."

I knew for years that Shamai had been working devotedly on his book about Holocaust survivors. Although in my opinion he was a gifted writer, whatever he wrote was never good enough for him, ostensibly because nothing he could say about the survivors would ever do justice to the depth, complexity, and poignancy of their experiences and conditions. Yet to someone close to Shamai, it became inescapably clear that he was also engaged in a powerful personal drama of striving for excellence. As Shamai's fame spread far and wide, including across America—*Time* magazine in 1972 reported his work on how "the effects of the systematic dehumanization [of survivors] are being transmitted from one generation to the next"—he proudly signed a contract with Simon and Schuster for publication of what was to be his life's work, yet he never finished the work for the publisher before he passed away.

I was stunned by Mrs. Davidson's request, yet I could not decline it, both out of appreciation of the unique importance of what Shamai Davidson had to say about survivors, and on a personal basis.

I also could not help but be struck by the paradox that Shamai Davidson had been uniquely skillful in evoking from survivors and giving voice and recorded memory to their most silenced stories, and now I was to do the same for Shamai by finally giving a publication voice to the manuscript he himself was unable to complete and release to the world.

Acknowledgments

Appreciation is given to the following for permission to reprint, in whole or in part, materials previously published by Shamai Davidson:

Ministry of Cultural Affairs, Recreation, and Social Welfare, The Netherlands: "On relating to traumatized/persecuted people," from *Netherlands-Israel Symposium on the Impact of Persecution*, Vol. 2, published by the Ministry of Cultural Affairs, Delfson, Holland, April 1980.

Israel Journal of Psychiatry & Related Sciences, Jerusalem: "Group formation and its significance in the Nazi concentration camps," published in *Israel Annals of Psychiatry* 22:1–2 (1985): 41–50.

Yad Vashem, Jerusalem: "Human reciprocity among the Jewish prisoners in the Nazi concentration camps," in *Nazi Concentration Camps*. Proceedings of the Fourth Yad Vashem International Historical Conference, 1984.

Journal of Marital and Family Therapy, Alan Gurman, Editor, Madison, Wisconsin: "The clinical effects of massive psychic trauma in families of Holocaust survivors," 6:1 (1980): 11–22.

Cruse, the National Organization for Widows, Widowers, and Their Children, Richmond, Surrey, England: *Bereavement in Israel from War, Holocaust, and Terror*, 1985, pamphlet.

Van Gorcum Publishers, The Netherlands: "Trauma in the life cycle of the individual and the collective consciousness in relation to war and persecution," published in *Society and Trauma of War*, 1987.

Mrs. *Shamai (Jenny) Davidson acknowledges with gratitude the devoted secretarial assistance of Sylvia Gefen to Professor Shamai Davidson for many years.*

Foreword

Robert Jay Lifton

Thinking of Shamai Davidson, I see before me eyes that are a little sad, a facial expression that is open and warm, curious and somewhat tentative, puzzling over problems that must be pursued but cannot quite be solved. He seems mostly boyish but at times a man aged by burdens he has assumed.

I was introduced to Shamai Davidson in 1978 by Phyllis Palgi, a legendary anthropologist and one of my oldest Israeli friends. Shamai stepped right into a twenty-year conversation between Palgi and myself, talking animatedly about Holocaust survivors of course, but also about Israeli struggles, his love of the country, and his disapproval of certain things going on in it, about Jews, America, England, but always from the perspective of humankind.

My most memorable experience with Shamai occurred during two interviews he and I conducted together with survivors. The interviews had been scheduled as part of my study of Nazi doctors, and when, at the last minute, the scheduled interpreter (from Hebrew to English) was not able to appear, Shamai insisted upon serving that function, despite my protestations that this was not the proper use of his valuable time. Of course, we quickly became co-interviewers, and I was treated to an extraordinary lesson in responding to Holocaust survivors.

There was something maternal about Shamai in his soothing tones and nurturing demeanor toward the survivor. At the same time he was intent upon evoking every nuance of the survivor's past experience and present feeling, asking further questions that evoked in turn additional clarifications. He seemed to give over his entire being to the survivor sitting next to him, but never to the extent of surrendering his own exquisite instrument—his emphatic imagination—for understanding and recasting what he was observing. His energy was limitless as he tracked down details and combinations of feelings and then sensitively conveyed everything to me. Each of the survivors immediately sensed Davidson's special combination of knowledge and sympathy and derived visible therapeutic benefit from the exchange.

How can one best describe Davidson's relationship to Holocaust survivors? Davidson himself wrote that "in the presence of a sensitive, encouraging and attentive listener, survivors . . . often reach a universe of unarticulated feeling seeking expression." He was surely that kind of listener, and much more. He seemed virtually to merge with survivors in his identification with them, but he could sufficiently separate himself from them to carry out his healing function. Devotion is the word that comes to mind, in something close to the religious meaning of that word. *Devotion* means fidelity and love; its etymology suggests having taken a "vow" and become a "votary," one who lives out a life of religious service, a monk or a priest or, in Shamai's case, a special kind of rabbi. Shamai brought a secular version of all this to his work with survivors.

His own history—the loss of most of his father's family in the Holocaust—was a powerful influence on that evolving relationship. Shamai was not just a survivor by proxy, but was himself a survivor of Nazi persecution, even if he had never been himself subjected to that persecution. But more than that history was needed for what Davidson came to do. I believe that, over the course of his life, he came to a profound inner decision, however inchoate, to expose himself to the full range of what he spoke of as the Holocaust therapist's "fear, anxiety, guilt and shame, helplessness and hopelessness"—emotions not very different from those of the survivors one was treating. That is, it was his choice to take on many of the searing emotions that actual Holocaust survivors had no choice about experiencing. It is not too much to say that such a therapist shares with the survivors he treats their burden of the dead.

That burden can never be fully lifted, and one who takes it on engages in a continuous Sisyphean struggle to undo what cannot be undone. Davidson did that and in the process made himself vulnerable to every form of pain. But one should not forget the strength that he brought to, and derived from, that struggle. When he talks about the deep satisfaction of survivors' confirmation of one another—"I was saved and you were saved"—he is talking about himself as well. His life work received profound confirmation from the survivors' response, as well as that of colleagues. And that work so consumed him that, concerning the rest of existence, he might well have shared words he quotes from a survivor: "I don't belong to this reality."

Davidson required a certain perspective on the Holocaust for him to do what he did. He understood the Holocaust to be "an absurd phenomenon in the history of Christian European civilization," and he further saw the effort "to give meaning to the meaningless"—an effort he had to make constantly—as "absurd in itself." Absurdity at this level suggests more than just incongruousness, more than a general philosophical characterization of human life in the face of our inevitable death. It is closer to what theologians speak of as "surd evil," meaning evil closely related to chaos, evil from which there is no redemption. This view of the Holocaust, though it hardly lightened Davidson's or anyone else's burden, perhaps did offer some spiritual protection. Even if the Holocaust could not be fully grasped, one could call forth a judgment on it. One could place it in a certain realm of depravity rather than being inundated with its evil to the point of personal despair.

In this and other ways, Davidson never succumbed to a merely technical approach. He followed, and contributed greatly to, work done internationally on post-traumatic stress disorder, but insisted that Holocaust survivors had "important additional and specific characteristics." Therapists and researchers always require categories within which to understand their observations, all the more so when concerned with issues as painful as the Holocaust. Davidson too constructed categories, but always with the awareness that they were only approximate, and that individual survivors could defy any single category. And he could place his entire project within the larger context of the "special meaning of Israel" in serving as "a gigantic rehabilitation project for a traumatized people."

Yet it was never just Israel that concerned him. I had many

discussions with Shamai about Hiroshima and Vietnam, about the kind of genocidal mentality that can operate anywhere. Davidson focused on the Holocaust but his moral concerns knew no boundaries. He could readily extend his extraordinary talent for empathy to survivors of Hiroshima and to both American and Vietnamese veterans of the Vietnam War.

In a sense Shamai Davidson was in continuous mourning for people killed by other people's cruelty. But that mourning, that sensitivity to pain, rather than immobilizing him, animated his perpetual struggle to heal.

This book is a precious legacy of Shamai's struggle and the wisdom he derived from it.

Introduction: Shamai Davidson's Vision of Survivors

Israel W. Charny

This is Shamai Davidson's book, and clearly the pity is that he did not live to complete it himself.

He worked on this book for many years. It was a dream of his to write an authoritative work on the life experiences of the Holocaust survivors and their families. It was to be, and is, a gift to the mental health professions he loved so much, and to the survivors for whom he felt so passionately.

He worried about this book a great deal because, he well knew, it sought to encompass and make comprehensible a subject that grows out of the totally incomprehensible. Shamai feared to be inaccurate, and he also feared deeply the possibility of doing any harm—even in a symbolic sense—to any survivors because of what he wrote. Yet he also believed passionately in the importance of making intellectual and scientific progress toward understanding the minds and souls of people who had been through the worst hell humankind has ever created.

He had an almost reverential feeling for each and every survivor. It was well known in mental health circles in Israel that he was always there for survivors and would respond to them with unusual graciousness in their dark moments of mental health anguish. He met with them far beyond the fixed hours of traditional psychiatric appointment schedules. He was there as a professional, but from the first he also simply and unabashedly cared for them and conveyed the warmth of his concern to them. And thus it was that many survivors who had never before told the story of their awesome experiences in the Holocaust told that story for the first time to him. One patient said to me after his death, "He was the only person to whom I could tell my story. I knew plenty of other psychotherapists, and had even worked for some years with a psychiatrist whom I admired, but it never occurred to me to be able to tell him. Dr. Davidson was the only person who made me feel that I could speak about what I had vowed I would never talk about."

There was always a vibrato of emotion in his voice as he spoke about survivors of the Holocaust. He sounded as if he were trembling with the combination of his sympathy for their suffering and more than a trace of rage at the bestial human beings who had made them suffer so. As he listened to survivors, he looked and sounded horror stricken at each and every manifestation of the unthinkable and unfathomable human evils that were done to them. And at the same time, he was moved and awed at the courage and creative power he saw in so many of the victims who had survived with spirit and dignity beyond what one could possibly have anticipated under such overwhelming adversity. Most of all, he wanted to help, and it was as if he wanted to take each and every one of his emotions of involvement, caring, and empathy and give them as gifts to each of his survivor-patients who had endured so much, so that perhaps in this way the survivor would have some relief from his terrible burden.

The manuscript of this book is based on a combination of thousands of pages of incomplete manuscripts and notes towards manuscripts that Shamai Davidson left behind him as well as papers and chapters he published in books and journals during his lifetime. They have been woven together to create a tapestry—as close as possible to that which I intuited was the tapestry he intended to weave for his magnum opus. There are, inevitably, repetitions of phrases and of ideas, and while I have made arduous efforts to eliminate as many of these as possible, I have also chosen to allow a certain degree of repetitiveness for a number of reasons. The simplest was that I did not want to disturb the context in which a topic was being treated. More importantly, many times when Shamai Davidson repeated himself, it seemed as if he were remembering and echoing still another and another of the many survivors whom he had treated, and I also felt that I did not want to cut off these voices being heard through him. Shamai also repeated himself because, characteristically, his was the kind of mind that looked at the same phenomena from many different vantage points, each time holding up the survivors' descriptions of their suffering to examine them from the different viewpoints of what they had endured, how they mentally survived their incredible privations, how terrifying experiences of death and threats of death were cushioned by personal courage and the supports of group identification in the very midst of the hell of the concentration camp, and how the spiritual relationship of victims with their Jewish people gave some of them strength to carry on. Finally, to my eyes and ears, as I read Shamai Davidson, many times I felt him move into a kind of poetic prose, in which certain choral stanzas are repeated, over and over again, as he fulfills the spiritual commandment of telling the story of the Holocaust and its sequellae, over and over again, for this person and that, and from one vantage point to another.

The most important issue of inconsistency that comes up in reading the Davidson papers is how to reconcile the contradictory voices that are heard in Shamai Davidson's assessments of the emotional and psychiatric damages inflicted on survivors. One "hears" Shamai Davidson say a number of times that the *majority* of survivors were damaged; and, in fact, he argues that even those survivors who denied that they were in any way traumatized or distressed by the Holocaust, and lived their lives functioning quite well, nonetheless carry within them a long-range vulnerability that more often than not will be activated, typically in the later years of their lives when aging robs them of their ability to maintain their sense and appearance of power. Yet one also "hears" Shamai Davidson say, more than once, that it has to be emphasized that the majority of survivors were not psychiatric patients, and that in fact they showed unusual strength in their coping. Moreover, as regards the many who indeed did display manifest psychiatric symptoms, such as periods of agitated anxiety when they were triggered into flashback memories of their terrified pasts in the Holocaust, these anxiety states and the reliving of memories were not psychiatric manifestations in the sense of representing *pathologies*, but were natural, and in effect *necessary and desirable reprocessings of traumatic events*, whose purpose was to free survivors to be that much more intact and emotionally healthy.

How does one handle this running thread of contradiction in the Davidson papers?

On the level of concrete meanings, the simplest answer is to distinguish between observations of the emotional impact of the Holocaust on survivors—virtually all *were* necessarily hurt by the incredible events they underwent—and the epidemiological question of how many became identified psychiatric patients. Here the point is that the majority did *not* require psychiatric assistance. By making this distinction, we have seemingly resolved the contradiction.

Nonetheless, tracing the coloring and resonances of Davidson's words, it also seems that he is not only making the distinction between inner impact damages to the survivors and their actual objective entry into psychiatric-patient status, but that he really is also vacillating back and forth as to whether and to what extent the Holocaust did cause permanent damage to the real understructure of emotions and spirits of Holocaust survivors—that is, to what extent survivors were damaged in their long-range ability to function with trust in other human beings, to endure intimacy and love, to feel empathy and compassion for their loved ones, and so on—to retain the most sensitive qualities of being human. I think this is what Shamai Davidson was struggling to map, honestly and accurately, as he struggled back and forth between observations that most survivors retained their ability to function free of actual psychiatric disease, and that most survivors of course were distressed and traumatized.

I also think that he was worried about how to convey his findings. To my personal knowledge, Shamai Davidson was a gifted, astute clinical observer who was capable of baring and identifying with unusual perspicacity, in very nonstandard ways, some of the truths about how people are put together that are not at all summarizable in the standard psychiatric language of diagnosis. At the same time, he was also a person who was deeply, even exquisitely sensitive to human hurt, and who genuinely sought to avoid hurting others, certainly the people for whom he felt so deeply, survivors. I think there was a continuous battle between these two sides of his personality, the discoverer-scientist and the compassionate healer, which affected the ways in which he was formulating his observations of survivors' emotional status, because heaven forbid that he should hurt even more those who had already been so hurt, yet he also had to report the scientific observations he was making responsibly.

This contradiction is also exemplified in the fact that Shamai Davidson is the only person that I know of who dared to observe and conceptualize the considerable emotional damages that await latently even in survivors who have coped externally "entirely healthily" and have been highly successful in their business or other status positions in society. Davidson described in many of these survivors a pattern of driven overactivity, hypercoping, and hyperpotency, their being on the go at all times and at any cost, and he observed that these are people who can never let their guard down to their emotional neediness, or experience and acknowledge humility and imperfection, because to do so would thrust them back on a huge well of denied vulnerability as survivors who had been exposed in the madness of the persecutory Holocaust world to the most extreme vulnerability that human beings have ever known. Indeed, Davidson goes further to dare to identify some such overactive survivors as officious, arrogant, overbearing, and dismissing of the sensitivities of others—including those closest to them in their own families—and to point out how in many cases, they end up driving everybody away from them.

On the other hand, as I said earlier, Shamai Davidson was forever sensitive to the possibilities that any of his observations, including observations of the known incidence of clinical cases of psychiatric disturbances among survivors, might be taken in any way to defame them or place them in any kind of embarrassing light. He needed to return time and again to referring to them as deserving and wonderful people, and he needed to make the observation over and over again that the majority of survivors were not bonafide psychiatric patients. At various times in his writings, he emphasizes the considerable strength that so many survivors showed in their abilities to carry on life with considerable degrees of success following the Holocaust, to such an extent that he seems to be implying that there was nothing emotionally hurt or damaged in them, which of course is a direct contradiction of the point he was making at other times that it was inescapable that there had been damage to the capacity for tenderness and intimacy in virtually everyone who had undergone the persecutory brutalization and systematic torture of the Holocaust odyssey of evil.

I think that Shamai was under the greatest strain whenever he was delivering statements on these issues to *live* audiences. There was, first of all, always the concern that there were survivors present, and also inevitably children of survivors, who might be symbolically wounded by observations about damages to the emotional wholeness of virtually all survivors. Moreover, as Shamai spoke, he was pulled first and foremost by his heartfelt emotional empathy and celebration of the heroic triumph of survivors over death, and it became almost a matter of superhuman skill, which he could not manage fully, to be simultaneously able to describe the extensive damages and weaknesses that the Holocaust had wrought in survivors and the life-long vulnerability of most of them. One "hears" Shamai in many of his talks reaching a height of celebratory poetry as he, in effect, offers homage and congratulations to the survivors for their incredible courage of survival during and following the Holocaust. He always enjoyed confirming the fact that the majority of the survivors did reconstruct their lives and families, and that no small number did so with credible success by any standard in our everyday world. Having sung this ballad of congratulation and blessing over life rescued and restored, he found it hard to "take back" his gifts and blessings and confront his audiences with harsh emotions. Yet, the nature of his real judgments about these issues emerges clearly enough from a careful reading of his texts.

As editor of the Davidson papers, I considered the possibility of rewriting, if only just a bit, the various statements that express Davidson's conclusions about the mental health of the survivors so that they would be consistent with one another, but I decided not to do so and instead to leave the texts of his various observations and conclusions about this subject intact as they are, so that the readers will experience and process the flow of contradictions for themselves. As I stated earlier, my own judgment is that Shamai Davidson's basic conclusions were that the majority of the survivors were torn and damaged in some basic aspects of their humanity by the terrifying Holocaust, *and* that a majority of the survivors did not become bonafide psychiatric patients, but that even among many of these there are/were serious hazards and vulnerability to breakdown in later years, due to the existential weakening that accompanies all aging and the unfolding losses that take place normally for those who are fortunate to live full lives—and that considering all, it is amazing how well many survivors were able to function for so much of their lives.

Davidson's epidemiological conclusions as to how many Holocaust survivors were emotionally damaged in effect runs into complexities that have never been solved by psychiatry in general as to the distinction between known or observable psychiatric damages that force a person into being a declared patient, and problems in the inner personality and character of a person's ability to love, enter into intimacy, share, befriend, and interact with integrity with other human beings. It is little wonder that the horrendous complexity of the Holocaust also forces us into the lion's den of the unresolved complexities of psychiatry's basic image of human nature.

In the chapter "Recovery and Integration in the Life Cycle of the Individual and the Collective," we find fairly explicit statements that tie together the range of his judgments on these issues. I shall sum these up and in each case cite a direct quotation from that chapter.

1. The majority of survivors were penetrated and wounded in their emotional souls by the terrors of the Holocaust, and the traces of these wounds accompany them for years to come after the Holocaust.

> Probably a majority of the survivors have suffered one or more of the traumatogenic and grief components of the survivor syndrome and their somatopsychic manifestations.

2. Many of the symptoms survivors suffered, including particularly flashback reexperiences of memories and distressful emotions about these memories, were in their essence psychologically necessary reviews of terrible events that did occur; the purpose of the normal reactions, however upsetting the reactions were in themselves, was to help the survivor put the past behind him or her in order to go on living more fully.

> In many survivors these [traumatogenic and grief components of the survivor syndrome and their somatopsychic manifestations] seemed to me to represent potentially normative responses to the traumatic experiences and losses rather than psychopathology. Many of these "symptoms" often gradually subsided during the course of the years. It appears that in many of these survivors recurrent fearful flashback associations and depressive preoccupations represented episodes of

grief work and cathartic working through of traumatic memories while at the same time struggling to integrate and to organize new external and internal worlds and to find meaning in life.

3. The majority of survivors of the Holocaust did not become identified psychiatric patients. In general, focusing solely on the negative consequences of the trauma of the Holocaust is likely to blind us to, or cause us to ignore, the remarkable strengths survivors showed for recovery and living new lives.

The vast majority of the large survivor population in Israel and elsewhere did not become psychiatric patients. Focusing solely on the pathological consequences of trauma obscures the remarkable potential for new adaptation, recovery, and integration throughout the lifespan.

4. Nonetheless, the basic vulnerability attached itself to virtually all survivors, including those who were free of symptoms.

The memories of the traumatic experiences were "held off" and to a greater extent or lesser degree "walled off" and encapsulated by avoidance and denial mechanisms from the rest of the psychic functioning. However, this meant that vulnerability was always present though often quiescent for long periods.

5. In fact, each survivor must be looked at individually in every case. Each specific clinical evaluation of survivors, and also the summary judgments of survivors as a group, must take into account *both* strengths and inevitable damage.

Generalizations must be avoided that simplify the complexities of survivors' lives, which often demonstrate considerable strengths and resources in facing life's stresses. Toughness and reduced sensitivity may coexist with specific vulnerability that may only be revealed in particular periods in the life cycle.

A very welcome result of the tension in Davidson's thinking is the emergence of new understanding of the naturalness and potentially health-supporting purposes of various kinds of emotional distress that we have otherwise been trained to think of in the mental health professions only as symptoms and markers of disturbance. Shamai Davidson points out, in effect, that *although these are moments of disturbance, they are also intended psychobiologically as a process to detoxify and desensitize terrible traumatic experiences in order to free the person to live more healthily in the future.*

The practical clinical implications of this kind of view are enormous, for they call on clinicians to enlarge their view of mind toward much greater *respect* for certain acute disturbances of the human spirit, and to know much more about how to accompany many people who are undergoing natural processes of detoxification even though they are in acute distress while doing so. So many mental health clinicians are wont to turn to therapies and management stratagems that neutralize and overcome anxiety and distress at their first appearance, as if the prime responsibility of every mental health professional is to overcome and banish all emotions of suffering, when in fact many aspects of anxiety and distress accompany one's natural potential for growth.

Personally, I know no clinician who gave so much thought and creative struggle to the task of accompanying survivors, both emotionally and conceptually, through the full range of their grief and suffering as well as triumph, wisdom, and emotional potential. I think that for many years most mental health professionals stood in such awe of the survivors, in the incredible survival that they represent, that relatively little understanding developed of the complexity of the survival experience. Those who were obviously damaged were objects of traditional clinical observations of symptomatology, and while in this respect there did develop important new insights into the nature of survivor guilt and damage to the capacity for basic trust, few clinicians succeeded in approaching the evidences of weakness in apposition to strength as Davidson ultimately did.

I believe that in his clinical work Shamai Davidson touched this drama of contradiction and complexity more deeply than anyone else I know, and that this is what his survivor patients sensed and were grateful to him for. He touched them, and even hypnotized them, with his uncanny ability to ferret out pain and problems and to bear listening to them and giving names to their problems while, at the same time, extending friendship and compassion and helping them search for better ways to go on living with their memories and burdens.

It took the clinical genius and largeness of heart of Shamai Davidson to struggle with these dilemmas and to forge new knowledge for the profession of mental health without hurting the human beings he cared about. That, I believe, was the overriding meaning of his life and work.

Author's Preface: Notes of Self-Analysis: Shamai Davidson's Thoughts on Himself and the Holocaust

Like many people who are devoted to a very special subject that has become the center of their work and even personal life, as the Holocaust became for Shamai Davidson, he tried to understand what was it in this life quest that so totally drew him and captivated him?

This is the natural curiosity of a man about himself, not to speak of the fact that the well-trained psychoanalyst and psychiatrist that Shamai Davidson was could not resist asking himself what were his personal motivations in his profound commitment to study of the Holocaust and devotion to Holocaust survivors.

The following material was assembled from a variety of handwritten notes that were found in Shamai Davidson's papers. They were written on different dates, and are clearly in the voice of a man speaking to himself. I have edited these notes to create a measure of continuity in the text, but the real continuity lies in the fact that in each note it is the same person looking for himself. [Ed.]

My life obsession with the Holocaust relates to a drive to deal with the stark, extreme, massive, naked tragedy of life. What most concerns me are the black-and-white issues—not the greys of everyday reality of problems of human interaction, and the necessity for compromises.

There is in me a deep desire to demonstrate the ever-present reality of human suffering and its life-long and transgenerational results. The persecution and murder of the Jews of Europe has been a central theme in my awareness since childhood and throughout my life. It has colored my life. When the Nazis came to power, I was seven years old and their persecution of the Jews was a central feature in the Jewish periodicals that my parents regularly read. I remember vividly photographs of Jews being beaten in Germany from these early years, the boycott of Jewish shops, the humiliation of Jews in the street.

An intense Jewish consciousness prevailed in my parents' home, associated with traditional Jewish religious observance of a moderate degree and a clear adherence to the Zionist aims of the establishment of a Jewish homeland in Palestine. My parents were troubled and I could feel their pain. Two or three years before the war, when I was about eleven, there appeared in my grandparents' home a yellow and black colored book entitled (in large letters) *The Yellow Spot*. This book contained detailed accounts of the persecution, humiliation, tortures, and murder of the Jews in Germany. It gave detailed figures and described incidents, but the greatest impact was made by the lurid *Der Stuermer* caricatures as well as the blood-chilling photographs of terror against Jews. Week after week on our Sabbath visits to our grandparents, I would pore over this book, which both repelled me and held me riveted.

My father had left Poland for Britain in 1923. He was the only member of his family to leave, but he maintained contact by letters and visits until the war broke out in 1939 and no more communication was possible. I remember his futile attempts to trace the whereabouts of his two sisters and their husbands and eight children and his fearful preoccupation and agitation as to their fate and sleepless nights. They were never heard of again and all perished in the ghettos of Warsaw and Lodz and the gas chambers of Treblinka.

In 1941 and 1942, when I was in my early teens, there appeared the booklets *Stop Them Now*, with the early reports of mass murder of Jews in Poland. I remember the feelings of helplessness and infuriated frustration that were in me, and I collected and preserved these documents and pamphlets and newspaper writings as an agenda that had to be dealt with somehow. Meanwhile, my adolescent development and my school years (in Glasgow, Scotland) continued on throughout the war, yet I was always aware of what was happening a few hundred miles away in Europe.

We knew all along what was happening to the Jews of Europe.

An awareness of the atrocities and exterminations was ever present throughout my adolescent years. From 1942, pamphlets were distributed by the Federation of Polish Jews in Great Britian with extremely appalling photographs of the atrocities and the heaps of dead. These documents appealed to the peoples of the world to halt the extermination of the Jews of Europe.

My father's entire family had remained in Poland and Russia. Most of them, expecially his beloved two sisters and their children, were incarcerated in the ghettos of Lodz and Warsaw. Driven by apprehension, he had traveled through Germany in January 1939 to visit them and to persuade them to leave Europe, but he did not succeed and returned only with photographs that were placed prominently in the family sitting room. Our Polish relatives were frequently in our thoughts. I had met and played with some of these relatives when they visited us when I was six or seven years old, and so the memories of my young cousins intruded painfully into our family life for me as well.

My father suffered, preoccupied with the fate of his family after the last vividly remembered postcard arrived via an address in Switzerland, horrifically stamped by the Gestapo censorship. This postcard, written from the Lodz Ghetto, proclaimed that all was well with the family and that they were in good health. We realized that the content was meaningful only as a means of getting through the Nazi censorship, and it only served to increase our fears.

Thereafter, my father tried constantly to get information. We knew that he was preoccupied with the thoughts of his family, that he suffered from insomnia as a result, but although we felt his anxiety, he did not share his fears with us. After the war was over, we learned that both his sisters and their eight children had perished.

My father's suffering at the disappearance and loss of his family, his depressive preoccupation and irritability, are indelible memories of my early teenage years. As a result, although I grew up in the relative safety of Scotland during World War II, the Nazi extermination campaign was an integral part of my consciousness and my Jewish identity, later manifest in my need to settle in Israel and my motivation to work with survivors. I felt destined to identify with the survivors. I felt that I belonged with them in Israel.

I was also engrossed with the idea of what could have happened to me. There but for the grace of God go I. How would I have fared in the concentration camp? What would I have been prepared to do in order to survive? There were such terrible choices to be made, like having to decide whether to hand over parents or a spouse and children.

If my father had not come to Great Britain in 1923, I would have been born and grown up in Poland and died in the Holocaust. The Holocaust was so close by. I remember Berta and the children visiting in 1939, staying with us, and going back to Poland. What could, would, should I have done?

Why should there be such unbearable differences in the fate of people just as the result of mere accident?

Normally, people cope with the dramatic unfairness of life's differing experiences due to fate or accident or luck by denying that there are any real implications involved. But when major tragedies occur, then the limits of empathy seem to be overtaken. One curious tendency is to blame the victims of major tragedies and disasters, as if in some way they themselves are responsible for the events. In this way, it seems, human beings defend themselves from having to deal with the awareness of what could have happened to them, and from the guilt they feel about getting away free. But such defense mechanisms cannot operate when one bears exactly the same characteristics as one's cousins—those who were fated to be victims to the Holocaust. Avoidance mechanisms and denial break down in such closeness, and the mere accidental difference of place of birth bears down intensely on one's consciousness. Just because my father left Poland in the 1920s—the only one in his immediate family to do so—doesn't seem to be reason enough why I and we escaped the terrible fate of our family.

My father never verbalized his survivor guilt. He had been back nine months before the outbreak of the war to visit his sisters and their families in Poland and tried to persuade them to leave Poland and come to Britain. Did he try hard enough? Was there more he could have done? His sleeplessness during the war, after all contact with the family in Poland had been lost, testifies to his distressing preoccupation with these questions.

I experienced the Holocaust through my father's loss of his sisters and their children, whom I had met at age five or six. At the height of my own oedipal crisis, I remember insisting that I go out in the boat with the grown-ups, bawling until they gave in—I was the only child among the grown-ups, the elite!

For many years, into adult life, I had fantasies about killing the Nazi leaders—an invisible hand machinegunning them down. Many Jews of my generation who were affected by the Holocaust from afar through the loss of parents' families had such desires for revenge as surrogates of their parents who had lost so much! To be active instead of passive!

1.

Introductory Statement: On the Difficulty of Writing and Research about the Holocaust and Survival

What happened—really happened
What happened—really happened
What happened—really happened
I believe with perfect faith
That I will have the strength to believe that
What happened—really happened.

—T. Carmi, "Anatomy of a War," 1973

A famous Holocaust historian committed suicide. Clutched in his hand there was a letter in which appeared the words, "Hitler was victorious." This tragic event expressed in extreme form the despair of a man irrevocably and eternally involved in the Holocaust who, without adequate psychological insight, finally succumbed in confrontation with life's crises. At about the same time I saw an announcement in a Swedish newspaper, *Nugens Nyleter*, "Journey in the Footsteps of K.Z.: Treblinka, Auschwitz, Buchenwald, Matheusen, an interesting horror-awakening meeting in the places of history." In these two events the polarities of human reactions to the unspeakable are expressed: many people flee knowledge of the Holocaust at any cost, while others are drawn even hypnotically toward its seemingly unfathomable mystery.

The whole of mankind is still struggling with the evil of the Nazi era. The Holocaust is inevitably within us, not only in the

7

survivors but also in the spectators. The language of mankind today is congested with expressions of the Holocaust and its symbols—*Auschwitz, survivors, genocide, Nazis, Mengele.* The terms *survivor* and *Holocaust* have become overused in their application to a wide range of situations, from the banality of everyday expressions in relation to the everyday stresses of life in a technological society to their exploitation for radical political purposes.

Throughout the Western world there is a widespread use of psychological symbols of the Holocaust to express anxiety, fear, and guilt. Holocaust and concentration camp imagery of victims and perpetrators is often seen in the dreams and fears of people living in the safety of Western countries remote from the events.

Despite Auschwitz, poetry has been and is being written, and hope does exist, and love and laughter, just as they existed in the ghettos and concentration camps. No writer can adequately express the horror of the Holocaust because it would not be art. They can try to present the inner analogies of the victim in his despair and also in his hope. But there may never be the right expression in art for a man giving his bread to his friend as the ultimate in compassion, a deliberate choice to preserve the life of the other at the possible expense of sacrifice of one's own life.

For writers the dilemma is related to an inability to identify with the survivor in the Holocaust—an inhuman situation that one cannot internalize (incorporate into one's inner experience) because of the dimensions of the horror. One can only write about the Holocaust indirectly. Many historians, poets, writers, and psychiatrists studying one or another aspect of the Holocaust, within the framework of their own professional conceptualizations, are afraid of being overwhelmed with doubts, emotions, thoughts. To make understandable, to give meaning, to the meaningless is a paradox, absurd in itself—"contraditio in adjecto"—as the Holocaust was at the end an absurd phenomenon in the history of Christian European civilization.

It seems that however powerful the motivation to study, research, and attempt to come to terms with that which it is impossible to come to terms with, there are awakened in all of us a spectrum of threatening feelings, as men and women in our varied human roles, in our individual, family, and public lives, and in our relations to social and governmental institutions. In our work on the Holocaust, we experience fear, anxiety, guilt and shame, helplessness and hopelessness. All our basic premises for functioning become threatened. We are afraid of what we may uncover in our research. We are afraid to stand alone, lonely, before the ununderstandable.

The function of language as a tool for dealing with the awful reality is of limited help.

Kierkegaard's "dread and trembling in the presence of God" is perhaps the theological concept for universal trembling in the face of the uncontrollable, but it is still inadequate either to conceptualize or to diminish our anguish in the presence of *man*-made disasters. The "trembling" is still very much with us when we are confronted with the events of the Holocaust.

The widespread processes of avoidance and denial manifested in relation to the Holocaust are a reflection on the one hand of man's desperate struggle to survive physically in the face of the overwhelming threat of death, and on the other of the attempt to ward off knowledge of an inconceivable catastrophe that threatens his psychological survival. The subject is thus man's adaptive response to death and disaster in our culture.

It seems that the danger to life can be faced and attempts made to master and overcome it only up to a certain level of intensity. Beyond this level, and especially when the danger is unprecedented and inconceivable in terms of the individual's life experiences and system of values, avoidance and denial processes are mobilized as important protective and coping devices enabling the victims to carry on with the daily struggle for survival.

Avoidance and Denial by the Victims during the Holocaust

During the Holocaust, the victims needed to deny the full extent of what was happening and what evidently lay in store for them. The general pattern of denial was contributed to and reinforced by

1. the lack of knowledge and information available to the Jewish masses isolated in ghettos and camps;
2. the secrecy and systematic deception practiced by the Nazis in order to conceal the perpetration of genocide;
3. the collective historical "memory" of modes of "living through" past experiences of persecution and pogrom; and
4. the lack of the possibility of escape or of physical resistance for the vast majority of the trapped and helpless.

The denial of feeling manifested itself in emotional withdrawal and a blunting of feeling ("psychic numbing" or psychological closing off, as Lifton has described).[1] Such numbing was widely reported by the survivors as having enabled them to cope with the unbearable pain and horror witnessed and experienced daily in the ghettos and concentration camps. There was often also a closely associated cognitive constriction.

In the process of catastrophic trauma, as described by Krystal, "the blocking of the ability to feel emotions and pain as well as other physical sensations . . . is experienced with relief in relation to the previous painful affects" (of anxiety and panic).[2]

In the unbearable conditions of the Nazi concentration camps, suicide was a logical reaction. Many killed themselves on the electrified fence or by passive surrender to the "Musselman" state.

Denial and the maintenance of hope are closely associated, and, however illusory, can be looked upon as serving a life-preserving function in conditions of such extremity.

Leo Eitinger, in writing from his personal observations of denial in the concentration camps, describes how with the selection for work the immediate danger of death was reduced, and the complete denial of the initial phase could be painfully modified "to a more differentiated degree of understanding and emotional assessment of the real possibilities to survive."[3] This "awareness control" involved an intermixture of denial and hope with vigilance and awareness in accordance with the fluctuating dangers of the reality situation.

Denial processes, hope, and the motivation to continue the struggle to survive were sustained by the mutual support, solidarity, and encouragement of friendships and group relations. When verbalized in the group interaction, denial and hope become more powerful through suggestion and mutual validation.

The utilization of professional and vocational skills by ghetto and concentration camp inmates who were fortunate enough to have these possibilities also strikingly demonstrates the use of denial as a positive life-sustaining force. Prisoner doctors in the concentration camps were able to alleviate suffering and to give important medical help to fellow inmates, however limited, by using denial of the situation.[4]

In the Warsaw Ghetto, a group of doctors scientifically collected and collated their observations on the process of starvation while themselves starving to death.[5]

Rabbis have described how in Auschwitz and other camps they would concentrate on Halachic questions, rationally working out how they would in the future determine such questions as the marital status of survivors whose spouse had been selected and sent "to the left" (which meant certain death) without there being a witness to the actual death, as is required in normal life for the declaration of widowhood.[6]

The degree and complexity of these protective processes vary considerably in accordance with the different Holocaust situations —the conditions and particular individuals involved. Furthermore, because of the vast numbers and heterogeneity of the people involved, generalizations about psychological response should be looked at with reserve.

A striking description of denial processes in the face of catastrophic tragedy in the Lodz Ghetto appears in the *Chronicle of the Lodz Ghetto*.[7] This chronicle, written on a daily basis in the Department of Archives in the Lodz Ghetto, provides a unique account of a persecuted community caught in the Nazi vice. At the beginning of 1942 it was announced that twenty-five thousand people had to be deported for "resettlement." Rapid actions followed, involving the surrounding of buildings by Jewish police, firemen, and Gestapo representatives who collected all the inhabitants of several blocks and sorted them into those to remain and those to be deported. In commenting on these horrifying and tragic events a week later, the chronicler (Josef Zalkowitz) writes that it is worth noting the strange response of the population to these events. No doubt the actions caused a terrible shock, but it was astonishing to realize how apathetically the people whose loved ones were taken reacted (apart from those who weren't directly involved, who carried on as usual). One would have expected that with the events of the previous few days, the entire ghetto would be overcome with mourning for a long time. Yet even before the action was over, the population was again completely preoccupied in everyday problems—getting bread, food, etc., immediately reverting from the personal tragic events to "routine daily life" in the ghetto.

The use of avoidance and denial mechanisms by victims on entry to a concentration camp is described in the following personal account by an Israeli physician.

C. S-M, a 23–year-old Czech student, after one and a quarter years in a Gestapo prison for anti-Nazi political activities, was transferred with her group to Bergen-Belsen in November 1944. They arrived at the camp at night, and when they awoke in the morning "wild-eyed emaciated figures with shaven heads in rags" were hammering at the windows and doors of their wooden barrack telling them of the systematic mass killings in the death camps, and that their parents and siblings had been sent to their deaths in Auschwitz where there were gas chambers and crematoria. She and her comrades refused to believe them and thought that they were mentally ill and their stories of Auschwitz delusions. They took turns to guard the windows and doors so that "the crazy Belsen inmates could not get in and tell us such terrible stories and destroy our morale." Although she and her comrades had been isolated in prison and had no information of the Nazi genocidal activities, they had undergone systematic torture by the Gestapo and were fully aware of the brutality and murderousness of the Nazis. However, their humanistic value system, derived from their upbringing in Masaryk's Czechoslovakia, made them unable to believe at first the tales of systematic mass murder.

Denial Processes in the Post-Holocaust Years

The struggle to adapt to the new reality after the Holocaust demanded the maximal mobilization of the psychic energies of the survivors. The experiences of catastrophic trauma and loss could not be integrated into the psychic functioning. Avoidance and denial mechanisms were thus of considerable coping value for the survivors. In fact, denial of various degrees, forms, and complexities seems to constitute the psychic mechanism most fundamentally and widely used in Western culture for dealing with the effects of traumatic experiences (especially when of catastrophic dimensions and when "man-made"). The new social frameworks that the uprooted and traumatized survivors found themselves in after the war demanded great efforts of adaptation. In fact, surprising quantitites of energy seem to have been available in many of the survivors, especially those of the teenage and young adult age groups, in their determination to create new lives. This resulted often in the establishment of patterns of overactivity. When associated with a tenacity of purpose and the determination to succeed, this capacity for work resulted in considerable productiveness and economic and occupational success. The tendency to be constantly active and self-driving seems to be closely linked with avoidance and denial mechanisms, and emphasizes the primarily adaptive direction of the psychic functioning after massive trauma. Denial mechanisms and activity seem to mutually reinforce each other, and as long as the individual can remain active, they are likely to be maintained as efficient defensive systems throughout the lifespan.

The hunger for success and activity in some survivors has also been seen to serve omnipotent needs and attitudes that overcompensate for the impotence and helplessness experienced in the Holocaust. It should also be remembered that activity in the concentration camps after selection for various work situations of importance to the Nazis generally enabled postponement of one's death. This sense of the significance of work in warding off the danger of death continued thereafter into the normal working life and contributed to the anxiety experienced whenever the threat of loss of work arose. Limitation or loss of activity seriously undermined the denial defenses, with possible clinical consequences.

In the early postwar years, many survivors who later suffered from the clinical symptoms of the survivor syndrome were free of symptoms.[8] This apparently symptom-free interval is explained by several factors related to denial processes.

Undoubtedly the needs for readaptation to the new conditions and for coping with the many hardships during the early years after the war demanded maximal psychic energies. Furthermore, many of the survivors were preoccupied in the early months, and sometimes years, with processes of physical recovery from malnutrition, disease, and injury.

The hope that murdered family members were still alive, which sustained the motivation to survive in the concentration camps, involved many in a constant search and expectation that they would suddenly reappear after the war. Denial processes played a central role in maintaining these hopes with avoidance of grief and mourning.

Sooner or later the bitter truth could not be denied, with the realization by most that they had no basis for hopes that loved ones had survived. Depression and other symptoms of the survivor syndrome would then appear. In some cases the realization of the death of entire families proved too overwhelming and guilt pro-

voking, so that severe depressions resulted, and occasional suicidal acts. On the other hand, there are some who, although forty
years have passed, are still unable to accept that a particularly
loved and idealized relative (often a child, sibling, or offspring) is
dead, and continue to believe that he or she is still alive some-
where and that reunion is still possible.

Probably a majority of the survivors have suffered from one or
more of the traumatogenic anxiety and grief components of the
survivor syndrome.[9]

In the struggle to readapt to the demands of reality on their
emergence from the catastrophic trauma of the Holocaust, avoidance and denial mechanisms were central in survivors' attempts
to forget their agonizingly distressing memories of the recent past.
To recall them and tell them to others involved a traumatic reexperiencing that they wished to avoid.

Some were categorical about this, as in the statement, "I have
given up enough of my life and I don't want to take up any more
by talking about it." Others were conflicted between the longing
to forget and the need, which is also a commitment, to remember
and to bear witness.[10] Recently a survivor summed up the dilemma with these words:

> They brought us to the lowest level of existence, and we were made to
> feel the deepest shame. Our shame is greater than that of those mur-
> derers who did it to us. Therefore we want to forget it . . . also not to
> forget it . . . to remember it at the same time. We go over this broken
> bridge of our lives and try not to look back.

The reluctance to talk about the traumas of the past and the
longing (desire) to forget interacted with a general avoidance by
society of the survivor's personal experiences of death and extremity. This avoidance of the realization that "this could have happened to me" manifests itself in the observer's shying away from
confrontation with what he, the observer himself, could have experienced if circumstances had been different. In this way the
avoidance and denial of the past by the survivor were reinforced
and efforts for social integration in the present were encouraged
as the major task.

Ernest Rappaport describes how his determination to write and
publish his concentration camp experiences was weakened by the
fear of appearing abnormal, and he reflects wryly, "It is con-

sidered an attribute of normality to retain a resigned or acquiescent silence in the face of crime."[11]

The survivor is not only tacitly encouraged to forget the past in the service of social acceptance, but should he insist on telling about what happened to him, his traumatic experiences and their long-term effects are converted into psychiatric symptoms to be dealt with by an expert. However, since the experts also belong to the "denying society," by and large they too tended to avoid their patients' Holocaust experiences even in long-term psychotherapies and even in psychoanalysis.

The general difficulty in relating to the survivors' experiences of extremity and the avoidance and denial resulted in social attitudes to survivors deriving from split-off aspects of people's feelings. Referring to survivors as heroes (ghetto or concentration camp fighters or partisans), or to the dead as holy marytrs represents their glorification by "splitting off" the shameful, vulnerable, and helpless aspects of the Holocaust experience. The denial and repudiation of their own vulnerability were seen in disdainful attitudes toward survivors by the Sabra (native-born Israeli) who reveled in self-images of mastery and invincibility.

Blaming the victims as in some way responsible for the Holocaust events (for not getting out beforehand, or for not escaping or resisting) implies that "it couldn't happen to us." According to "defensive attribution" theory, when disaster strikes beyond a certain level, observers insulate themselves from the realization of the possibility of a similar danger occurring to them by assigning responsiblity to the victims.[12] For Israelis who had come from Europe, blame sometimes angrily directed against the survivors often was derived from guilt feelings for their having "abandoned" their relatives and friends by leaving Europe before the war. After the survivors began to receive reparations, a cynical and vulgar pragmatic attitude of denial of their experiences was seen in the provocative question posed to survivors with a concentration camp number tattooed on the forearm: "How much did you get for that?"

The social climate of denial in Israel in which the Holocaust experiences were dealt with in such a matter-of-fact way can, however, be seen also as having been sociotherapeutic for the rapid resettlement and adaptation of the hundreds of thousands of survivors who poured into Israel in the early years of the state.

Their main concerns were to create new lives and new families, which coincided with the central need of building the new state and enabled the survivors to achieve new identities.

Many mental health professionals have been driven to study survivors. Motivated by humanistic and empathic feelings, and their own guilt at being spectators or at best limited participants during the Holocaust, they make the error of using accepted everyday conceptualizations, models, and terms from medicine, psychiatry, and psychoanalysis, but the Holocaust and its aftermath cannot be reduced to conceptual clinical terminology. Some have been able to contribute important conclusions connected with clinical observations, but many of the studies are limited. After making their contributions, many students of the Holocaust become even more aware of the insurmountable nature of the Holocaust, and some give up the task as the subject retreats in the face of the methodological difficulties involved.

I have dialogued with many survivors and their families. I have attempted to hear, understand, and experience what they are telling all of us and our civilization, trying to make meaningful the meaningless. I have found that the old psychoanalytic conceptualizations can only give partial answers and limited help to the survivors and to their therapists. To answer the powerful existential questions the Holocaust poses, we have to be ready to grope in the darkness without any framework of conceptualization as a crutch. I often ask what Freud would have said. In spite of his pessimism, he did not anticipate the absolute principle of the evil —the autoclysmic discharge of the repressed aggressive forces in cultured nations of Europe.

In our culture, people are uncomfortable in the presence of survivors of man-made disasters. In the personal encounter with survivors, images arise of victimization and confrontation with death, humiliation and horror, helplessness, abandonment and loss, and the dreadfulness and misery of the struggle to survive in extremity. These images arouse feelings of anger, anxiety, shame, guilt, and blame in us, emotions that we prefer to avoid, although we also want to know what really happened. Our discomfort and avoidance are especially evident when both the victims and the perpetrators belong to our culture, as happened in the Nazi genocide of World War II.

In psychiatry too, the avoidance of the subject of the Holocaust was overwhelming—and I do not believe it has stopped occurring.

Through the 1970s, psychiatric cases were presented, and reports of psychoanalyses were presented in professional mental health meetings and *not a single remark* was made in respect of the fact that the patient was a survivor, or that the patient's parents were victims of the Holocaust. The extent of denial and dissociation even in mental health services in Israel was almost not believable. The phenomenon of denial clearly calls for more understanding.

1. The subject is often too painful for therapists to deal with.
2. Denials of the Holocaust identities of patients by psychotherapists illustrate the far-reaching extent of denial of massive trauma like the Holocaust by all human beings.
3. The survivors themselves resist removing the denial of their identities as survivors because of their own participation or fears of succumbing to the stigmatization they attribute to themselves as victims.
4. Psychiatric and psychoanalytic theory could not deal with the issue. There are no conceptual categories in psychoanalytic thinking for conceptualizing the damage to human personality on the basis of traumatization in real-life societal events of the nature of the Holocaust. Although there was always lip service paid to bringing in social and environmental elements to understanding one's patients, in practice this was not really done in psychiatric work.

For Whom Is the Holocaust Significant?

The Holocaust constitutes a collective trauma for all those who lived in its shadow, even those who did not experience the Holocaust directly. Obviously the entire Jewish people are deeply touched by the Holocaust, for we Jews were all potential victims. Although there can be no comparison of the experiences of the actual victim who suffered ineffable hell and the symbolic experience of other Jews who were not victims of the Holocaust, yet on a symbolic level, all Jews were potential victims. Jews who do not acknowledge and validate their potential-victim status are denying an essential component of their collective identity and collective self. Listening to survivors, speaking empathically with fellow Jews about the events that took place in the Holocaust and all that could have taken place to all the rest of us, is part of a complex, arduous process that is essential for the identity of all Jews.

But ultimately the Holocaust is an essential issue for *all of humanity* to share in the unbearable and unimaginable experiences, first of the possibility of being victims, and second of the possibility of participating as victimizers.

The bridging of the gap between our universal potential for long and fulfilling lives and the events that actually befell those who had the terrible misfortune to be the victims of the cataclysmic event of the Holocaust is a necessary step in the completion of a person's human identity. In addition, there are also in all of us sufficient elements of aggression and sadism—in other words, identification with the possibility of our having been victimizers in the Holocaust—that the completion of one's human identity also requires an encounter of the Holocaust and its survivors as an expression of not running away from the shadow of our own potential to be among the perpetrators under other historical circumstances.

Understanding the role of the Holocaust in the survivor's life means really coming to grips with the traumatization of human beings that was and is being done by human society.

2.
On Relating to Traumatized/ Persecuted People

For the survivors themselves, recalling and relating their experiences was, for most, excruciatingly painful and humiliating—hence the tendency to avoid and to forget. Moreover, the survivors were especially perceptive that even with the motivation of people in their new countries of settlement to accept them, they were not always ready to hear their tales of misery. The reluctance that survivors sensed in others to listen to the details of what they had been through in the Holocaust reinforced their tendency to avoid talking about their dreadful history, except when together in the special intimacy and solidarity of groups of fellow survivors. They justified their silence in the general society in terms of the inability of the others to understand what they had experienced. In this way both the survivors and the surrounding society interacted to maintain, by and large, a shameful silence.

However, this repression and longing to forget conflicted with the need, which is also a commitment, of the survivor *to remember and to bear witness*. A survivor summed up the dilemma in these words:

> They brought us to the lowest level of existence and we were made to feel the deepest shame. Our shame is greater than that of those murderers who did it to us. Therefore we want to forget it ... also not to forget it ... to remember it at the same time. We go over this broken bridge of our lives and try not to look back.

19

The will to bear witness—to tell the truth of what really happened to them and to their fellow victims—is described by some survivors as having been a motive in their struggle to survive. On bearing witness the survivor preserves the connection with his own past and identity, and he fulfills a duty to those who did not survive. Furthermore, bearing witness is important for the reintegration into society of the survivor of extremity. He needs to be heard and to be believed within the framework of the social community in order to feel recognition and validity for his experiences and for his having succeeded in the struggle to survive.

In most of the societies of the democratic world in the postwar era where the survivors settled and worked, they were accepted as citizens with more or less full rights and opportunities, but their survivor identities and experiences were avoided and remained shadowy and unexpressed.

Even in Israel, where the Holocaust has been given a central significance from the very time of the establishment of the state, and at important institutional levels (Holocaust Memorial Day, Yad Vashem, Holocaust teaching in schools, etc.), the experiences of the survivors *as individuals*, by and large, went unheard and were even avoided! On the other hand, ex-partisans and the few who had the possibility of active and heroic resistance during the Holocaust were idealized as heroes, but the vast majority of survivors of the concentration camps and other situations of death and destructive persecution were given little or no recognition and personal validation in their struggle with their memories of abject misery, horror, shame, and loss.

Altogether, Israeli society has been characterized by avoidance of individual experiences of helplessness and passivity. The orientation to the Holocaust on a collective level, therefore, has been through an emphasis on heroism. For a long time, Holocaust survivors were implicitly urged to forget their past, not to expect others to listen to them, to wipe out the shameful past identity of being "galut" (exile) victims, and to emerge from their background of powerlessness, helplessness, and defenselessness into a new Israeli identity. The Israeli ethos became a repudiation of the passivity of the European Jew and the many-thousand-year tradition of Jews of affirming the dignity of powerlessness and acceptance of one's fate at the hands of others as God's will. The Israeli was to be a self-reliant, active, masterful, aggressive fighter. Paradoxically, this admirable goal set the Israelis up simultaneously for secret fears of being in touch with and showing any vestiges of weakness. The Holocaust became a symbol for a sense of helplessness and also a rationale for using power so as not to be defenseless.

Whereas the survivors themselves often projected their experience as a struggle not only to survive but to *stay human*, the Israeli experience became one of regaining the power that was missing. For the average Israeli, overcoming the Holocaust meant overcoming all vestiges of weakness and powerlessness, a way of thinking that of course has been totally rejustified and "proven correct" while violence and hostility to Jews continue unabated from Arab enemies all around the remnants of the Jewish people in Israel. As time goes by, this Holocaust psychology has seemed the more confirmed in the actions and statements of Arab political leaders who refuse to recognize the permanence of Israel and the right to life of the Jewish people in Israel.

For many survivors who led active and, as we shall see, often overactive lives, in their successful achievement of social goals and in creating and bringing up their new families, avoidance and silence with regard to their sufferings and losses was the normal mode of coping with the catastrophic past. In this way they were socially acceptable and even became exemplary citizens in terms of personal, family, and social achievement.

Today, more than forty years later, many survivors who were adolescents or young adults during the war are showing a willingness and a need to talk about their past; to return to and even to attempt a belated "working through" of their Holocaust experiences. Now middle-aged and older, they are confronted with a flooding-back of repressed Holocaust memories as part of the normal process of reflection and review of past life at a stage in the life cycle that is associated with existential depression. In addition, after decades of avoidance, the upsurge of interest by society in looking again at the Holocaust, as well as manifestations of neo-Nazism, have also encouraged more survivors to come into the open. However, these memories arouse feelings of anxiety, loss, depression and guilt, and shame.

In the individual life cycle, age forty represents the transition into midlife. Similarly, in the collective experience forty years after an event represents a kind of midlife for people still closely connected to overwhelming historical events in their rememberable consciousness, yet already at a point of distance that enables new kinds of perspectives.

The passage of forty years is in the history of a people and its folk metaphors a particularly significant time dimension. It is not only a considerable period in the life of any human individual, but also a significant time period in the history of society. There are many instances in the Bible where the histories of societies are recorded in terms of forty-year intervals. It seems that in the ancient world a forty-year time lapse was understood to be required by society and a people in order to reach a perspective on past experiences and to make the transition to a new period successfully. In the life cycle of individuals who personally experienced the Holocaust, the passage of forty years enabled many of them to arrive at a degree of emotional distance that allowed a greater recalling of traumatic memories without the agonizing pain that a time closer to the events brought up.

There is a characteristic return of memories at this transition point. For some who needed time to forget the tragic losses of their loved ones, it is now possible to begin recalling and to mourn. For others, there is the press of the increasing awareness that life is not forever, and that one must remember before one ends one's journey. Moreover, in midlife or at least toward the end of midlife, there begins to be a reduction in the pattern of maximal activity that was used as a way of avoiding pain and mourning. The past now begins to emerge. It can become a resource or a menace. As an enduring repository of valuable memories, it can be drawn on and mobilized as a resource to maintain one's psychological equilibrium, or it can be a volcano that has long lain dormant and now spills forth its searing lava of memories, including delayed and neglected grief reactions. The reemergence of memory is a renewed challenge. The period of reconnection with the past can become a source for new creative activity, for individuals and for a collectivity, working through grief of the past through new regard for the survivor, the continuity of Jewish life, and the meaningfulness of all human life.

In the early years after the war, the attempt to come to terms with concentration camp experiences and Holocaust losses was so excruciatingly painful that it was avoided and postponed until this later period in life when the passage of time may have rendered the traumatic events more distant and less intolerably painful. Until then all the psychic energy of the survivor was mobilized for adaptation to the demands of reality.

Stressful life events in well-functioning, nonclinical groups of midlife and aging survivors may stir up traumatic memories and painful emotions of massive losses. Particularly devastating for survivors are disappointments, separations and losses, especially in relation to spouse or children, and the cessation of work activity such as at retirement.

Some of the survivors who now feel the need to talk see the return of Holocaust memories and their depressive mood as connected with an increasing disillusionment and disappointment with the state of society and the world. The optimism, hopes, and expectation for the creation of a new society and a just world was an important positive force in their adaptation and reintegration into society. Today in their sensitive awareness of continuing injustices, inhumanity, the lowering of values and ethical standards in man's relations with his fellow man, and recurrent wars and mass deaths, they feel that nothing has changed, that they have been cheated and their survival robbed of justification and meaning.

The modes of coming to terms with Holocaust trauma utilized by individual survivors are multiple and complex. Of central importance are the personality resources of the survivor, and the presence of a nurturing and supportive relationship in the survivor's life.

Each phase of the life cycle presented new opportunities for "working through" the war experiences and losses. Creative artistic expression (painting, writing prose or poetry) as well as communal and societal activity have been used successfully by many for working through their experiences in ways that constitute valuable communications to the rest of society. Self-help survivor groups have been of considerable help for many, and have enabled a slow working through of losses and other traumata in solidarity with other survivors who had similar experiences. Some of these groups, especially if families were involved, became substitutes for the lost extended families.

At the psychiatric center I direct, we set up a counseling service for survivors as part of our outreach community mental health service for *nonclinical* survivors, who avoid clinical services in which they feel stigmatized. Our object is to provide a suitable framework for survivors seeking to communicate traumatic experiences and express the hitherto inarticulated feelings of guilt, shame, helplessness, and anger. Many of those who have turned to us have been "waiting" for many years to deal with their Holocaust experiences and the associated feelings. They wanted to speak, but waited because they didn't know how and with whom.

In reconstructing from many survivors the overall fabric of an era such as the Holocaust, in some ways we get to know more about what an individual endured in the past than he himself knew, even though he was enduring calamitous events beyond our personal understanding of his experience. The cumulative evidence of many oral histories of the experiences of individuals who lived through the Holocaust gives us the possibility of a perspective that was denied some individual survivors as they were preoccupied by the bitter drama of their own battle for survival.

In the encounter with the massively traumatized person, our capacities both as human beings and therapists are challenged maximally, since the counselor-therapist has to undergo a personal confrontation with the traumatic situation in which the victim struggled for survival. This means a readiness to be involved within the therapeutic relationship with the death and the torture, loss and abandonment, humiliation and helplessness that the survivor experienced and still carries deeply imprinted within his self. This is an extremely painful experience for both parties. For the survivor it means a reexperiencing of horrors he has tried to forget, which also means that the therapist takes on himself the responsibility for exposing a traumatized person to retraumatization. For therapists it means a readiness to expose oneself by empathic listening to experiences of extremity beyond one's personal life experience, yet many therapists are not unlike the society to which they belong, and try to avoid personal confrontations with the extreme and the associated unexpressed affects of fear, grief, anger, guilt, and shame that are aroused.

As stated previously, the survivor has for many years struggled to repress and deny the painful affects associated with his traumatic experiences, and when he senses avoidance on the part of a therapist, his denial and repression are reinforced. In many therapies with survivors, there was an unspoken and tacit agreement between the therapist and the survivor to avoid opening up and dealing with traumatic Holocaust experiences. The same "conspiracy of silence" has also been seen in the therapies of children of survivors.

The establishment of *basic trust* in an individual whose trust in human beings was systematically undermined constitutes a challenge for a therapist that is much more demanding than the usual therapeutic situation. It means that he must be ready and able to listen empathically in a mode that conveys to the survivor a feeling of solidarity and hope, enabling him to relive the traumatic situations of extreme suffering with a person who, although he himself had not lived through them, is prepared to accompany him on the journey back. The therapist is not expected to be nor can he possibly be an "expert" on the Holocaust experiences. If he tries to appear as such he will be reacted to with scepticism, since for the survivor the only experts are those who were "there."

Each survivor is uniquely different in relation to the nature of his suffering, its meaning for him and the adaptive mode used to cope with it, so that each requires a special renewed effort of understanding and concentration. By establishing a relationship of trust with the survivor of man-made catastrophes, the therapist becomes a "significant other," who, by listening in an empathic mode conveys to the survivor that he is believed despite the fact that he has undergone the unbelievable, and that he is understood and accepted in his having struggled for survival in extremity. Receiving validation and recognition of his suffering, the survivor feels less shame, and can begin to recount and explore in detail experiences that until then he had been unable to verbalize, as well as express hitherto inarticulated affects of fear, grief, rage, shame, and guilt.

Considerable caution is required in encouraging the release from repression, denial, and isolation of terrifying affects. *Overwhelming depression may appear when the attempt is made to work through long-delayed mourning.*

Fears of abandonment and loss of the therapist can impede the development of the therapeutic relationship. It is essential to create a feeling of availability and readiness to maintain the relationship *unconditionally.* The fear of a new close relationship, the threat to the idealized concept of the pre-Holocaust destroyed family, and the threat to the sense of uniqueness and omnipotence are issues in the functioning of survivors that are connected with, and defend against, terrifying anxieties of death, abandonment, helplessness, and loss. These anxieties frequently result in feelings of disappointment with and accusations of lack of understanding and warmth in the therapist. The survivor may project on the therapist intense aggression and guilt and accuse the therapist of being a Nazi persecutor.

The therapist who is unable to share empathically and to identify with the victims of atrocities may defend himself against the painful affects aroused in him by adopting the role of the objective "physician" authority—but this is a role in which he again can be experienced as a persecutor by the survivor. On the other hand, if the therapist overidentifies with the survivor, he may be idealized as the longed-for savior.

Each therapist will have to deal with his own anxiety, grief, and guilt according to his background and the history of his own involvement with the Holocaust, and in relation to all of his own most painful life experiences. Listening to experiences of atrocity and genocide, which are so radically different from the life experience of most therapists, can create doubts about one's ability to help, both as a therapist and as a human being. Sometimes the therapist may want to share with the survivor his feelings of helplessness about presuming to be a therapist to the helplessness of the survivor-victim.

Trauma is an integral part of life in Israel. There is no end to the reality of traumatic experiences for people in the repeated wars of Israel for its survival and self-defense. The anxiey of repeated traumatization is characteristically avoided and denied, which is an adaptive way of psychic functioning after trauma that enables the society to maintain its forward momentum despite the fact that peace has never come to Israel to this day. Israel as a society is, in effect, a dynamic ongoing lifespan study of a people whose collectivity is a tradition of suffering in exile, which reached its zenith in the Holocaust of our century and then continues in the struggle to build and protect the new state in which Jews will be less vulnerable.

Israel is idolized by all the Jews of the world because it is seen as a substitute for the massive loss the Jewish people suffered in the Holocaust. On the positive side, the state of Israel is perceived metaphorically as the grandest rehabilitation project of a traumatized people that enables rebirth, revival, survival—the creation of a new society in which the family of the Jewish people will no longer be decimated. It reestablishes connections with the values and ideals of the pre-Holocaust Jewish family, and it opens the door to a new identity of belonging and meaning that is part of a healthier age in which Jews are no longer defenseless.

In Israel, there are unlimited opportunities for studying the two sides of responses to trauma. On the one hand, there are the cases of clinical decompensation of those who become overwhelmed with the objective intensity and meanings of the traumas with which they have been faced, such as repeated and overwhelming losses of one's dearest relatives from which one can never recover. Simultaneously, there are opportunities to study people's vital capacities to work through trauma and the remarkable number of people who are capable of applying flexibility and plasticity in developing a successful dynamic encounter with and mastery of horrendously stressful events.

Regrettably, the natural tendency of professionals in mental health is to study those who do suffer breakdowns, and in that sense there has been an excessive preoccupation with psychic damage in the wake of the Holocaust, and not enough study of the many survivors of the Holocaust who emerged more or less with psychological integrity and were able to build new lives, a new identity, and contribute so meaningfully to the regeneration of Jewish collective life in Israel.

3.

The Clinical Effects of Massive
Psychic Trauma

About half a million Jewish survivors of genocide were left alive
at the end of the war in the areas of Europe that had been occupied by the Nazis. About two-thirds of the survivors, over three
hundred thousand, including tens of thousands who had been in
concentration camps, settled in Israel after the establishment of
the state. They became an integral and highly significant part of
Israeli society.

In relating and verifying these events of mass murder and unprecedented suffering, the survivor commits us to become involved and even somewhat responsible for that which happened
and must never happen again.

Like many of my psychiatric colleagues in Israel, I began listening to survivors' experiences in the course of my work in the
psychiatric clinics and hospitals of Israel. Working with the survivors of the Holocaust in therapy and research meant relating to
human beings who had been exposed to massive psychic trauma.
This committed us to an understanding of the nature and effect of
the processes, intrapsychic and interpersonal, by which men,
women, and children lived through extreme experiences, and how
they have struggled in their attempts to deal with and overcome
painful memories and traumatic effects throughout their lives in
the years since the Holocaust. Studying the processes of such
inordinate trauma teaches us much that can be applied to under-

standing and handling phenomena of a less extreme nature in man's daily struggle to cope with stressful and tragic life events.

The Nazis had planned that nobody and nothing would be left, that all traces of the Jews of Europe would be erased, leaving an empty space. But a remnant was left—the survivors—and from them we know, beyond all shadow of doubt, the objective and subjective conditions, in all their horrifying detail, of the extermination camps, the forced labor camps, the ghettos, the extreme situations of flight and hiding for long periods.

Many of the survivors are tragically condemned by the massive traumatization process to carry within them the concentration camp world and continue to relive years later the persecutory experiences. In these survivors, despite their having created entirely new lives and new realities, a part of the self continues to exist in the reality of the concentration camp.[1]

In my contact with survivors throughout the years, I have seen how the deeply imprinted persecutory experiences are continually and compulsively aroused by the trivial stimuli of everyday life. A loud barking of dogs, sudden shouting, a bang at the door, a calling out of their names, a sight of a strange uniform, a newspaper article, barbed wire, even a certain smell can precipitate a photographic flashback—memory in which present reality is exchanged for the reality of the concentration camp world with all its terror. Some of my Haifa patients could not travel past the chimney stacks of the Haifa bay cement factory. An experienced nurse, an ex-Auschwitz inmate, unexpectedly exposed to a skin cautery, suddenly ran out of the clinic in horror when she smelled the burning flesh. States of great mental distress arise in this way, often requiring emergency psychiatric treatment. At night, many survivors awaken, overwhelmed with panic and rage from persecutory nightmares.

Teaching Mental Health Students about Psychic Trauma in Adult Life

Never before have the victims of social catastrophe been the subject of such systematic study—both in history and in the behavioral sciences.

The new concepts yielded by our study of Holocaust survivors become a new paradigm for understanding the recent-long-term adverse effects in victims of other serious violence, especially when an overwhelming and repeated threat of death has been experienced.

Today when we meet refugees who have been brutalized during imprisonment, victims of prolonged torture and brutal rape, and others in the seemingly endless and ongoing list of variations of man's inhumanity to man, we understand their plight more through the paradigm that has emerged from our understanding of the prolonged suffering and aftereffects of survivors who emerged from the Holocaust. This paradigm now links all victims overwhelmed by terror, brutalization, and pain.

The Nazi concentration camp is the most extreme situation of adversity known to man, and *in a sense has replaced the state of nature as revealing the "true nature of man."* The interpretation of the victims' behavior in the concentration camps has become a test case for our vision of humanity.

Concepts

1. *Trauma* and *stress* are terms used frequently in clinical psychiatry to describe events experienced by individuals and groups that can precipitate the onset of a variety of mental disorders.

2. The student should know the meaning of these terms and understand theories of their use in psychiatry.

3. The student should understand the meaning of the traumatic situation and its relation to threat to life. He will learn the significance of the traumatic process and appreciate its possible after-effects.

4. The student should be familiar with common events in civilian life such as work and road accidents, violence and death, separations, and stress of warfare and combat, which can result in post-traumatic reactions.

5. The student should understand the normal coping mechanisms in the encounter with stress and trauma, and the attempt to master them.

6. The student should understand the nature of the grief reaction to the loss of a significant person, should know the stages of the mourning process and appreciate its

significance as a model for "working through" and mastery of a wide range of traumatic experiences.

7. The student should know the general symptoms of the post-traumatic reactions, acute and chronic, as well as the specific features involved in the post-traumatic reactions of civilian life and of warfare and combat.

8. The student should be able to make a differential diagnosis from other neurotic reactions in relation to the pathognomic features of the post-traumatic reaction.

9. The student should understand the factors influencing the responses to stress and trauma, such as personality structure, predisposition, and vulnerability, age, psychosocial aspects, etc.

10. The student should study the importance of the compensation motive in the post-traumatic reaction.

11. The student should understand reactions to disasters involving large numbers of people and the significance of communal trauma, uprooting, and the refugee experience, as well as individual trauma.

12. The student should appreciate the difference between man-made and natural disasters.

13. The student should understand the significance of the concentration camp survivor syndrome as the paradigm of massive psychic trauma. He will learn the specific psychosocial events and reactions in relation to the varied traumatic situations of the Holocaust, which a large part of the population of Israel underwent. He should appreciate the effect of the trauma of the Holocaust experiences on the life cycle of the survivor and of his family in terms both of coping and vulnerability to such events as anniversary reactions. He needs to understand the possible influence of Holocaust and catastrophe on the children of traumatized survivors due to the effect on their functioning as parents.

14. The student is to learn management and methods of treatment of post-traumatic reactions, acute and chronic. He is to understand the technique of crisis intervention, including appreciation of the significance of catharsis and abreaction in the treatment program.

15. The student needs to appreciate the specific problems and different implications of treatment of civilians, soldiers, and survivors suffering from post-traumatic reactions.
16. The student needs to understand the psychosocial needs of traumatized, victimized, and persecuted individuals as a major aspect of their rehabilitation.

Long-Term Psychological Effects of Massive Psychological Trauma in the Holocaust

There is an overwhelming of defenses that leads to impairment of the regenerative capacity of the psyche, which results in permanent psychological effects.

Clinical manifestations include the following:

1. Traumatogenic Anxiety Syndrome: Reexperiencing of traumatic events triggered by memory associations
2. Anxiety phenomena
3. Psychosomatic manifestations
4. Persecutory experiences and fears, for example, persecutory nightmares
5. Prolonged–Interminable Mourning Syndrome: *Loss and suppression of mourning for massive losses of loved ones and community. It was impossible to mourn in the concentration camp or on liberation, and thereafter the mourning continued to be postponed.* Symptoms include

    a. Depression and preoccupation
    b. Grief over life and death
    c. Guilt at survival (active and passive)
    d. Inability to enjoy pleasure

6. Difficulty making new relationships. Symptoms include

    a. Fear of separation
    b. Psychic numbing—affect is "lame" or black, denial

7. Blocking of aggression. Symptoms include suppressed rage, irritability and free-floating rage, an inability to deal with aggression in one's family
8. Ontological insecurity: Insecurity resulting from a massive constellation of uprooting, loss of community, de-

humanization, undermining of basic trust and identity in the face of relentless persecution, and in many cases even a further ("double") uprooting after the Holocaust

9. Difficulties in aging: Aging in itself is further traumatic for the survivor: the shift from doing to thinking and from preoccupation with everyday events and long-range planning to reviewing and thinking over one's life make old age specifically more difficult for survivors if they haven't come to terms with the past.

   a. Aging intensifies and magnifies past trauma. "Who loves me, who cares if I love?" The survivor who has not mourned cannot experience love.
   b. An inability to review their lives: it is too painful to remember one's life, or the survivor doesn't have words to describe and give meaning to over-whelming experiences of loss, grief, and rage.
   c. The experience of aging may recapitulate the Holocaust experience, especially as children leave home and distance themselves, and deaths of friends and family take place, leaving the survivor alone.
   d. Loss of activity, adaptive capacity, and physical power is dreaded—in the Holocaust these meant loss of one's capacity for defense and certain death.
   e. Approaching death—death is at last catching up with them.

The survivors are scattered among the nations of the world, but the great majority of the seventy-five thousand remnants of the extermination and other concentration camps, and another quarter of a million who survived the many other extreme situations of forced labor camps, hiding, and flight settled in Israel. For mental health professionals in clinical practice in Israel, the Holocaust and its long-term effects has always been and is still a constant presence, a constant content in daily work with thousands of survivors and their families in our clinics and hospitals.

The psychiatric disabilities and psychopathology of the concentration camp survivors, when first encountered in the 1950s, could not be understood in terms of existing psychiatric terminology and theories of psychic trauma, and so a new diagnostic conception—the *concentration camp survivor syndrome*—was created. Psychological traumatization of such a degree and of so many people had never before been described in the behavioral sciences. The concept of concentration camp survivor syndrome signified the discovery that psychic traumatization, once it exceeds a certain degree of intensity and duration, can cause irreversible damage to fundamental psychobiological processes and to the recuperative capacity of the psyche. This can result in chronic mental changes that are often resistant to treatment and may be progressive.

There have been many examples in the long history of man's inhumanity to man of mass murder of peoples with survivors. The slavery process of the African peoples, the decimation of the Indian peoples in North America, the extermination of one million Armenians by the Turks in 1915 are a few examples that in recent years have received public attention. However, the consequences of genocide on the psychological functioning of the survivors has not been a subject of study. Thus, the delineation of the concentration camp survivor syndrome established a new awareness and insight into the long-term effect of massive traumatization and focused interest for the first time on the plight of survivors from many different kinds of disasters. Robert Jay Lifton's studies in the 1960s of the survivors of the atomic explosions in Japan added important insights to our understanding of the psychological plight of the survivor.[2]

Unique, however, to the Nazi Holocaust was the systematic dehumanization process that accompanied every stage of the Nazi murder machine. This process had started long before the setting up of the extermination camps with a deliberate indoctrination campaign of vilification of the Jews portraying them as evil, degenerate, and dangerous subhuman creatures who had to be gotten rid of for the good of society without any need for remorse or guilt feelings. In fact, for some of the Nazis the killing of Jews was a sacred task of a paganistic religious nature.

The journey to the concentration camps and finally the arrival and life in the concentration camps involved deliberate, systematic, maximal debasement, degradation, and humiliation of the victims, who were stripped naked, shaved, whipped and brutalized, forced to brutalize each other at gunpoint, forced to drink out of toilet bowls and become covered in excrement (Terrence

Des Pres called this "excremental assault").[3] The inmates were quickly made to look and feel subhuman. This dehumanization process had the double aim of

1. crushing all manifestation of resistance in the victims, resulting in their complete subjugation; and
2. conditioning the perpetrators, making it easier for them to do the job of mass murder of the less than human "cargo," who were made to look inferior and subhuman—"unworthy life" to be destroyed for the good of society.

Franz Stangl, the ex-commandant of Treblinka, when asked what, if they were going to kill the inmates anyway, was the point of all the humiliation and brutalization, answered, "to condition those who actually had to carry out the policies," and "to make it possible for them to do what they did."[4] When pressed more specifically about the nakedness, the whips, the horror of the "cattle pens," he answered that "this was the system, it worked, and because it worked, it was irreversible."

This dehumanization process was accompanied by

1. constant confrontation with imminent death;
2. persistent and unabated arbitrary brutality and sadistic torture;
3. degradation; and
4. loss and destruction of family, community, and the entire familiar world.

Psychiatrists have to deal with the casualties of rapid social change and social cataclysm. For many of the survivors who suffered this massive traumatization, the results were devastating. I am referring to my experience and that of my colleagues in Israel (see works of H. Klein,[5] H. Z. Winnick,[6] F. Brull[7]) as a psychiatrist and psychotherapist working with severely damaged people. I am not speaking of all survivors—although we believe that very few if any emerged unaffected despite successful social and vocational adjustment, not all developed the characteristic survivor syndrome symptomatology. In those who did, some of the common manifestations of the concentration camp survivor syndrome were

1. chronic anxiety, irrational fears, chronic depression;
2. perpetual feelings of loss, emptiness, and preoccupation with the idealized memories of families who were murdered and could not be adequately mourned;

3. inability to enjoy (anhedonism) or obtain real satisfaction from anything;
4. guilt feelings (survivor guilt); and
5. a peculiar form of psychic numbing that had started in the camps and that prevented survivors from feeling real contact with their environment. This was an adaptive, protective suppression of feeling that enabled many concentration camp inmates to go through the camp horrors in a state of detachment and unreality.

The following is an example of one of my survivor patients who suffered from concentration camp syndrome.

He had been brought up in Warsaw in an assimilated family with no Jewish consciousness. After many persecutory experiences in the Warsaw Ghetto, culminating in his separation from his mother, to whom he was very closely attached, at age thirteen he was incarcerated in Bergen-Belsen. After the war, he continued to long for his mother, unable to accept her loss, searching everywhere for her in pictures, including heaps of corpses. He became a successful writer on the Holocaust. He suffered from his inability to form relationships with women. Emotionally immature, he continued searching everywhere for maternal love, until eventually he became increasingly depressed in his early thirties, seventeen years after the end of the war.

In therapy, after successfully working through the blocked mourning and loss of his mother, he could at last begin to develop emotionally and form a successful love relationship. He wrote a letter to a friend toward the end of the therapy (after three years) that illustrates how, despite the passage of many years after the traumatization, he had remained fixed in the state of depersonalization that was originally a protective and adaptive reaction in the concentration camp and now had become a disabling symptom nearly twenty years later.

"During one of the first times that I came to the doctor, I told him that I don't feel any contact with reality. I told him that when I look at the environment around me—the streets, the houses, the trees, people or objects in the room, I feel that they are separate, that I don't belong to this reality. It is as if everything is like a film and I am only an observer. Only as a result of an effort of will can I behave as if I belong to this, as if this is really my life. During all the time that I've been in treatment, I could not really speak with the doctor about the war because with him I would need to relate the events of the war in a different way, not like I tell the others, as if I am an observer, as if it did not affect me—the child. With the doctor, I shall have to tell him about the war as it really was, to live it as it really was. I am not able to give validity to this. I am not able to admit that there really was a war like this, and the things that happened really happened. I am not able to accept the reality of the war because to accept that reality means to admit that I am alone, that I have no parents, that strangers to whom I did not do anything came and killed all my family, killed all the people that I knew in my childhood. They destroyed the streets, the houses, the roads, our playgrounds, the hiding place that we had behind the house, our apartment—they burned everything. Nothing remained. I am not able to admit that they brought me here [to Israel] and that I am speaking Hebrew, and that I am called [his Israeli name], because to admit this means to really accept that there was a war and that mother was really killed. To admit reality means to accept that I am no longer a small child that the grown-ups, the parents, have to look after. To admit reality means to take responsibility for my actions, alone, to look after myself. And above all, to admit that there was a war. My problem now is that because I love, really love, my girlfriend, I am forced to recognize reality. It is difficult for me to love my girlfriend because this drags in with it reality, and this reality forces me to make a step, to move forward. Perhaps for the first time in my life, by choice, I admit and accept that I am in Israel, that I speak Hebrew, that I am a Jew. I love my girlfriend in reality, and I am ready in reality to do everything for this love, even to admit the war."

Various personality disturbances were prominent in survivors. Many suffered from feelings of emptiness and a lack of a sense of meaning in their lives. An impaired self-image often resulted from the imprinting of the Nazi attitude of their inferiority and worthlessness. The inability to trust others resulted in isolation, suspiciousness, and a difficulty in relating. A further dehumanizing trauma was the destruction of home, family, and community, and in fact the entire familiar world, which further undermined identity and basic security and the sense of continuity with the past.

Many had nowhere to go back to and remained in D.P. camps for years until they could emigrate to Israel (1948–51).

The final blow—"the eighty-first blow"—was the attitude of society, an attitude toward survivors of avoidance, denial, and a desire to forget.[8] Many felt uncomfortable and guilty in the presence of survivors, and these feelings were often transferred onto the survivor, with the implication that he was in some way responsible for his own fate (e.g., that he went passively to be slaughtered) and was suspect and guilty in some way for having survived. It is easier for society if there are no survivors, only dead victims. This attitude reinforced the aggressors' imprint of inferiority and impaired self-image. As a result, many survivors felt ashamed of their concentration camp experiences and refused to talk. Niederland called this "the Schweige agreement."[9]

I have had the privilege of treating many massively traumatized survivors. No matter how we seek to classify types of survivors for purposes of increased scientific understanding, each is uniquely different and no two have suffered the same. Each demands a special effort of attention, understanding, and empathy. The challenge is to establish a relationship of basic trust in people whose ability to trust and self-image have been shattered.

In every survivor there is a universe of inarticulated feeling, blocked mourning, and rage and guilt feelings seeking expression. To succeed in creating an atmosphere of trust in which the survivor can release and work through these destructively pent-up emotions is indeed a great privilege for a therapist and has often required long-standing efforts to maintain the relationship until such a time as the survivor feels himself ready to discharge and relate. Many are doing this now, having acquired distance and some degree of integration of the experiences with the passage of the years.

The Concentration Camp Survivor Syndrome

The first clinical descriptions of the psychiatric disabilities found among concentration camp survivors appeared in the 1950s from countries in Europe that were occupied by the Germans during World War II. During the ten succeeding years, reports of these disturbances came from a variety of countries, cultural backgrounds, and psychosocial conditions where the survivors had settled. By the 1960s, the concentration camp survivor syndrome

(CCSS) had been clearly delineated as a new diagnostic category for the psychiatric disabilities resulting from massive traumatization.

There have been many examples of man's inhumanity to man, of genocides and massive traumatization of peoples. However, these catastrophes of extremity occurred before the era of modern psychiatry and the systematic collection of behavioral data, and we can only make retrospective generalizations regarding their long-term psychosocial effects.

The definition of the CCSS established a new diagnostic and conceptual entity that changed our understanding of the nature and effects of massive psychic trauma. It became clear that the psychic traumatization process, once it exceeds a certain degree of intensity and duration that stretches the psychic functioning of the victim to a breaking point, leads to severe impairment of the fundamental psychobiological processes that were hitherto thought to be inexhaustible. As a result, the recuperative capacity of the psyche may become irreversibly damaged, manifesting in chronic mental changes that, often, may be resistant to treatment and may be progressive. Many clinicians believe that no one of the concentration camp survivors escaped the consequences of the traumatization and, although superficially many appeared well, careful scrutiny revealed some psychological scars and personality change.

Psychoanalytic theories of trauma were woefully inadequate in the face of the massive psychic traumatization experienced by survivors of the Holocaust in World War II. These theories were based on Freud's original concept of infantile trauma, with the later inclusion of the cumulative effect of childhood traumata of everyday life creating vulnerability to subsequent traumatic events. Descriptions of traumatic neurosis and battle combat reactions described in the two world wars was a further important stage in the development of the psychodynamic theories of trauma. However, these conceptualizations fell far short of encompassing the massive traumatization encountered by the victims of the Holocaust. Incarceration in a Nazi concentration camp emerged as a universally accepted criterion of the most massive traumatization possible. Other situations in the Holocaust outside the camps, in the ghettos, and in the various situations of flight and hiding, resulting from the Nazi persecution and murder program, took their place as lesser but still severely and uniquely damaging conditions, all deriving from a unique program of prejudice, persecution, and torture leading to an unappealable sentence of death in a mass program of death never before seen in human history.

In recent years, increasing interest has been focused on the long-term effects of severe environmental stress of many different types and deriving from a wide variety of situations that threaten survival. Natural catastrophes like floods, shipwrecks, or the Aberfan disaster in Wales in 1966, and man-made disasters such as Vietnam War experiences of U.S. soldiers and the trauma of terrorist attacks on civilian populations in Northern Ireland and Israel are examples of man-made disasters being studied. Other situations of traumatization endemic in society, like the Black poverty ghettos in the U.S., poverty families in Britain, long-term incarceration in coercive institutions, prisons, and mental hospitals, chronic malignant disease, child abuse, early loss of parents, etc., are being subjected to this new interest in and awareness of the importance of traumatization studies.

The importance of these states cannot be denied, but it is essential to differentiate between man-made and natural disasters, and to avoid the tendency to broaden the concept of survivors to include everyday social stresses of life, illness, and death. This tendency leads to a loss of the essential meaning of the Holocaust and results in a simplification of complex psychological reactions. It is an attempt to dilute and avoid the narcissistic trauma of genocide for mankind. A full confrontation with the cruel and fearful realities of the Holocaust, due to the perpetration of systematic murder and suffering by one human group on another, demonstrates the instability of all human civilization and progress, and the possibility of social regression at any moment. This is especially so when the perpetrators were human beings who belonged to a leading culture and civilization, a realization that induces feelings of disappointment, pessimism, doubts about the basic moral sense of mankind, and loss of faith in human beings and in the future of humanity. The significance of genocide committed by other human beings is thus of an entirely different order than destruction and suffering from natural disasters.

Freud's psychoanalysis, which grounded mental life in the psychophysiological reality of man's savage instincts, was cruelly corroborated in the Holocaust. However, Freud himself, with his great involvement and identification with Western culture, tended to see the instinct as a mental representation to be changed and sublimated—"Where id was, ego shall come into being." This ideal realization of man's potential through the progressive sublimation of his instincts to become a "whole person" was cruelly shattered in the Holocaust and shown to be an illusion.

Concentration camp survivor syndrome has many elements typical of post-traumatic stress disorder, but with important additional and specific characteristics. A central component of the concentration camp survivor syndrome derives from the repeated and frequent confrontations with violence, murder, and death that became deeply imprinted in the psyches of the survivors. These imprinted memories have accompanied them throughout their lives, manifesting themselves by day in flashback associations to trivial stimuli in which present reality is exchanged for the memory of horrifying scenes from their Holocaust past, or by night in persecutory nightmares. A certain noise, knocking at the door, a smell, the approach of a barking dog, a man in a strange uniform, seeing tall chimneys, hearing a certain word, reading a name in the newspaper or news of some atrocity can arouse intensely distressing associations.

The confrontations with death during the Holocaust were accompanied by a state of utter helplessness to resist the perpetrators and to intervene in relation to one's own suffering and the suffering and deaths of others. This helplessness was a dehumanizing experience in itself, adding a further dimension to the memories of degradation and shame that the survivor has had to struggle with and that may have affected his self-image. The impossibility of mourning the many deaths of loved ones resulted in delayed or interminable mourning with depressions and preoccupations. The effects of long-suppressed hatred and rage, and a feeling of guilt at the mere fact of survival were further components of the survivor syndrome.

Accompanying these processes of individual psychic trauma was loss of the community, which is particularly important in relation to the problems of refugees and displaced victims, especially with regard to their rehabilitation. The destruction of one's community means the loss of an important source of strength and support in coping with trauma. These two major dimensions—the individual traumatic process in the confrontation with death and dehumanization, and the communal traumatic process that disconnects the survivor from his individual, family, and community past—are manifest in the survivor syndrome.

As a result of my experience with survivors in psychiatric and psychotherapeutic settings, I developed a schematic division of survivor patients into three main groups and a small fourth group based on clinical observations:

1. severely damaged survivors;
2. symptom-free survivors;
3. survivors with "typical" neurotic and character problems unrelated to concentration camp survivor syndrome; and
4. survivors who have remained "Musselmen."

1. Severely Damaged Survivors. The first group, which contained the majority of survivor patients, suffered and have continued to suffer from different degrees of the CCSS, which has been well described in the psychiatric literature. The varying symptomatology and personality change includes chronic fluctuating anxiety and depression with somatization, hypochondriacal tendencies, and persecutory nightmares. Innocuous daily events can stimulate associations of a compulsive, vivid, photographic-like nature of presenting experiences, causing acute exacerbations of anxiety.

In this state, present reality is overshadowed by deeply imprinted memories of events from the concentration camp past with overwhelming feelings of fear, terror, and sometimes aggression. These spells of acute anxiety are often followed by a feeling of emptiness and exhaustion and a need to be comforted and protected. Many of these patients created the impression that in part of the "self," nothing of real significance had happened since the concentration camp—it is as if they are still living there and are continually reexperiencing the deeply imprinted horrors that they are often unable to verbalize.

Feelings of loss and preoccupation with the memories of murdered parents, brothers, sisters, wives, husbands, and children are often associated with severe feelings of guilt at having remained alive when so many died, what has been called "survivor guilt." The experience of overwhelming losses of murdered family and friends is closely associated with the feeling of inability to have done anything to save them and then, finally, guilt that one has continued to live and to feel alive. In the mind, there results a conception that one's survival actually depended on the deaths of others. This is the central existential theme expressed in different shades of survivor guilt. Spells of survivor guilt often well up during reunions, which are always of special emotional meaning for survivors, or during joyful happenings and celebrations connected with the development of children. These events become overshadowed by ever-recurring pictorial memories and images of the dead. The inability to enjoy or obtain real satisfaction from anything is thus a manifestation of identification with the dead, of living as if dead. It has prevented many survivors from fully participating in the happy events of family social and occupational life, and such occasions are experienced as unreal and guilt provoking.

Among the most damaged patients in this group are those who went through the severest forms of psychomotor regression in the concentration camp, to automatonlike states with loss of identity —the catatoniclike "Musselman" state. Psychic numbing or depersonalization, originally an adaptive mechanism in the concentration camp situation, often remained after the liberation. It sometimes became a chronic state in spite of the complete change of circumstances, impairing the capacity for appropriate feelings. Feelings of emptiness and a lack of ability to feel a sense of meaning in their lives are often prominent. Moreover, an impaired body image, which resulted from long periods of relating to one's own body as distorted, emaciated, or disfigured, undermined the survivors' belief in the possibility of their being loved by members of the opposite sex and even by their partners in marriage.

Sometimes there was a feeling that the whole range of horrors of what they had experienced was continuing to be expressed in their faces, and they then feared contact and rejection by others in their new environment. Some felt as if there were a special aura of estrangement around them. These body-image changes were related to experiences of dehumanization and deep humiliation. A total system of attitudes and behavior on the part of the perpetrators relegated the victims to the status of a subhuman species. This manifested in deeply humiliating tortures such as being shaved of all body hair and having to remain naked, being beaten on the genitals, having to stand for hours naked in the roll-call square with diarrheic faeces streaming down their legs, or being forced to eat and drink from toilet bowls. Repeated daily humiliations of this kind in the presence of the jeering perpetrators damaged the self-image of the victim, undermined his trust in other human beings and in himself. Many of the survivors never returned to their previous self and body image; they felt themselves permanently damaged and unable to relate satisfactorily to themselves or to others.

The experiences of psychological rape, humiliation, and brutalization were, of course, associated with tremendous hatred and aggression against the Nazis and their collaborators. However, any expression of hostility and opposition was dealt with by inevitable death, often preceded by terrible tortures, so that the survivors had to completely suppress their natural aggressions. As a result, many remained throughout their lives passive, timid people unable to be assertive or to show aggression in any direct way. Others became chronically irritable individuals with inappropriate outbursts of rage. Sometimes such a survivor suffering from the prolonged blocking of his aggressive impulses would create around him—in his home or at work—an aura of free-floating rage. Some, partially awakening in the middle of the night in terror and hatred of their persecutors in the concentration camps, would aggressively attack their spouse lying in bed beside them.

The impossibility of mourning the loss of loved ones in the midst of the Holocaust situation in ghetto, camp, hiding, or flight also resulted in a blocking of the normal mourning process with its important reparative functions. Mourning was thus postponed, and for many the losses were never worked through. This inability to free oneself from dead loved ones prevented the full development of new emotional bonds. In many of the women, mourning became possible for the first time only *after* they gave birth to children. It seemed that giving birth to new life enabled them to face and work through the losses of the past, including by giving the names of the dead family members and friends to their children.

The inability to relate positively and to trust other people, along with tendencies toward isolation and suspiciousness, are sometimes the most prominent of all the dimensions of the survivor syndrome. They constitute a serious interpersonal disturbance. The final irony is that for some such "asocial survivors," there is simultaneously a tremendous need for warmth and supportive relationships in their own social groups of survivors, but not with anyone else.

2. Symptom-Free Survivors Who Deny Having Been Traumatized.
A second group of survivors remained symptom free despite their

concentration camp experiences and loss of all their family. These people claim that they suffer from no psychological effects whatsoever. They deny that they suffer any effect of their traumatic experiences. They possess an unusual ability to deny, to isolate emotion, to avoid, and to rationalize. They often have very rigid personalities with obsessional trends and are emotionally restricted. They suppressed and repressed the painful emotions associated with the Holocaust memories, often refused to discuss them, and managed to "armor" themselves against vulnerability. Some have even presented themselves as possessing special strengths and tended to look upon those who suffered from the fears and depressions as being weak. This armoring, however, often restricted their emotional functioning and, however socially adequate, their interpersonal relationships were often unsatisfactory. In family interaction they may adopt an intellectual, emotionally sterile approach.

Many of them would rather forego financial compensation than upset the delicate, fragile equilibrium they have established, which would be threatened by undergoing the psychiatric examinations required by the indemnification boards. Some of these survivors, by dint of extreme self-driving, single-minded dedication to external goals, have made considerable achievements in business, industry, or the professions. They feel no real satisfaction, nor have they any significant activity or involvement outside the restricted sphere of their chosen field, upon which their adaptation is entirely dependent. One sometimes sees individuals of this group in psychiatric practice because of marital, family, child, or sexual problems. They deny any relationship between these problems and the persecutory experiences. Usually they cannot be dealt with therapeutically because of their phenomenal ability to deny and their insistence even on their supernormal ability to withstand difficulties.

As indicated, they are often disdainful of their weaker complaining brothers who suffer from overt survivor syndrome symptomatology. However, I have seen many of these survivors eventually breaking down after years of symptom-free apparent health when they have had to suffer an additional trauma or stress, often of a relatively minor nature, which causes the collapse of their whole defense system. Examples of such stress are separation from children or spouse, business and economic failure, marital stress, and physical disability.

3. Survivors with "Typical" Neurotic and Character Problems Unrelated to Concentration Camp Survivor Syndrome. The third group of survivors seen in clinical practice is a smaller one. In this group one encounters individuals who present typical neurotic and character neurotic states in which traumatization symptomatology is present only to a relatively minor extent, without the severely impaired functioning of those suffering from the typical survivor syndrome described in the first group. The various specific phenomena of the survivor syndrome are missing. The symptoms for which they seek help relate essentially to their present life situation in a similar way to the usual neurotic patient who comes for psychotherapy. We understand these clinical states largely as linked with predispositions existing in the individual before the trauma and reinforced by the massive traumatic experiences. Many of these survivors were adolescents or young adults during the Holocaust, and in contra-distinction to the previous two groups that have been described, have often responded well to systematic psychoanalytically oriented or other deep psychotherapy, or even psychoanalysis.

Many of this survivor group had an unusual ability to remain psychologically *as if outside* the traumatic experiences of the Holocaust, and were able to observe what was taking place almost objectively in a peculiar, depersonalized state, and to store the details of the experiences in memory. They often possess rich sublimatory powers, and if they are also talented creatively, they have been able to express the stored Holocaust experiences in artistic or other creative intellectual activity in a vivid fashion many years later. The level of regression in the service of survival during the period of traumatization in these survivors often remained at a level of depersonalization and psychic numbing without their succumbing to the deepest primitive level of narcissistic regression, to the "Musselman" state, as occurred in the cases suffering from full-blown survivor syndrome.

The intensity of the traumatization may have been relatively mild, or there may have been protective, mitigating external factors that protected a survivor from the full intensity of trauma. The opportunity of skilled artisans and others to have work situations needed by the Nazis for the running of the camp, occasionally the presence of a friendly SS man or friendly Aryan, the presence of a member of one's family, friends, and the formation of social bonds not only helped physically but also enabled the victim to maintain hope and some sense of individual existence. In the therapeutic situation, the preexisting neurotic developmental difficulties and preoccupations became interwoven into the experiencing of and adaptation to the traumatic experiences. As a result, sometimes these developmental problems even were seen to fulfill a certain defensive function during the Holocaust experiences as well as being complicated and aggravated by them.

Many survivor patients manifested mixed forms and varied constellations of physical and psychological symptoms and interpersonal disturbances. Interpersonal problems related to undermining of basic trust as well as an increased incidence of psychosomatic disorders were present among many of the survivors seen in the medical, neurological, and psychiatric clinics in Israel. In followup studies, they have shown specific vulnerabilities to many of life's stresses. Psychosomatic disturbances were frequent during stressful situations. With advancing age, there was often progressive deterioration in their psychological states. People who tended to be suspicious became increasingly so in the midlife period. When children left home, some reacted with paranoid reactions and severe depressive reactions. In fact, psychotic episodes usually showed an increased incidence among the survivors in reaction to situations of life crisis connected with separation and loss. The inability to cope with loneliness, which meant confrontation with inner emptiness, resulted in a binding of and clinging to their children as the sole significant source of meaning and purpose and nurture in their lives. Thus, many survivors were unable to adapt to the new situations of children growing up and leaving home permanently. With old age and loss of occupational activity, some have become chronically depressed, preoccupied with their past experiences, and suicidal.

4. Survivors Who Have Remained "Musselmen." Another group, albeit small, was made up of the most severely damaged survivors who have remained as chronic mental hospital inmates ever since their liberation. They were unable to recover psychologically from the *"Musselman"* condition and have remained cut off from life, as living dead, walking corpses. Many older survivors who had lost spouses and children remained in a chronic state of depres-

48   *The Clinical Effects of Massive Psychic Trauma*

sion. Unable to reintegrate and build new lives, their feelings of hopelessness and emptiness could not be overcome.

The Latent Vulnerability of Many Survivors Who Did Function Well

As the years passed, we saw many survivors who did not fit into any of these three groups; these were survivors who were functioning well and who seemed well adjusted, but who in encountering various stressful life situations would react or decompensate with manifestations of the survivor syndrome. We realized that survivors of massive trauma and uprooting may be left with specific vulnerabilities despite their apparent recovery. A major vulnerability is related to the fact that chance occurrences in everyday life can arouse memories of the traumatic experiences and return the survivor to the horror of experiences deeply imprinted in his memory.

A second area of vulnerability relates to confrontations with illness and medical situations involving physical examinations with instruments, surgical procedures, and hospitalization, which can trigger terrible associations and memories. It is important for medical professionals to be aware of the fact that memories, fantasies, and images of traumatic experiences even in the distant past may be aroused in refugees and survivors, and that they require special consideration in these situations.

Another area of vulnerability relates to separation. Separation during the persecutions and the genocidal process meant death for the majority of the Jews in Nazi-occupied Europe. The vast majority of the survivors never again saw the relatives and friends from whom they were separated. Therefore, in survivor families there is an understandable hypersensitivity to separation, a tendency to cling to and bind the children. Separations that are accepted as a natural part of life by most people often cause serious decompensation in survivors. There is also vulnerability with regard to loss of activity. Activity, and frequently overactivity, is an important adaptive defense mechanism seen throughout the lives of survivors. In general, keeping constantly active, as is typically seen in the so-called workaholic, is a frequent adaptive defense among people who have been traumatized, enabling them to avoid thinking about and reexperiencing the traumas of the past. There is, however, a further important and specific dimension in relation to the significance of activity for the Holocaust survivor. The ability to work in the slave labor camps and even in the extermination camps was often a means of postponing death. When concentration camp inmates could not go on working, they were usually selected for the gas chambers or other forms of death. Thus, there is often a compulsion to maintain activity and overactivity throughout the life cycle and into advanced age. Illness, accident, or old age, which prevent the survivor from carrying on with work and being active, can result in the breakdown of the important denial defenses and precipitate psychiatric decompensation. These clinical states often manifest as severe depression and paranoid states.

A further vulnerability relates to the significance of death for the survivor because death often carries with it the arousal of the memory of the murder of those whom the survivor had not been able to mourn. When death occurs in the survivor's family or among his close friends, there may be a prolonged mourning reaction, which has to be understood as including delayed mourning for those who had not been mourned during the Holocaust.

Another issue relates to disappointments in the family and crises in relationships. For some survivors, the search for validity and meaning has been a recurrent theme throughout the life cycle. They felt a commitment and even guilt for having survived when so many, whom they considered more worthy than themselves, had died. Their survival has thus always required validation and meaning, and children often represented to them the fulfillment of these needs. Therefore, disappointments with children often reduced the personal validity of the survivor's life as manifested in depressive self-accusations such as, "It would have been better if I had died in Auschwitz—I shouldn't have lived to rear children who are failures." Furthermore, disappointment may be deeply felt in relation to societal events of human tragedy and inhumanity in society, such as the Vietnamese boat people, to which survivors may be especially sensitive. Their hope and often strongly held beliefs that a new and better world would be created after World War II were not realized. On the contrary, they see repetition after repetition of the horrors of injustice and inhumanity. This existential dimension may be particularly felt at certain stages in their life cycles that coincide with disappointment and frustration in their personal lives.

The Majority of Survivors Did Not Become Patients

However, the vast majority of survivors did not become psychiatric patients and have shown remarkable capacities in overcoming the effect of the extreme experiences and multiple losses, creating new lives and healthy and successful families. Unfortunately, generalizations to the whole survivor population were made from those seen clinically, which did not do justice to the strength and complexity of the lives of survivors and their families. Research studies are needed that are concerned with understanding the processes and strengths within the survivor and in the environment that made for recovery, adaptation, and integration.

Those who were in their teens and early twenties at the end of the war seem to have been less adversely affected by the traumatization and have made the best recovery despite the fact that their adolescent years were spent in ghettos and concentration camps. Survivor syndrome symptoms were present to a much lesser extent and survivor guilt was often absent. It was much more possible for this age group to resume development, education, and occupational training. As a result, marriages that occurred years later were usually formed on a more solid basis than with many of the older survivors, who made hasty liaisons and gave birth to children very soon after liberation. The healthy new families they created have shown remarkable strength and resilience and the children are often very successful achievers.

Many survivors who were adolescents or young adults during the war still feel a need today to talk about their past, to return to and even to attempt a belated working through of their Holocaust experiences. Now middle-aged and older, they are confronted with a return of suppressed Holocaust memories as part of the normal process of reflection and review of past life at this stage in the life cycle.

In the early years after the war, the attempt to come to terms with concentration camp experiences and Holocaust losses would have been so painful that it was avoided and postponed until this later period in life, when the passage of time may have rendered the traumatic events more distant and less intolerably painful. Furthermore, until then the psychic energy of many survivors was largely mobilized to meet the demands of work and growing families, which provided purpose and meaning in their lives.

The need for validation of self by survivors was often postponed by them in the service of their efforts to appear appropriate and adequate, coping successfully just like others. As witnesses to the incomparable madness of man in the course of a period of horrendous genocide, some feared that if they remembered this past in later years they would appear abnormal, and so they avoided remembering and representing their past. Many survivors did not believe that there would be others, especially "significant others," who would be able to understand and accept what they had gone through. In some cases they were particularly concerned about how others would understand their history of moral compromise, including the way in which they had decided to go on living despite being forced to experience degradation and degrees of dehumanization that are virtually impossible to explain in the context of later human interactions when people are again people to one another. Many survivors feared that if they expressed their intense feelings of anger, guilt, shame, depression, and grief—all *negative feelings* in conventional social conceptions—they would be made to feel weird and different, and would be isolated by other people.

Survivors' ways of "coming to terms" with and "overcoming" Holocaust traumata are multiple and complex. Each phase of the life cycle presented new opportunities for dealing with the traumatic memories and losses, with great variations in individuals. Creative artistic expression (painting, sculpture, writing prose or poetry, etc.) and testifying and bearing witness at community groups, schools, and universities had been of considerable value for survivors in working through their experiences as well as constituting meaningful communication of real importance for the rest of society.

In a counseling service for survivors and their families that was a part of our Study Center for Holocaust and Psychosocial Trauma, under the auspices of Bar-Ilan University and the Shalvata Mental Health Center, we have provided a framework for those seeking to communicate their Holocaust experiences and express the hitherto unarticulated feelings of fear, guilt, shame, helplessness, anger, etc. Many who have turned to us have been "waiting" for forty years to deal with these memories. They wanted to speak but waited because they did not know how and with whom. This need often manifests itself in somatic symptoms or depressions triggered by stress in everyday life, especially stresses that arouse the traumatic memories. Physicians and other health-care professionals in all sections of the spectrum of medical and psychological and social services need to be aware of survivors' long-term need to relate to their suppressed agonizing experiences of the past.

Validation of the survivor is possible through a variety of situations, including peer support groups of fellow survivors, collective discourse in a society that is respectful of the survivors' experience, and of course personal relationships with one's most significant others. Survivors found with one another opportunities for consensual validation of their extreme feelings and thus were able to confirm for their own selves that they were not deviants, and indeed to give meaning to their roles as bearing witness to the Holocaust.

In peer support groups of fellow survivors, some Holocaust survivors were able to experience feelings of solidarity because they were able to share and compare emotional reactions with those who had similar experiences. These groups enabled them to overcome feelings of isolation of being unusual and unique, and also provided hope and meaning in looking toward a future as members of a collectivity. These special feelings of solidarity were originally experienced by many in the course of the actual traumatic experiences through friendships and groups in the ghettos and concentration camps, which played a central role in enabling the preservation of motivation to continue with the struggle to survive. For those who had been fortunate enough to experience life-sustaining connections with fellow victims during the Holocaust, renewed feelings of solidarity with other survivors in the years following the Holocaust had greater power to validate them in the continuation of their lives as meaningful.

There are any number of survivors who could not benefit from peer group experiences with their fellow survivors. Some would come away from experiences with other survivors feeling that much more deviant and depressed, and would need to renew their efforts to isolate themselves, block off their memories, and deny their connection to the perished at whatever terrible inner price.

The social context or collectivity in which the survivor continues life after the Holocaust represents a highly powerful significant other that can normalize and validate the survivor's experience, or contribute to his estrangement and isolation. There is no question that the society in Israel has proven far more healthy for survivors than any other in the intensity of their emotions of suffering. Ironically, as history provides repeated evidences of new dangers of victimization, and the realities of renewed genocides of peoples in the world confirms the reality of the almost unbelievable that took place in the Holocaust, a new level of confirmation of the survivor emerges.

In a group context, especially one that is devoted to tasks of learning about the Holocaust, the survivor is able to feel the largest degree of consensual validation because of the sense he gets not only of bearing witness to his contemporaries but of *transmitting* to future generations the knowledge of what happened and can happen. In my experience of several years of teaching the Holocaust experience and its significance to university students, the effect on survivors of the empathy they feel from young people is particularly illuminating and heartwarming. Both parties feel changed by the experience and each feels gratitude for it.

The individual experience does not end with the survivor himself—studies of the impact of the Holocaust on the second and third generations and the possible transmission of the effects in the families of survivors are ongoing. In survivor family studies we have often found a characteristic family atmosphere and pattern of parent-child interaction. On liberation from the camps, many women believed that they had been damaged genetically, and that they were physically and psychologically unable to bear and rear normal children. In parent-child interactions, overanxiety, overprotection, and intense emotional investment, idealization, and overidentification with one or more of the children occurred frequently. Children were identified with murdered siblings or parents as if they were a symbolic reincarnation. Many survivors have brought up healthy, well-functioning children, but in the families of many other survivors, children have suffered from fears, depressions, and interpersonal difficulties that mirrored similar manifestations in their parents, and we have seen reenactments of the parents' persecutory experiences in their children. Problems with regard to separation from parents and the struggle for autonomy and identity have been encountered frequently in adolescents.

For the majority of survivors and their children, there is much evidence to suggest that Israel has had a special meaning. In Israel, social recognition and meaning was given to their persecutory experiences and losses. In the "rebirth" of the Jewish people in a national homeland, Holocaust survivors found hope of their own "rebirth," thus encountering their identity impairment. In

Israel's fight for survival, they found a common theme with their own struggle to survive and constructive channels for expression of their blocked aggressions and mourning. The availability of new, active patterns and models for identity modified the influence of the parents' impaired identity on the second generation. In many ways, Israel has served as a gigantic rehabilitation project for a traumatized people and has provided them and their families with a positive sense of identity not found in other countries where survivors settled.

4.

Surviving during the Holocaust and Afterwards: The Post-Liberation Experience

When the Dreadful has already happened, we can hardly expect other than that the thing will echo externally the destruction already wrought internally.
—R. D. Laing, *The Politics of Experience*

The survivor syndrome can be formulated as an adaptation syndrome to the Holocaust situation that continues into the post-Holocaust life of the survivor in his attempts to integrate the traumatic past into coping with the realities of present-day society. For the survivor, the worst possible fears of being human have been realized; thereafter, he is condemned for the rest of his life to live with the dreadful and the impossible.

Terror and anguish about murdered family and friends and the destruction of one's entire familiar world is actualized in nightmares, guilt feelings and psychosomatic symptoms, aggressive feelings toward oneself and the world, and repetitious acts in which the survivor is aggressor as well as victim. In contrast, triumph over death is expressed in positive acceptance of motherhood, fatherhood, work, new relations, and the joys of life. The paradox or true challenge of survival, after the Holocaust, is in accepting the challenge to remain alive while still being transfixed in the encounter with death. Emotional survival of the Holocaust is in its own right a transcendence of death successfully achieved.

Lifton has dealt extensively with the phenomenon of the "death imprint" as seen in the survivors of Hiroshima and also in the

Nazi concentration camp victims.[1] He calls this imprint of death the key to the survivor experience. It seems to me that for Holocaust survivors, more than fear of death, the situation of overwhelming helplessness and powerlessness in life was the central destructive experience. In many it led to complete surrender, "giving up" and "giving in" that ended in death soon after arrival in the concentration camp or after some time in a "Musselman stage," with the exhaustion of the victim's emotional and physical resources.

A decision to go on trying to remain alive had to be made by each and every survivor. This issue arose many times in the everyday life of the survivor, and following the Holocaust it arises again. It is an issue that has to be dealt with in psychotherapy with survivors. In the fact of their survival survivors represent a coming back to life emotionally and spiritually, a unique test of the universal choice between life and death that all people must make in their lives.[2] In the Holocaust this choice had to be made in opposition to the obvious intentions of the perpetrators. It was a conscious and continuous choice that emphasized existential freedom as a reality even in the inferno of the Nazi concentration camps. The survivors who decided to live in the camps represent the ultimate triumph over death. This inner psychic choice was often connected with and made the more possible by empathy, relationships, and friendships in the social bonding and group situations that existed in the ghettos and concentration camps.

There were many survivors who did not decide to live, but also did not succumb to death. They blotted out experience and existed in a kind of hibernation. As such they were in sight of and closer to giving up than those who did will themselves to live, but they were still, cleverly, far from surrender. The meanings of life and death in the camps were unique.

The low suicide rate in the concentration camps can be explained by the fact that if somebody had no desire to continue to live, no suicidal action was required—the victim just had to give up the terrible struggle for life, the struggle to do everything possible to obtain food and keep up his morale, and death would then come by itself. Furthermore, as Lifton puts it, "The active suicidal attempt can, in fact, represent a desperate effort to emerge from psychic numbing to overcome inactivation by the act of killing oneself." It is a gesture of defiance and condemnation, the manifestation of one's last shred of freedom and autonomy and an act of affirmation of life.

Determinants of Pathology and Nonpathology

With the passage of years in my followup of clinical groups and studies of nonclinical survivors, I have been able to see how the events of the life cycle before, during, and after the Holocaust experience have modified the different clinical pictures and influenced the course of survivors' lives after the liberation.

Many factors were involved that interacted with each other in determining the long-term effects of the Holocaust trauma in the life cycle of the survivors. Here are the main ones I would document:

1. previous (pre-Holocaust) personality, dependency, depressive tendency;
2. the specific Holocaust experiences and the modalities of survival;
3. age of the survivor in the Holocaust;
4. family structure before the war;
5. physical illness. (In the concentration camps and ghettos, physical illness often resulted in the victim's isolation and intensification of his confrontation with death. People would see their emaciated bodies as being close to corpselike or skeletonlike states. In addition, physical illnesses were always associated with the possibility of immediate selection for killing in the gas chambers. The body image was often permanently impaired as a result of these experiences in the camp or at liberation, and these survivors were more prone to develop late survivor syndrome symptomatology.);
6. post-liberation experiences;
7. post-Holocaust family, including the choice of marital partner. (When losses were unusually massive in terms of family, nuclear and extended, and friends and community, there tended to be a greater severity of depression.)

The groups described above were defined from the viewpoint of my clinical experience with a focus on psychopathology. In the ensuing years, as a result of longitudinal and followup studies and especially my encounters with nonclinical groups of survivors, I have expanded and developed my original clinical approach in terms of a broader existential concept of how people adapt after massive trauma. I have become increasingly aware that schematic clinical categories do not allow for understanding the normal spectrum of life functioning of survivors who do not present themselves as patients.

People have different kinds of adaptive styles to past and present events. Some use their Holocaust experiences in a way that incapacitates them, and others are able to use their Holocaust experiences in a way that even enriches their human functioning as individuals, in family life, and in the society in which they have chosen to live.

The question arises of what meaning or significance the survivor syndrome has today. The survivor syndrome as a clinical diagnosis was derived from medical psychiatric concepts that push toward schematic unifications of observed symptoms and attempt to give them meaning in a clinical sense by reduction to a common denominator. These schematic medical classifications, based on familiar psychiatric symptomatology, render the survivor acceptable in terms of concepts of specific medical damage or disability, that is, invalidism deserving of our compassion, therapy, or material compensation. But this is also one of the ways used by our society in order to avoid a real coming to grips with the existential significance of the survivor and of society's responsibility for the Holocaust.

The Survivor's Previous or Pre-Holocaust Personality

In discussing the outcome of the individual survivor, I believe that we need to take into account the vicissitudes of his previous or pre-Holocaust internalized world and life history.

There exists much controversy around this issue. Most clinical authors consider that the preexisting personality was an insignificant factor in the face of the massive trauma of the Holocaust, which overwhelmed all defenses. This approach was also encouraged by the German indemnification laws, which demanded that the survivor suffer from overt psychopathology in order to justify his claim for reparation.

Nonetheless, it seems to me that the personality and the dynamic conflicts before and at the onset of the Holocaust were undoubtedly an important factor in relation to the outcome of

Holocaust trauma. The great variety of responses seen in survivors is unquestionably related to the personality variables of the victims. With adolescents, for example, the resolution of the developmental crisis had an influence on the style of adaptation during the Holocaust and on the quality of reintegration after liberation.

Individuals who had passive personality features were inclined to accept a fatalistic enigmatic sense of the persecutory experiences more easily than those who had a basic need for mastery and activity. Which style was to prove more effective for survival varied with conditions that were beyond the choosing of the survivor. In some phases of the Holocaust, activity and mastery were very important in the service of survival, such as in a capacity to run away suddenly, but in others passivity, clinging, and deindividuation allowed survivors to become an anonymous part of the crowd and to merge and regress in the service of survival. Although activity helped in many cases, in others it resulted in immediate death of the survivor and his family, sometimes preceded by unimaginable tortures.

The Specific Holocaust Experiences. The concept of the Holocaust is a holistic one that does not take into account the vast spectrum of different experiences undergone by different individuals. *Holocaust* refers to the common denominator of persecution of the individual as part of a group designated for extermination —every individual man, woman, and child, and also every family and every community—as the fulfillment of bestial Nazi ideology, but this does not mean that all survivors experienced the same suffering.

We have to be aware that the different vicissitudes of individual experience in ghetto, hiding, flight from place to place, living under a false identity, forced labor, concentration camp, or extermination camp demanded different specific personality defenses that revealed themselves during and after the end of the persecution. It is a constant finding in all studies of man facing extreme conditions of inhumanity and degradation that regression of the personality inevitably occurs. This regression is in the service of psychological and physical survival, and even states of severe regression can be partially or completely reversible if they have not progressed to the stuporous "Musselman" state that was usually followed by death.

In the destructive milieu of the concentration camp and ghetto hunger, there was a cumulative process of dehumanization and degradation and a constant fear of one's death by murder and the destruction of one's family and community. However, in the Holocaust human relationships of mutual aid and cohesiveness were often still possible, even in extreme conditions including the presence of starvation. Perhaps the fact of a common murderous enemy in contradistinction to natural catastrophes arouses such cohesiveness as well as resistance, however humble and unseen, especially when there are shared values and a common ethic. A moving example was a group of doctors in the Warsaw Ghetto who meticulously observed the starvation process in themselves.

The extremity of the conditions in the camps as well as in the ghettos fluctuated from time to time in relation to various factors such as (1) personality of the *kapo*, (2) dyadic or group belonging, (3) specific work conditions, and (4) physical state.

The *kapo* was a mediator between the victim and the perpetrators and much of the fate of individuals was dependent on the benignity or malevolence of his intentions. In spite of the rigidity of his role and function, many *kapos* saved their comrades by influencing the SS men and preserving and encouraging group solidarity. On the other hand, some *kapos* behaved to their fellow victims solely in terms of increasing their own chances of survival, which meant readiness to exploit and to sacrifice the other inmates without hesitation, including active participation in cruel beatings and tortures in order to impress the SS. Their rationalization was that the victim was not pulling his weight at work and thus the lives of all the others, including his own, were endangered. Sometimes a deteriorating situation was temporarily improved for the individual or group by a change of the *kapo* or a new work situation, a chance meeting with a helpful person or transfer to another camp.

In the early stages of regression, with the beginning of the apathy and withdrawal of the "Musselman" state, the regressive process could still be held in check and could be reversed by a supportive group situation. In the fully developed regressive, semistuporous "Musselman" state, these changes in external conditions could hardly reverse the inevitable process towards death. However, sometimes long-standing regression with withdrawal to very constricted relations with other inmates could have positive value in the service of survival as long as the physical state was not too depleted.

In general, the longer the period of massive traumatization, the more likely were exhaustion and death to ensue, with irreversible psychic damage in those few who survived. But we know also that some groups of people exposed for only brief periods to conditions of massive trauma rapidly became "Musselmen" and died in large numbers. Those who survived from such groups suffered from severe psychiatric sequelae for the rest of their lives because of the irreversible psychobiological damage. This occurred among Jews from stable and protected psychosocial conditions (e.g., Holland and Hungary) who were exposed abruptly to the concentration camp world without previous phases of severe persecution gradually allowing some degree of preparation and resistance to develop, such as occurred among the Polish Jews who spent long periods of persecution in ghettos before their transportation to the concentration camps. Sudden isolation from stable and secure social environments, especially of assimilated groups of Jews, was conducive to rapid exhaustion of psychic and physical resources and musselmanization.

Living under a False Identity during the Holocaust. This mode of survival was possible for some Jews in Europe who managed to conceal their Jewish origins and to live with forged papers as Aryans—the only category of humanity permitted life, according to Nazi ideology. This involved the ability to cut off from all other Jews in an entirely alien environment. A non-Jewish physiognomy was essential and entailed the conscious deliberate acquisition of appropriate gestures and movements, changing the intonations of the voice, etc. In short, an entirely false presentation of the self to the outer world had to be developed. The learning of Christian liturgy, rituals, and catechism was often an essential requirement in Catholic countries such as Poland, Hungary, France, etc. The local population was often as hostile and anti-Semitic as the Nazis themselves, and as a result the acquisition of an unquestionable non-Jewish identity and behavior became a precondition of existence. Sometimes these new identities could not be easily shed off after the war and became a source of much conflict for the individuals involved and for their families, especially if they were children or adolescents during the Holocaust and the natural parent or parents remained alive.

Some of those who survived in this way decided to permanently remain as Aryans and never again to return to their former Jewish identity or to have contact with anything Jewish. In some extreme cases this even involved a revulsion and hostile suspiciousness toward Jews and the concerns of the Jewish people, such as Israel.

Very few who tried to achieve "Aryan identity" accepted the Christian religion and its values. The hundreds of people who went through formal conversion to Catholicism didn't go through a spiritual conversion. It seemed for them a cynical irony to be embraced by a religion of love that preached centuries of hatred to the Jews in the name of one of them (Jesus). Only a few cases, one of them a cause célèbre, Father Daniel, who became a monk in the Carmelite Monastery on Mt. Carmel, Haifa, and is today a professor of philosophy at Hebrew University, went through a spiritual conversion connected with a transformation of his former identity while hidden in the monastery of Beil in Cracow.

Children who were forced to reject their parents' identity were confronted with tremendous psychic difficulties after the liberation, trying to achieve the old-new identity again. Eventually, for most of them, with the passage of years their former existence disappeared and a new one began, but there are also no few cases where the disruption of the emotional bonding to their parents left damages to the ability to love that could never heal. There are also cases of children who became genuinely attached to Christians who took them in, and then were traumatized by the need to separate from their surrogate parents, in some cases again at the expense of their ability to love and to trust continuity in subsequent years.

Here are three different clinical examples of teenagers in the Holocaust who survived under a false Christian identity and what their postwar style of adjustment has been:

> He had been a 16-year-old adolescent from an assimilated Jewish family that was closely identified with the Polish national identity. His father had been an officer in the Polish army, and he was very proud of him. During the Holocaust he succeeded in escaping from the ghetto after his parents had been sent to an extermination camp, where his father died and from which his mother and sister were sent to other concentration camps. He succeeded in living under Aryan identity with forged papers in a small Polish town where he invested his musical talents in becoming the local church organist, a pillar of the Christian community for four years.

After the war he decided to continue in his non-Jewish identity and persuaded his mother and sister after their liberation from concentration camps to live as non-Jews. However, he then married a Jewish girl who had been liberated from the concentration camps and was from an orthodox Jewish background, who had been his girlfriend before the war. Now he persuaded her also to drop her Jewish identity and in the 1950s they emigrated to the U.S., where he became a successful professional. He has lived in the U.S. ever since with no contact with Judaism whatsoever, and he is an active member of the local church.

Jewishness for these survivors became identified exclusively with danger, death, and Holocaust, and they decided to bring up their children with no knowledge of their Jewish origin. No book or written material dealing with the Jews or the Holocaust was permitted in the house. TV and radio programs on these subjects were also taboo. The atmosphere in the house was distinctly Polish Christian, U.S. style.

When their son became sixteen years old, the age at which the father escaped from the ghetto, the son developed an acute anxiety state with fears of ghosts and darkness, and as a result the family came into therapy. During the course of therapy it became obvious that the shameful and fearful family secret connected with the ghosts of the Holocaust had manifested itself in this family through the transmission of the parents' buried fears to their son. The father was suspicious, emotionally restricted, reserved. In effect, he had continued throughout his whole life to maintain the patterns adopted for survival during the Holocaust.

In the therapeutic situation, the father expressed many feelings of aggression. His hostility was projected onto Jewishness, which was made responsible for the suffering, killing, and destruction. In this way, he thought he had found the solution of avoiding such a fate for himself and his family. We also discovered a concealed motivation for his professional choice of surgeon: he wanted to be a savior of lives after he had failed to do so during the Holocaust and then had suppressed the inevitably associated guilt feelings for same.

Moshe is a sixteen-year-old adolescent from a traditional shtetl background. After the destruction of the shtetl and the murder of most of the Jews there, including his parents and three sisters, he and a younger sister succeeded in escaping and lived under false Aryan papers for three years in a Polish town. Throughout this period he was very active in helping other Jews despite the danger involved for himself. He had many narrow escapes when forced by Polish hooligans ("Shmalovnicks") to reveal his Jewish identity—by having to show his circumcised penis.

In 1944 he escaped through Slovakia and Hungary to Palestine, where he immediately returned to his previous traditionally Jewish way of life. He married an Israeli girl and adopted a very patriotic and politically chauvinistic position, created a religious home, and was active in the synagogue. He pursued a successful army career with enthusiastic participation in all of Israel's wars, feeling that he was filling a role of saving and defending against total destruction, "to defend that which I was unable to in the Holocaust." Although no overt psychopathology is evident and he is a congenial and warm person always ready to share and to help others, his Holocaust experiences have had their effect in his suspiciousness and rigid adherence to chauvinistic political loyalties.

Sara lived in Eastern Europe and was fifteen when the Russians entered the war. She was an only daughter. Her family was middle class, cohesive, cultured, with musical and literary interests. Thousands of refugees fled from German-occupied Poland to her town, but she avoided contact with them because it was too painful. She continued to busy herself with music, sport, and social life until the German occupation, when she was age sixteen. The Ukrainians and Poles started pogroms and her parents were removed to Yanowska camp. Prior to their transportation, they gave her false Aryan papers and instructions. She escaped Warsaw, and lived under false identity as a factory worker in Germany. During the Holocaust she resolved that she would never relate to or marry a Jew who had been through the degradations and humiliations, and she scorned the "galut mentality" of the survivor, which for her meant surrender and nonresistance.

After the war, Sara wanted to return to Poland to rebuild Poland but instead went to Germany, where she studied at a university, and then to Israel, where in the War of Independence she became a member of the crack Palmach force. She completely assimilated to her new Israeli Hebrew identity. Proud, ambitious, and hiding her feelings, she chose the slogan, "If I am not for myself, who will be for me." She maintained an external facade of good humor, kept smiling, and hid her emotions even in adversity and life crises. Like many of those who survived under a false identity during the Holocaust with the danger of being discovered, she always kept control and never let herself go. She became a well-adapted professional with a very responsible job, married an Israeli, and had two daughters, one of whom is an architect. The family style is built on pragmatism, with an avoidance of any emotional expression apart from keeping on smiling. She cannot express gratitude but has always to say thanks.

Survival through Hiding. Those Jews who survived the Holocaust by hiding constitute a very heterogeneous group. They experienced the most diverse situations. There were those who lived in the constant terror and inhuman conditions of perpetual flight through forests and hostile villages in Poland and the Ukraine, and there were families like that of Anne Frank, who lived together hidden by non-Jewish friends in their attics for long periods. The "Righteous Gentiles" who risked their own and their families' lives in order to save Jews by hiding them out of purely ethical or ideological motivations were few in number. A unique example of such an act of heroism on a large scale, of good in the face of evil and readiness for self-sacrifice, was seen in the population of the little French village of Le Chamban-sur-Lignon. Unfortunately, this was a rare and isolated example. Throughout the villages and towns of Nazi-occupied Christian Europe, the population did not share in the moral imperative of the dictum carved on the lintel of the Protestant church in the village of Le Chambon —"Love One Another."

The family who hid Jews was usually in opposition to and isolation from the community influenced by the Nazi anti-Semitic propaganda. The interaction between host and the hidden was complex, ambivalent, and fluctuating according to the external conditions. In Eastern Europe, in contradistinction to Western Europe, the agreement to hide Jews was often entirely based on a financial transaction, and with the passage of time extremely ambivalent feelings, including dependence and suspicion, were often manifested in both parties to the transaction.

If a group of Jews were in hiding together, then communication between them, the sharing of fears and doubts as well as hopes and celebrations, was possible, and the survivors were less traumatized.

The interactions within the group, the dyadic/tryadic relationships, resulted in tensions and antagonisms as well as friendships. The atmosphere was very intense because of the limited physical living space and the constant danger of death. Sometimes the physical confinement was extreme when people were forced to hide for long periods in bunkers, cellars, or, literally, holes in the ground.

Individuals in hiding were often completely isolated, felt helpless, and as a result tended to become extremely dependent on the host. The extreme loneliness experienced by many in hiding became especially excruciating when their hosts gloatingly expressed hostile sentiments based on anti-Semitic hatred. Longings to return to the ghetto with the closeness of bonds despite the dangers became overwhelming.

People living under false Aryan identity experienced similar feelings when hearing the expression of such sentiments toward Jews. The lack of any possibility of communication with the outside world sometimes created a situation similar to that of sensory deprivation, with disorientation in time and loss of identity, and even delusional thinking. As a result, many individuals eventually found the hiding situation insufferable and preferred to give themselves up to the ghetto or concentration camp despite almost inevitable death. They chose any situation in which there was some human contact and warmth with the sharing of common feelings and some feeling of mastery over one's body, however minimal.

Bluma was the second of three daughters from a middle-class traditional shtetl family. She was an adolescent when the Germans occupied. After systematic mass execution of Jews in the area, she managed to survive by building a bunker together with four other family members, which they entered on leaving the ghetto a few hours before the final liquidation. After a few weeks they all had to flee into the forests, pursued by the local Ukrainians and SS. They hid in the winter in severe frost conditions in caves. Eventually the father was killed when leaving the forest to find food in a neighboring village. Bluma then took over the leadership of the family group in the forest. They built another bunker. They had to hide and run for their lives all the time, digging and hiding themselves in bunkers.

In one episode she was left alone with her nine-year-old cousin. When a wild boar roamed into their hiding place, the child was terrified and started screaming hysterically. Sara, fearing that their hiding place would be discovered by the Ukrainians and Germans who were close by, hit the child and threatened that she would strangle her if she would not stop screaming.

After the war she married a concentration camp survivor, a rather passive-dependent, depressive personality. She has continued to function until now as a very capable, overactive, energetic person. In her relationships, she is overprotective, authoritarian, always the savior, giving the impression of alertness to danger, helping the other members of the family as her father had. Her only child is a 25–year-old daughter, overdependent on her mother and reluctant to leave her mother, showing anxiety about coping with independent life despite successful professional functioning.

The Younger Survivor. In my clinical experience, the generalization can be made that the younger the exposure to massive traumatization, especially if accompanied by the loss of key family figures, the more the personality development was disturbed, and the more difficulty was experienced in interpersonal relationships and in finding satisfaction and meaning in life later in the life cycle.

This generalization applies to survivors who were prepubertal children during the Holocaust. Tragically, few survivors who were infants and children survived. Those who did were hidden under the most diverse conditions by their parents and others. Sometimes a child was lucky enough to be under the protection of and in contact with an adult who was well disposed and acted as a "good enough parent" figure with whom a relationship of basic trust existed so that emotionally positive experiences could occur, permitting later healthy personality development. Many, in order to escape detection by the Nazis, which would have meant instant death, were hidden in situations of isolation. Isolation in hiding meant, in addition to constant fear, a lack of emotional support, a lack of meaningful human transactions in a framework of trust, and a lack of the possibility of identification with others. Furthermore, those in hiding lacked the possibility to be in direct free contact with nature. In addition, many children were impaired in their motor development because of actual limited possibility of movement in the cramped living conditions. Many of these children later developed claustrophobic symptoms and could be relaxed and free only in open spaces, feeling constricted and anxious in closed rooms and in work situations with rigid boundaries.

The classic work of John Bowlby (separation and attachment) and Rene Spitz (hospitalism) on children separated during the first two years of life from their mothers with no surrogate figure demonstrated the resulting reactions of grief and mourning and the permanent impairment of emotional and personality development.

Anna Freud and Sophie Dann studied a group of six children, aged three and four, whose parents soon after their birth were killed by the Nazis.[3] They were found in the Theresienstadt concentration camp at the end of the war, in a ward where they had been looked after by adult camp inmates for about three years, since their arrival at age six to twelve months. They were brought to England in August 1945, and a special nursery was set up for these six children where they were brought up as a group for a period of one year. They clung to each other and showed an intense sense of belonging to the closely knit group, with a striking awareness of each other's sensitivities and feelings. Their unusually strong group identification and the warmth and spontaneity of friendship they showed toward each other went far beyond ordinary sibling bonds and were considered to be a reaction to and a protection against the effects of the total lack in their lives of the experience of having parents or a family structure. They were described as being hypersensitive, restless, aggressive, and difficult to handle the first year after their arrival in England, but the group bonding had enabled them to master some of their anxieties and develop social attitudes and they were able to learn a new language without undue difficulty.

Survivors who were prepubertal children aged five to twelve during the Holocaust and thus had experienced parental upbringing in a family structure during the first five to seven years of life tend to suffer throughout their lives from emotional instability and anxiety that may be phobic in closed-in situations such as cinemas, meeting halls, etc. They experience considerable difficulties in interpersonal relationships because of their demanding, clinging dependence, are easily disappointed, and feel rejected. They may never have achieved a stable relationship. As a result many suffer from chronic bitter, depressive states.

It became clear to me in my clinical experience with such age groups that the first impact of experiencing the helplessness of their parents in the presence of the perpetrators undermined their basic trust and belief in the omnipotence of the parent and in his ability to save them from pain and destruction. Furthermore, they manifested feelings of chronic anger at parents for this helplessness, as well as self-destructive tendencies that could be understood as aggression toward the internalized image of the parent who abandoned them to terror. The loss of basic trust and security resulted in deep confusions about needs to receive and to give. Their eternal unsatisfiable search for nurturing comes to expression in their relationships with their own children, with direct and indirect wishes to be nurtured by them, and dissatisfaction with their own parenting roles. We often see in these families manipulation of the children into a reversal of the parent-child roles.

In addition, the witnessing of the brutal traumatic death of parents or other adults by young children, as so often happened in the Holocaust, can predispose them to difficulty throughout the life cycle in controlling the excitation of impulses connected with aggressive acts, and also in the anticipation of their aggression toward others. This could result in rage and violent behavior or acute anxiety when encountering stimuli associated with violence and death.

I have seen some survivors react with inappropriate outbursts of rage at their children and spouses and authority figures (such as doctors) who have acquired a special significance as omnipotent parent figures fused with components of the aggressor–SS-man–murderer. Some of these rage outbursts have terminated in delusional acts of paranoiac dimensions—with physical assault. In one extreme case, the situation ended tragically in murder of the spouse accompanied by mental associations to Hitler and

Mengele, who acquired the mystical dimensions of demons who must be destroyed in revenge for the horror and humiliation perpetrated in childhood on the survivors and their families.

The Adolescent Survivor. A large part of the survivor population were adolescents during the Holocaust. They were in the different developmental phases of adolescence—early adolescence, middle adolescence, or adolescence proper, or in late adolescence and in transition to adult life. In spite of different psychosocial backgrounds and individual differences, a common feature was the intensive involvement with ideological issues—from assimilation and complete estrangement from Judaism through intense striving and longing for Jewish and personal identity, and in the belonging of most of the Jewish youth to the contemporary youth movements of all sectors and ideologies. Many of the youth movements were based on the Wandervogel movement in Germany of the 1920s, with its emphasis on the romantic approach to life and idealization of nature. Intrinsic in the Jewish youth movements was a rejection of the old patterns of life of the Jewish communities in the shtetls and towns of Europe, and a longing for a future free of the grinding poverty and struggle against then rigid psychosocial structures. The success of this movement among all sections of the youth was also connected with the discovery of physical and psychic resources. Furthermore, the group affiliations enabled catharsis of the age-oriented conflicts of adolescence and created a framework for intersexual experiences, for protest against the parental home, and for trials of autonomy and identity.

At the beginning of the Holocaust these movements tried to carry on after the initial shock, but the continuous and repetitive deportations destroyed their psychosocial structure and decimated them and their leadership until only some nuclei remained in the ghettos. These became foci of resistance for ghetto uprisings such as in Warsaw, Cracow, Vilna, Bialystock, and Kovno.

However, in the ghettos the main emphasis of the survival struggle was on mutual aid, saving activities, and the attempt to establish communication with the silent, hostile, alien outside world. Youth were in a basic conflict between their solidarity to their families—the desire to save them and to remain with them despite the knowledge that their chances for survival were all the time diminishing—and their awareness that staying with the family was alien to their adolescent system of values, which called for activity and active resistance.

In my longitudinal life cycle studies, I have found considerable difference in the modes of survival and life style and ego adaptation in relation to the age of the survivor at the outset of the Holocaust. The self-conception and self-realization in the gradual return to normal life varied greatly among the different age groups.

The physical and psychological stamina of youths made them particularly suitable for the German slave labor camps and enabled them to have a greater capacity to survive. The group phenomenon that was a major factor in survival in the camps was particularly evident in this age group, where peer group bonding is normally so central.

The adult life of many of these adolescents commenced after the Holocaust after they had lost the rich, elaborate communal, ideological, traditional, and religious frameworks in which they had grown up as children in the very cohesive Jewish communities that existed in the towns and villages. The Holocaust motif can be traced in their later development as young adults facing the dissolution of the external familiar world and the loss of family and community models for identification. Instead of the normal developmental involvement with clear goals of adolescence (autonomy, mastery, and identity), they found themselves in an unreal chaotic world. This situation led in the displaced persons camps after the war to various primitive behavior patterns, patterns with no real goal orientation and manic defenses against the losses and bereavement. Phenomena of psychic numbness, withdrawal, drifting in a pleasurable passivity from one day to the next, luxuriating in eating, sexual acting out, and sleeping were all observed. The emotional life of many of them was constricted to the needs for food, sexual acting out, and material satisfactions. Some engaged in grotesque hoarding of foods; others were involved in dubious business activities and other excessive, narcissistic self-indulgences. Serious interests such as studies were avoided because of difficulty in concentration and a lack of connection with the outer world.

The lack of structure in the D.P. camp society as well as in the early settlements of Jews in the German towns encouraged acting-out tendencies of a sexual and aggressive nature related to the adolescence that had been missed, with extreme polarization of instinctual and interpersonal life. This complex emotional existential situation of the young survivor expressed itself in various patterns of behavior. Survivors differentiated into characteristic roles and styles, for example, the provider, the passive-dependent victim and welfare client, the naive adolescent craving for culture and emotional warmth, the cynical, materialistic, power-driven opportunist, and the compulsively sexual person who was promiscuous with German girls—among other things in connection with his revenge fantasies.

Intense group living, often as in extended families, prevailed in the D.P. camps and reinforced these regressive tendencies. Unfortunately, there were many survivors who had to remain in Europe, and who were exposed to and influenced by the chaotic situation of postwar Germany and the complex psychosocial situation involved in continuing to live in the world with yesterday's perpetrators, whom they feared, hated, and despised. On the other hand, groups and individuals who were fortunate enough to be adopted by the Jewish communities in the U.S., Britain, Canada, and Palestine avoided or moved out of the D.P. camp experience and had the opportunity for a formative framework and a "good enough" environment (as in the ego psychology concept), which played an important part in enabling the possible establishment of a new identity.

The looseness of structure in the D.P. camps also allowed for a wide range of positive individual initiative and trials at achieving autonomy in constructive activity. In the more healthy and active adolescents, living without family structure and parental models allowed for a diverse experimentation of roles. Within the D.P. camps there were many diverse attempts at organizing social life into different political groups centered around Zionist ideology or religious organization. Schools were established, mostly with instructors from among the survivors as well as from the Yishuv (Jewish community) in Palestine, and Jewish committees were set up in the German towns to organize social and religious life and allocate material help.

An outstanding manifestation was the need for pairing dyadic relationships, which was also a continuation of the pairing that had been so important in the concentration camps. This pairing was often expressed in early impulsive marriages connected with the desire to reconstruct the lost family, a flight from loneliness, as well as, on a psychodynamic level, an inability to mourn the losses of many loved ones.

One can see in many cases the leitmotif of Orpheus who wishes to bring to life Eurydice from the Kingdom of Death in the concentration camps. They fell in love in the pale of the infernos of ghettos and concentration camps and married soon after liberation, only to lose their partners later to a realm of emptiness. The awakening from the dreamlike hell brought with it illusions of a heavenly future, but then the return to normal everyday life brought the inevitable disillusionment and deidealization. There were tragic instances of projection of the internalized bad object of the Nazi perpetrator onto the spouse, who was experienced as a *kapo*, a Nazi, or even Hitler. Later on, this same process of projection took the form of relating to some of the children who were born to these marriages as if they were "Nazis."

Many of the survivors suffered a vacuum of the loss of religious belief, which was sometimes filled by empty ritualistic practices rather than morality. Emptied of the God who had failed them, many of the survivors were left with lacunae in their superego personality structure. This void was filled by ideological strivings. At this period in history the need for ideology coincided with the struggle for an independent Jewish state as a legitimate expression of autonomy, fight, and aggression against mankind, which had been silent. The battle for Israel connected with magic fantasies of restitution and restoration of that which could never be restored—family and community. The need for ideology as a cohesive libidnal force was connected with a fantasied mother-and-fatherland that would permit revenge and triumph over the evil and hostile world. Zionism meant "to build and be rebuilt." The rebirth fantasy of an idealized, extended family of the Jewish people was expressed in the song of a Cracow poet who perished in the Holocaust: "Our poor little shtetl is burning with folded arms; do something to save and rebuild the destroyed shtetl." It came true now in this posthumous act of rebuilding their destroyed communities and shtetls in the reborn homeland of Israel.

The Zionist ideology and the longing to go to Palestine was widespread among the adolescent and young adult survivors as an expression of fidelity to their family and people, as a reaching back into the destroyed pre-Holocaust life and its family and community ethos, as a means of realizing themselves as human beings again, as a transcendental triumph after years of struggle for physical survival. Palestine represented the old-new symbolic homeland Zion in the midst of the disappointing emptiness of the postwar reality in Europe around them. It was an expression of the overcoming of death and their uprooted existence and an attempt at renewed human spirituality.

In their pioneering zeal to contribute to building the Zionist homeland for "the rebirth of the Jewish people," many of the young survivors also felt the associated urge for revenge. "I wanted to take a gun and to defend myself." To possess a gun was longed for by so many in the wake of murder and humiliation. During the Holocaust one of the motivations for survival was coming to life again in Zion. The fighters of the Warsaw, Bialystock, Bendzin, Cracow, and Vilna ghettos saw beckoning them the Promised Land. Revenge was dreamt of again and again and fantasied in all stages of the Holocaust. It was expressed in some poems—"The day of revenge will come" ("Es will kummon der tog fun nekama")— and in partisan songs ("Don't think that you are going on your last way"). The fantasy of revenge was an existential leitmotif aiding in survival, but however vivid it was in imagery, it was rarely manifested in action. Despite their hatred, few survivors took advantage of the helplessness of the Nazi criminals after the liberation. They had the feeling that in the destroyed cities of Germany revenge had been meted out and further revenge "would only dirty their hands." They wished to leave the burnt-out cemetery of Europe to go back to an unsullied old-new homeland for their own rebirth in identification with and on behalf of their lost brothers and sisters. This was in itself an act of revenge and at the same time a triumph over Hitler's image of the Jews and the fate he planned for them in the "Final Solution." The country of pioneers, with its collective settlements and its myths of fight against the desert and malaria, coincided with fantasies of their own rebirth and restoration in joy and love. "The eternity of the Jewish people will not be denied" ("Netzach Yisrael lo yeshaker") became a popular slogan in the D.P. camps.

After the liberation, demands and expectations for restoration and restitution from the outside world reached unrealistic proportions. This resulted frequently in conflicts with the allied military administration, UNRRA and Joint Distribution Committee and, inevitably, deep disappointment at the relative indifference of the various authorities and rescue organizations. Many survivors were sole representatives who remained from destroyed communities and large families and had expectations of being compensated for all that was lost, human and material. This expectation of restitution reached almost magic proportions, for instance when it was applied to physically disabled survivors who aspired to a complete renewal of their physical constitution, bodies, and organs and not just improvement in their health. They attempted to deny and erase all traces of injuries and illnesses perpetrated on them.

They longed for magic restitution of their bodies to consummate pre-Holocaust body images of healthy adolescence. They were unable to accept that their physical constitutions were impaired and that they could no longer achieve the lost body images of adolescence. For many of these survivors, their magical need for restoration was to manifest itself in future years in chronic hypochondriacal symptoms.

Compensation for Psychopathology. In my opinion, generalizations based on statistics of morbidity among survivors who were psychiatric inpatients and on results of compensation examinations are not relevant to an understanding of the complexity of the life of survivors who were adolescents in the Holocaust. Focusing exclusively on disturbances and clinical findings is a means of avoiding the complexity of human functioning, which morbidity statistics can never give. Derived psychopathological and psychiatric concepts are not only distorting, but enable a new mythos of mental illness and disturbances in the survivors to be created. The motivation of many papers and reports that studied psychopathology in survivors was undoubtedly a positive one designed to facilitate the survivors' indemnification claims. However, they are based on false premises.

In my opinion, acceptance of the German restitution laws, which were based on accepted medical and psychiatric illness categories, in order to receive indemnification was amoral and amounted to a post facto recognition of Nazi policy of physical and psychological destruction of the Jews. *It seems to me that there is a right to indemnification of every Holocaust victim for all his losses and that indemnification should not be based on proving mental damages. In many ways the German restitution laws have forced the survivor to emphasize his disabilities and not his positive functioning, and has even constituted a retraumatization experience for many survivors.*

Surprisingly, many of the survivors themselves were concerned that their psychological damage and disabilities be prominently stated. They wanted to demonstrate and prove to the world what the Nazis perpetrated according to tangible and accepted criteria.

They wanted to accuse those who had stood by passively during their sufferings.

Post-Liberation Experience. The long-term effects of massive traumatization are intimately related to events immediately after the liberation and to the degree of acceptance or nonacceptance of the survivor by society. This varied in different countries, from the enthusiastic welcoming of the survivor as a returning hero in Holland, France, and Scandinavia to suspiciousness and hatred in Poland and Hungary and an admixture of fear, hatred, and acceptance of their survival in Germany.

Israel as a pioneering society had a special significance, encouraging and accepting new citizens who could contribute to the rebirth of their homeland. In Israel there was a specific situation where intense emotional ties to lost families and identification with the survival of the Jewish people awakened a feeling of solidarity with the pain and losses of the survivors. At the same time, there were also anger and accusations about why the survivors, and all Jews in Europe, had not come to Palestine before the Holocaust. This was accompanied by accusations of shame at the victims having gone "passively as sheep to slaughter." Only years later, with the Eichmann trial and then the Six Day and Yom Kippur wars, were these ideas about survivors changed and bridges developed across the gap between the general population and the survivors.

The United States was seen by many survivors as an historic country of immigration with rich resources, a country of freedom and of fulfillment of "all" of one's needs for personal achievement and success, that is, all the needs so long frustrated in the Holocaust years. Uncle Sam represented the strong liberating image that could save them and restore their depleted resources. The U.S. helped many young survivors in particular to realize their working potential to the full, while weaker survivors found a supportive framework of "landsmanschaft" with groups of earlier Jewish immigrants from other communities, with whom they could keep the traditions of loyalty to the memory of their communities and the Jewish community and its communal caring for all Jews.

The Psychiatric Needs of Survivors. Although more than forty years have elapsed since their liberation, the flow of people needing help is undiminished. In one survey conducted at the Shalvata

Psychiatric Center near Tel Aviv, of the total population of 120 adult inpatients (over age eighteen), 20 percent were survivors and 10 percent were children of survivors whose mental states were related in one way or another to their war experiences. In one period of a few months, I became aware of instances of six survivors committing suicide—two aged forty, two aged fifty, and two aged sixty-eight; of them four had never undergone any form of psychiatric treatment. Many survivors have refused to seek any mental health treatment for fear of being stigmatized, and for many years few possibilities existed for obtaining help other than psychiatric facilities. Many well-functioning, symptom-free survivors, on reaching midlife and its known crisis period (forty-five to fifty-five) experienced a flooding of Holocaust memories that aroused deep anxiety and anger. The attempt to come to terms with concentration camp experiences and Holocaust losses is often postponed until this midlife period, all energy having been mobilized until then for adjustment to reality and social integration. In the presence of a sensitive, encouraging, and attentive listener, survivors in this age group often reach a universe of unarticulated feeling seeking expression.

Children of survivors often also require psychiatric attention. Adolescence has been particularly difficult for many of them. Among young adult offspring of survivors, there are existential-type depressive states, often with suicidal ideas, in relation to feelings of a lack of meaning and significance in their lives despite successful social adjustment and achievement. As indicated earlier, some cases showed mental states that mirrored their depressed, emotionally depleted parents. In survivor family studies, I have often found a characteristic family atmosphere and parent-child interaction conducive to the transmission of the effects of Holocaust traumatization to the offspring. Studies of the impact of the Holocaust on the second and even third generation in the families of survivors are ongoing, and we will need to track their needs and provide appropriate mental health services to these groups for years to come.

Over the years of my clinical work with survivors and my formulation of classificatory concepts, I have become ever more convinced of the limited significance and indeed inadequacy of an approach to the functioning, experience, and therapy of survivors based only on the one-dimensional concepts of psychopathology and clinical psychiatry. I now believe that the only satisfactory approach to understanding the long-term sequelae of massive traumatization is through longitudinal studies of the lives of survivors. Such studies of individual survivors and the families they have created are especially indicated in the large, nonclinical population of survivors. Here the emphasis should be on the definition of the adaptive and protective factors involved in preventing the appearance of negative effects of traumatization and in enabling successful social integration, rather than on psychopathology.

I would recommend the following projects be undertaken:

1. *Nonclinical* counseling services are required for social advice and assistance to survivors. These could be part of already existing community outreach programs, provided they are separate from psychiatric services, which are often avoided by survivors because of the feelings of stigmatization that clinical frameworks arouse in them.
2. Psychiatric staff require systematic training to help them understand the significance of persecutory experience, since otherwise their reaction is often one of incomprehension or denial of the influence of the traumatic experiences.
3. Peer discussion groups for children of survivors are needed in community centers and outreach programs in order to help them deal with specific difficulties such as separation from parents. Advice and guidance for parents with regard to appropriate communication with their children about their Holocaust experience is clearly indicated for survivors with young families.
4. Research is indicated in the following areas:
   a. Studies of patterns of adaptation and protective integrative factors such as community and other support systems in nonclinical populations. Many survivors are healthy, well-functioning individuals who have reared healthy children despite their having experienced massive traumatization. Survivor symptomatology need not interfere with normal living, and its significance has often been exaggerated with unfortunate and unjustified generalizations invidious to survivors.
   b. Study of the influence of traumatization on different character structures.
   c. Epidemiological studies of the incidence of disturbance

in survivor populations, including second and third generations.

d. Study of the transmission of the effects of traumatization from parents through the parent-child interaction to their children and possibly to future generations, as well as the protective factors making for healthy child-rearing despite massive traumatization in the parent.

e. Family studies related to the varied reactions of different children in the same family circumstances.

f. Comparative studies of the influence of different psychosocial settings on Holocaust survivors and their children. In this connection, findings to date that Israeli society has posed unique sociotherapeutic and rehabilitative qualities for the mass of survivors and their children who settled there requires further validation.

The understanding to be derived from such studies of the long-term effects of traumatization and their transmission has important implications and challenges for community mental health programs, with regard to both treatment and prevention, for many years to come.

Life Styles of Survivors

During the Holocaust each survivor experienced the struggle between the desire to live and the desire to die. There were fluctuations of hope for the renewal of life interweaving with desires to die. Charny has written about this alternation as a universal process in all human beings, and has applied it as a framework toward understanding the psychology of the persons who commit genocide as an attempt to sacrifice their victims to the death they fear.[4] For survivors, in the inferno of the Holocaust and its overwhelmingly real dangers of death, this universal metaphoric-experiential process was transformed into a deadly real challenge to hold on to wishes for life as long as possible in the face of deadly conditions. Furthermore, this theme continued to accompany survivors throughout their lives after the Holocaust, again not only in the sense that it is part of every person's life, but also with the ineradicable special meanings that are carved into the survivor's memory and consciousness forever.

Having escaped physical extinction against all odds in his encounters with death in its manifold forms within the inferno of the Holocaust, the survivor now had to meet the challenge of the renewal of life in himself, and for his reconstructed family, in order not to surrender to the process of death to which the perpetrators of the Holocaust had originally sentenced him.

The survivor's special knowledge of death awakened in him two antagonistic tendencies:

1. a hunger for life expressed in activity and powerful quests for achievement and pleasure seeking; and
2. an opposing tendency to regression and an acceptance of passivity, minimal activity and achievement, and dependency in object relations.

The first is transcendence and triumph over the persecutor; in the second, the survivor continues to manifest the passive victim role allotted to him in the concentration camp world. Thus, in studying the life cycles of survivors we can see styles and modes of adaptation that can be understood as a direct continuation of behavior patterns of survivor coping mechanisms developed during the years of the Holocaust sufferings in the ghettos and concentration camps and situations of hiding and living under a false identity.

However, in contradistinction to clinically related studies, my predominant approach to the life styles of survivors is from the standpoint of "meaningful life experiences" rather than from a standpoint of psychological damage—although there is some inevitable overlapping between the two sets of concepts. I see the survivor as perpetually trying to come to terms with and overcoming death in order to embrace life, a life characterized by a struggle that never ends to incorporate the trauma.

Some of the coping patterns used in the struggle to survive during the Holocaust, which were originally adaptive and of survival value while in the grip of the Holocaust trauma, persisted as life styles despite new and totally different conditions of life, and now proved constricting and limiting in the survivors' personal relationships. Thus, suspiciousness, which had been adaptive in the grip of the destructive persecution, persisted in the survivors' relationships. Similarly, many survivors—including especially successful ones—showed a constant seeking of security in grandiose material achievements as disguised desperate efforts to replace their irrevocably lost security and basic trust. Such attitudes and patterns of behavior derived from the attempt to come to terms with having experienced "the utterly impossible and the unforgettable" that the Holocaust constituted, as well as from the need to adapt to a different reality than that which they had lived in before the Holocaust. Furthermore, after liberation, the survivors' confrontation with a world that had not gone through these experiences and that was utterly different from their fantasies, hopes, and expectations was often traumatic in itself.

Bereft of family and very often surrounded by an alienated or a hostile environment in the various countries of Europe, survivors developed secondary adaptive patterns of coping with the various challenges of reintegration into society. Two dynamic dimensions of secondary adaptive defenses and coping can be identified. On the one hand, there was the task of interpreting the Holocaust experience into the post-Holocaust psychosocial realities of Europe, which often included continued rejection of Jews and renewed anti-Semitism. On the other hand, there was an intrapsychic task of reintegrating the Holocaust experience into one's reemerging previous personality, which of course by now was also molded and affected by the traumatic experiences. For all survivors, an integral task was the need to live up to their previous self-ideal in proving to themselves and also to the environment that they were not destroyed and damaged but alive and valuable human beings.

In many survivors suspiciousness, overalertness, and hypervigilance can be observed in their behavioral patterns. These patterns derived from the adaptive imperative to be constantly alert to danger. These reactions enabled the mobilization of all energies to face the real dangers while survivors were in the grip of destructive persecutions in the ghettos and concentration camps. Such personality trends can be sublimated and expressed in extreme solidarity with kin and nation for better and for worse. They are a basis for a deep, satisfying identification with one's own people, but they can also create a constant suspiciousness and hypervigilance toward other people who have not declared their unequivocal friendship.

Within the complex interactions of interpersonal relationships, these suspicious and hyperalert tendencies can be constricting and limiting. At a societal level, this can lead to reactions frequently associated with fear and hatred with regard to potential enemies, and a tendency to be overpatriotic and overchauvinistic. Survivors are often unable to stand the ambiguities and ambivalences of reality. In relationships, they tend to experience the extremes of loving-hating, and of being loved-hated. They will be excessively loyal to their friends, with a tendency to suspiciousness toward those who have different opinions and who could be a threat to their newly achieved post-Holocaust security. One sees in such people not only the traditional suspicion of Jews toward the "goy" (non-Jew) but also suspicion toward those Jews who did not experience the Holocaust ("were not there"). As indicated, security may be sought in perpetual and insatiable material achievements as an intended replacement for the irreplaceably lost ontological security and basic trust of their pre-Holocaust lives. With misfortune and isolation in old age, if and when children leave or, worse, abandon the parents, or after the death of the spouse, this suspiciousness can develop into full-blown persecutory feelings and ideas. These hyperalert survivors tend to be constantly on their guard by day and often sleep lightly at night because of their deeply imprinted experiences and their fears that they may fail to be on alert to face new dangers lurking at any time.

Sometimes the marital relationship may reinforce tendencies in each partner toward fear and lack of trust. When both spouses are survivors, there are probabilities of stereotyped dyads that replay aspects of the persecution in the Holocaust. They may constitute passive, clinging survivor-victim dyads or an aggressor-victim dyad, and there are also marital transactions in which both of these models are interchangeable—namely, an alternation between survivor-victim and aggressor-victim patterns.

These survivors show an inability to relax and to enjoy pleasurable situations, with a compulsion to be constantly working or actively achieving. They fear to relax. They are alert to the constant dangers of exposure to an enemy who is always about, who knows where. Related to this is the tendency to see in any rival or competitor an "enemy" against whom one has to fight for one's life in competition for the basic ingredients of survival, such as food and shelter. This everyday rivalry and competitiveness in turn threatens to reveal the survivor's basic feelings of inadequacy and helplessness, driving him always to seek to be more successful and achieving. Achievements thus can become overcathected with the need to overdefend one's achievements and the quest to achieve, and business and work situations can be related to as if they constituted real situations of danger.

The Hyperactive Survivor. Constant activity and the perpetual drive for achievement is a common pattern among survivors and is related to the need to prove to oneself and to the world that survival had meaning. New goals are set in a constant search for security as a replacement for the irrevocably lost ontological security. Replacements for a lost basic trust are constantly sought in social relationships, in occupational and academic achievements, and in material goals and possessions.

In some survivors, a need to have a feeling of open space ("lebensraum"), as well as an avoidance of closed and fenced-off places, is seen in a desire for frequent traveling to new places. This pattern reminds one of the pattern of the Jewish *luftmensch*-type caricaturized by Sholem Aleichem in the figure of Mendele, who always has a hundred projects to achieve security and wealth. It is different because it is much more rooted in reality needs and connected with the survivor's traumatic past.

The workaholic (hyperactive) survivors usually have difficulty in taking vacations. They cannot relax from their constant driven activity, which gives them a feeling of security and a diminution of the fear of being helpless and vulnerable to danger. They often are unable to enjoy real pleasure and a relaxation of tension, but engage in a repetitious running after success in the service of a security that is never really attained no matter how successful they are in their professional and financial attainments.

In the concentration camp, activity was a behavior pattern of considerable importance in the struggle to survive. Occupational skills that were sought after by the Nazis either for the German industrial machine or for the construction and maintenance of the concentration camps themselves were an important factor in staving off selections for death. Many of the survivors, when in the ghettos and camps, understood this and did everything to ensure that they would be selected for a specific occupational working group ("arbeit-kommando"). Quickly realizing this soon after arrival at the concentration camp, many would claim to be plumbers, electricians, carpenters, locksmiths, and so on when they had no experience whatsoever; they would have to know how to simulate, improvise, and appear to be constantly productively employed. After the Holocaust, the continued maintenance of activity throughout their lives represents a continuing flight from the passivity, dependency, and helplessness that so often were associated with inevitable death.

Some of these hyperactive people who have since invested their energies single-mindedly in a particular direction have achieved great success in professions and considerable wealth in commerce and industry in many countries in the Western world.

The emotional life of these survivors is often restricted and rigid since they avoid feelings that could threaten their overactive life style. Reaction formation in the form of exaggerated optimism and hypomanic behavior helps them to avoid the delayed confrontation with mourning for their lost families and the feelings of depression that would come forth from the store of their traumatic memories. Basically escaping contact with the inner core of their being, they demonstrate in their psychic functioning a "hypomanic defense" against mourning and depression.

Their imperative is to be "know-it-alls," the most successful. A false self is developed—an "as if" personality style—in accordance with how they think their environment would most appreciate them. They thus may appear to others as conformists and conservatives.

In middle age or later, when forced to become inactive and dependent on retirement or because of accidents or illness, they may break down into suicidal depression. This process may also occur as a result of hospitalizations for surgery. Since their successful achievement is a constant preoccupation and a necessity in defense against depression and loss, any encountering of failure can result in psychological crisis or even major breakdown. This is seen also in relation to failures and disappointments in the children of survivors, whose lives for the survivors are a direct extension of their own.

Intrinsic to this life style is an unbounding appetite for life and a tremendous vitality, as if the survivor is dedicated to the attempt to compensate for all the massive losses he suffered of family and of the sources of gratification and security that he once had. This hypomanic pattern seems to be most prominent in survivors who were young adults or adolescents in the Holocaust, so that "replacement" and compensation for the lost years of life in their youth is a driving element throughout the life span. In some, personal life styles reach gargantuan dimensions of grandiosity and extravagance.

Passive and Victim Styles. At the other extreme are seen austere life styles as a continuation of life under minimal conditions despite material success. These survivors cannot allow themselves to emerge from the Holocaust level and to have freedom for pleasure and gratification. They are always hoping for reparation for the injuries and losses and easily feel rejected when not accepted and loved. These survivors are reminiscent of orphans who lost parents in early childhood and who then have a tremendous need for love and acceptance, and continue to be vulnerable, with lifelong sensitivities toward real or imaginary rejection.

Situations also may arise with the survivor accepting servile, submissive, dependent roles according to a slave-master bond. The pattern may be played out in a marital style of being a dependent spouse who is a slave to the other. In the marital relationship of a survivor, such a slave pattern of dependency takes on additional echoes of one's history as victim. The expression of the master-slave relationship may be projected into other relationships. Total expressions of this style may be seen in survivors who sought out compliant, submissive, slavelike roles in society, for example, street sweepers. Living for so long under oppression by the cruel aggressor, losing their entire families, unable to create a new family, the sum total of Holocaust experiences caused a serious impairment of vitality and identity and the survivors remained as if "living dead." All they could now do was to continue stereotypically in a passive, submissive role of "psychological Musselman" until their physical death.

In those survivors in whom previous personality structures were characterized by lack of strong enough male figures for identification in their early life, the Holocaust trauma reinforced their tendency in transactional processes within their family structure for clinging, submission, and passivity and for manifest submission in their posture and presentation of self in all situations as a "nebich" (good-for-nothing).

Some survivors live out of their suitcases, unable to commit themselves to one place where they will feel secure enough to grow roots and to accept it as their real home. They long after their lost pre-Holocaust home that was destroyed. They cannot adopt new nonmaterial values that would give them a sense of security, and cannot believe in the continuity of their lives and achievements, but live from day to day as if tomorrow there will be another Holocaust. Thus, there are large numbers of survivors who emigrated with their families from Israel to the U.S. and Canada without succeeding in achieving inner security despite material success and achievement.

Other Defensive Styles of Coping. Other styles of coping that may be exaggerated in the lives of different survivors include defensive overawareness of others, preoccupation with injustice, and a need to be in control of situations. Defensive overawareness of others' attitudes and behaviors toward the survivor are frequently manifested in hypersensitivity to possible injustice by others, violation of human rights, anti-Semitism, racial prejudice, neo-Nazism, and political oppression. These preoccupations with injustice can be transmitted to the survivors' children, who may express them directly in their professional and occupational choice—psychology, social work, medicine, and other helping professions—as well as in their personal lives and ideological affiliations. Another modality of behavior observed in survivors is the need to be always in control of situations. This can be seen in a wide range of situations in relation to children when unhappiness or lack of success is interpreted as a major catastrophe in which the survivor reacts as if submission to another's opinions or authority could result in helplessness and "disaster." These tendencies frequently create difficulties in interpersonal relations and especially in relationships with authority figures. These survivors cannot accept a submissive role in work situations and need mobility and autonomy both in the physical and social sense. They tend to prefer professions and occupational situations that allow freedom of movement and do not require having to answer to superiors. They generally avoid any role or situation with clear, rigid boundaries, as in traditional institutional frameworks where roles tend to be authoritarian. Similarly, they can create difficulty in their own families.

Grouping Together. During the Holocaust, the survivors developed strong, cohesive relationships with comrades, who replaced their lost nuclear or extended family and became the basic determining factor in their survival. Furthermore, in the early period after their liberation, these relationships continued with small groups living close by each other together as small "families" in the D.P. camps and cities of Europe. This form of living signified the attempt to restore their pre-Holocaust homes and to set up a

disorders, and psychotic breakdown. It is our impression that there is a high incidence of emotional disturbance and serious psychiatric disturbance among the children of concentration camp survivor parents. This impression is shared with clinicians in the United States and Canada.[1] Statistically, we have found that as many as 20 percent of the children referred to some of our child psychiatric and adolescent outpatient services in Israel had at least one parent who was a CCS, but systematic epidemiological studies have yet to be carried out. We are now also seeing increasing numbers of the grandchildren of survivors in our child psychiatric clinics, and we are studying the specific effects in the transmission of traumatization within the parent-child interaction.

Knowledge of the long-term effects of massive traumatization of different groups and comparison between the effects of different kinds of traumatization and the influences of different psychosocial settings on the lives of the individuals, their families, and future generations is rather problematic because of the complexity and number of variables involved, and much work remains to be done. There is increasing awareness of the importance of such studies and their implications and applications. However, I feel it is important at this stage to register our clinical impressions.

On scrutinizing the large amount of clinical material that we have amassed over the years in Israel, it is obvious that disturbances would have had to be found in the children of grossly disordered survivors. These are the families in which both parents underwent massive traumatization and one and often both parents have suffered from severe, although often different, manifestations of the CCSS.

Many of these survivors have been in therapy for years. Their anxiety and depressive states have been relieved symptomatically by tranquilizers and antidepressive drugs. More important, however, has been the therapeutic relationship, which, with its basis of trust, has helped decrease the basic insecurity feelings and has served the survivor well in his moments of crisis when fear and depression exacerbate. They are dependent on therapy and the feeling of availability, reliability, and hope that they receive from the relationship with an empathic therapist. This continuing therapeutic relationship, although essentially supportive, makes it possible from time to time for cathartic discharges to occur. Such discharges are cumulative in their effects over the years, and enable some degree of working through of blocked aggression and

grief, and sometimes they make it possible for parents to communicate their traumatic experiences more appropriately to the children. In addition, such an ongoing therapeutic framework with
the survivor parents existing over many years has made it possible, when problems arose in the development of the children, to
deal with them by appropriate interpretations, guidance, referral
for child therapy, and referral to family therapy. The treatment of
the survivor parent(s) often has been significant in modifying the
pathogenic influences of the parents on their children. In addition,
therapy has often been helpful to the survivor parents in those
critical periods when they have had to face separation from children or when problems in the children's development have aroused
guilt, hostility, and depression.

Some of the most disturbed children we have seen had survivor
parents belonging to the group of survivors we have described as
denying that the Holocaust had any impact on them. In these
cases personality distortions and emotional restriction are often
present, and psychopathology is frequently massively expressed
in the parent-child relationship without the moderating influence
that a successful therapeutic relationship can provide.

The Concentration Camp Survivor Family

It is important to recognize that there are also occasions when
exceptional personality qualities of warmth, support, and ego
strength have been seen in a survivor mother or father that have
compensated for the pathological influence of the damaged spouse
and made for healthy functioning in the children. Some survivors
are surprisingly successful parents and appear to be unusually
well endowed for child rearing. Those factors that make for healthy
family functioning despite traumatization of parents merit deeper
study.

In order to understand the transmission of the effects of traumatization to children from parents, one must examine the structure and history of the family created by the survivor. On release
from the camps, the ability of many of the survivors to make
satisfactory human relations was seriously impaired. Many suffered from psychic numbing and depersonalization states. Their
capacity to trust others was undermined and they feared to love
because to do so would mean exposure to the danger and pain of
further object loss. For some, to love again meant betrayal of a

previous relationship in which the partner had died. They were thus unable to make new cathectic investments, and would remain so until and unless they could work through their losses; otherwise they could not create the possibility of making new object relationships without encountering depression and guilt. Motivations for making liaisons on a defective basis, however, were not lacking. Many survivors finding themselves entirely alone after liberation rushed hastily into marriage on release from the camp in an attempt to overcome loneliness, fear, loss of the prewar family, or just because of the basic lack of everything. Typical is the statement of one woman survivor: "I married him because he had a room, a bed, and a blanket."

Sometimes the object choice was based on a superficial resemblance to the longed-for lost parent of the opposite sex or some tenuous connection with the survivor's earlier life, or similar camp experiences. A common background of camp experiences sometimes resulted in the creation of a dyadic victim unit in which the couple clung together in the face of a hostile, threatening environment, thus reinforcing persecutory and even paranoid feelings in each other. The desire to save the other also was an important motif, so that some relationships showed an anaclitic protective quality with extreme dependency. When the marital relationship was based essentially on the attempt to reconstruct a previously destroyed marriage and family with an inability to accept the destruction of the first wife and children, the memory of the first unmourned partner and children overshadowed the new marriage and prevented the establishment of a satisfactory relationship.

Sometimes the inability to mourn a lost spouse and children and the desire to keep them alive intrapsychically resulted in the choice of an older partner who could not bear children and who was not a survivor, and was emotionally remote or cold. Such a marriage lacking in warmth and anything in common between the partners increased the feelings of loneliness of the survivor. When based on the unconscious longing for reunion with the lost parent of the opposite sex, problems arose because of the fixated, immature oedipal component.

Some survivors chose nonsurvivor partners with an impaired self-image like their own, although deriving from entirely different cultural and other circumstances of childhood traumatization or deprivation. In some cases the nonsurvivor partners showed schizoid or other severe personality disorders or were passively withdrawn people. Many survivors reacted with guilt and depression on realizing that the marital choice was inadequately based, and that they lacked the capacity for developing the relationship, which was essentially a desperate attempt to overcome their feelings of isolation and emptiness.

Usually, however, the survivors clung on to these unsatisfactory marriages rather than having to face separation and physical loneliness again, and they continued to live in a state of hostile stalemate or shared loneliness. Lacking warmth and meaning in their lives, they then concentrated all their hopes of finding these by bearing children, although again the motivation for children was often related to the attempt to deny the destruction of pre-camp families. Many mothers had periods of amenorrhea and several miscarriages before finally carrying a full-term pregnancy. During pregnancy they often suffered from depression and fears that they were abnormal and damaged, and therefore were not qualified to marry and bear children. Their negative self-image also made them fear that the child born to them would be abnormal.

The family atmosphere, because of the parent survivor's mental state, was often a very pathogenic one for child rearing. Because of their depression, pessimism, and general emotional depletion, parents were unable to enjoy family events together with their children; they isolated themselves from social life and family life lacked vitality, zest, and warmth. Sufferers from the survivor syndrome preoccupied with traumatic memories, fears, inadequacy feelings, and the memories of lost relatives were not emotionally available for the children. In the opinion of Sigal, this parental and especially maternal preoccupation is the essential pathogenic influence on children in the families of survivors and other severely traumatized individuals.[2]

In many of the families seen, although both parents have experienced massive traumatization, only one parent, usually the mother, manifests the survivor syndrome symptomatology. The father remains symptom free but shows a defensive pattern of overactivity outside the home with personality rigidity and emotional restriction inside the home. The mother is seen as the identified survivor patient expressing the symptomatology of traumatization for both of them. Furthermore, the father may be weak, withdrawn, and passive, leaving all the child rearing to the mother, who appears as the dominating influence. Thus children are excessively exposed to the maternal disturbances. Other survivor fathers showed irritable-moody patterns in the home, with frequent aggressive outbursts against their wives and offspring. The free-floating rage present in some families was a direct derivative of parents' persecutory experience.

Interpersonal functioning within these families was often intensely disturbed with rigid pseudomutuality, and schismatic or skewed marital relationships.[3]

Against this background of parental and intrafamilial disturbance, a wide range of distortions have been seen in the parent-child interaction, including destructive projective identifications and distorted communication patterns. The most characteristic ones that I have seen are as follows:

1. *Overanxiety.* Overanxiety permeated every aspect of the mother-child relationship. From the moment of the child's birth, these mothers feared that some harm would come to the child from outside forces, with resultant extremely overprotective behavior. They were constantly on the alert in case some catastrophe would occur. They overfed their babies, slept with them beyond the appropriate age, and examined them frequently during the night to see that they were still breathing. Any illness, however minor, caused an exacerbation of fear. Many of these preoccupied mothers felt emotionally and physically inadequate in the maternal role and overcompensated by excessive "giving and doing." Separation anxiety showed itself throughout childhood, resulting in constant clinging behavior, which interfered with the child's ultimate separation-individuation.

2. *Intense emotional investment in the child with idealization and overidentification.* These patterns resulted from the survivor parents' attempts to restore their damaged self-image and identity, and to validate and give meaning to their survival. The children, or parenting them, represented the survivor-parents' renewal of life, but as a result enormous burdens were placed on the children, who became the receptacles for all the shattered dreams and hopes of their parents. Patterns were established from early childhood of overindulgence and exaggerated overcompensatory expectations with regard to behavior and achievement. It was as if the psychological survival of the parents depended on the child's conformity with their idealized wishes. As a result, these parents are unable to respond appropriately to the specific individual needs of the child, who is seen entirely in terms of the parent's psychic needs.

3. *Identification of the child with siblings and parents lost in the*

camp. This was often seen strikingly in the names and nicknames given to children who were expected to replace, as a symbolic reincarnation, significant figures in the parent's family who were murdered. Thus, again, they became receptacles for the identities of others, together with the associated, inappropriate longings and expectations on the part of the parents and idealized as a link with the lost relative.

4. *Projective identification onto the child of the parents' experiences and affects.* Projective identification resulted from the utilization of the child by a parent attempting to work through and free himself from tormenting memories and affects by splitting them off from himself. In this way, persecutory fears and blocked aggressive impulses, feelings of guilt, low self-esteem, and loss were transmitted to children with subtle cues to act them out, thus vicariously gratifying parental needs. The whole gamut of survivor symptomatology that the parent is experiencing can be reexperienced by a child in identification with a depressed, depleted, fearful parent. We have seen such children appearing almost as if they themselves were concentration camp survivors. These affects can also be signaled to the child by nonverbal means, and many survivor's children are ultrasensitive to the look on the survivor parent's face, which opens before them the misery and horror of the parental experience, which has never been verbalized or directly expressed.

In many cases we have seen one child chosen as the main object for these destructive projective identifications because of sex or physical appearance or merely because he is the first child to be born. This child later becomes the identified patient in the family, absorbing the major impact of the parental pathology, and the other children may then remain relatively free of the pathogenic parental influence. However, in many of the cases we have seen, there is only one child on whom the full onus of bearing the parental pathology fell. In some cases a lonely, isolated parent actually allocated to the child the role of intimate companion, subjecting him from early childhood to a recounting over and over again of the traumatic experiences he had undergone. In these cases, reminiscent of the folie à deux phenomenon, the child internalized, experienced, and acted out, sometimes delusionally, the parent's persecutory experiences.

Denying, silent parents have also often raised disturbed children, perhaps the most disturbed. The Holocaust experiences have acquired the aura of "shameful family secrets" in relation to which children often weave fantasies about what was done to their parents and how they survived. Information derived from the media and by nonverbal cues from the parents, interacting with the intrapsychic needs of the child, have resulted in fearful and shameful fantasies.

Psychiatric Disturbances in the Children of Concentration Camp Survivors

In childhood the full range of emotional disturbances have been seen. Most common were early sleeping and feeding problems, nocturnal enuresis, fear of leaving the mother, school refusal, and spoiled, demanding, aggressive behavior. Phobias and recurrent nightmares related to parents' experiences were also frequent.

Many children of the survivors were referred first for psychiatric help in adolescence on facing the identity and autonomy challenges of this period. Adolescence also had special significance because this was when many of the parents were traumatized. The parents experienced a flooding back of memories when the child reached the age when they had gone through the Holocaust. Furthermore, the parents who had gone through the Holocaust during adolescence had lost their own parents at that time and, as a result, lacked parenting models for dealing with the problems of this age group. Anxiety and depression were precipitated by the need to begin to separate from the home or by interpersonal or academic frustrations or failure. The internalization of the parents' poor self-image and lack of identity was manifest in feelings of alienation, emptiness, and lack of meaning to their lives.

Many of these parents who realized early on the deficiencies in their parenting capacity had reacted with overindulgent behavior, attempting to gratify all the material needs of the child. As adolescents these youngsters became aware of the parents' inability to give them real security, love, and support and realized that instead, they had been recipients of overanxiety, overprotectiveness, and extreme, uncompromising demands and expectations. Many children had carried enormous burdens of parental needs and had submissively conformed with successful school performances in the attempt to prove themselves to their parents before eventually giving up when they realized that they could not satisfy the unrealistic parental aspirations invested in them. Hostile feelings would then be expressed towards the parents with aggressive, overdemanding behavior. The parents, struggling with their own problems of aggression, could not cope with this, and either gave up or tried to impose rigid controls, sometimes with displays of destructive verbal outbursts that were both critical of the youngster and self-blaming. The adolescents were often guilty about expressing their aggression directly against their suffering parents, and instead displaced their aggressive impulses onto siblings or outside the home, or they reacted with self-punishing depression, apathy, and withdrawal.

Difficulties in relating were frequent and these youngsters tend to feel isolated and unable to trust others. Their parents had been unable to transmit feelings of basic trust in early childhood and the children internalized a model of lack of trust in others. I have seen several cases of closed family systems in which both parents were survivors with an only child whose whole raison d'être was to justify and give meaning to the parents' existence. These parents, suspicious of others, isolated and clinging together, indoctrinated their child from early life not to trust outsiders and to avoid talking with anyone outside the family about anything intimate. On entering situations demanding closer interpersonal relations outside the home such as army service, they frequently reacted with acute anxiety states and phobias. These youngsters showed a marked inability to communicate feelings and thoughts and an inability to form intimate relations.

The impaired self-image and identity of the survivor parent, which was transmitted to the child together with destructive self-criticism, frequently resulted in sadomasochistic parent-child interactions. Failure of any kind, and especially psychiatric disturbance in children, caused an exacerbation of guilt feelings and depressive reactions in the survivor parents. Failure meant that the child could not fulfill the role of validating the parental existence and confirmed the parents' impaired self-image.

Typical was the case of a thirteen-year-old boy showing severe behavior disorders in school and complete oppositional withdrawal from the mother.

The mother had been in Auschwitz at age eighteen and her parents and four siblings were killed there. She was depressed and preoccupied with her losses, and her only child was clearly given the role of compensating for all her losses. Her husband was an obsessional, rigid individual with an impotent intellectual attitude to everything. She had made herself a helpless doormat for the child and continually demonstrated how much she was suffering because of him. She felt herself deeply impaired and that her only reason for living was her child. Preoccupied with guilt feelings, she stated, "We the survivors should not have given birth to children because the Nazis changed us genetically and our children must inevitably be sick and damaged."

In the course of therapy, it became clear that the boy had persistently received conflicting messages from his mother—despairing statements of inadequacy on the one hand and tremendous expectations on the other. This mother had never been able to talk about her persecutory experiences with anyone, but her child would guess the nature of her suffering from the expression on her face. In his demeanor, he mirrored his mother's withdrawn, joyless, suspicious, austere appearance, and his voice was always sad.

In another case, a sixteen-year-old girl made a suicide attempt following school failure and interpersonal difficulties, and her mother then stated, "I've never wanted and do not want to live. I have no joy in life because of 'the camps.' But all my life I wanted my children to be happy, and my greatest failure is that despite this, I have succeeded in transferring to them the feeling that there is no point in living."

We have frequently seen the sudden appearance of fears in adolescents whose parents suffered from chronic fear and persecutory nightmares—an only son of sixteen was afraid to stay alone at night in his own home in case his heart stopped beating. His father, who had to bury several members of his family, including two brothers who died during their flight from the Nazis in Eastern Europe, had frequent screaming nightmares.

We have seen several cases of depression in childhood and early adolescence where a survivor parent is preoccupied with the unresolved loss of a child from a previous family. Although the parent had never talked specifically about the loss, the child is exquisitely aware of the parent's preoccupation.

In one case, a thirteen-year-old reported that he had felt guilty as long as he could remember because of his father's previous child. The child would pore over old photographs that the father had preserved of his former family and he would think to himself, "I shouldn't be here, his son should be alive. I am here only because Hitler killed his son."

Separation anxiety is a common problem in the families of concentration camp survivors. The parents bind and cling to their adolescent children, discouraging and often blocking their attempts to develop autonomous activities, peer friendships, or heterosexual relationships. Survivor parents became ill or had outbursts of self-denigration and suffering designed to arouse guilt feelings in youngsters when they tried to participate in peer group activities that would take them away from the home. One sixteen-year-old describing her mixed feelings of aggression and guilt whenever her mother would try to prevent her from going away from home for any length of time stated, "My mother is weak, half dead. I feel that she doesn't really live after what happened to her in the war and she does everything in order that I also won't live." On the other hand, she felt that she had to do everything not to hurt or disappoint her survivor parents and especially the mother because "I am the only thing that remains in her life." She felt guilty and conflicted between her desire to always be with them and look after them and her need to struggle on to realize herself independently from them. This case exemplifies also the failure of the survivor as a parent to respond to the needs of the young adolescent. Instead, the parents' needs take precedence and the child assumes the nurturing, protective role.

Sometimes the fear of separation is transferred entirely to adolescents so that they are unable to be outside the home or the community without being overwhelmed by fear. I have seen several cases of young men after army mobilization who had to be discharged because of severe anxiety associated with the feeling that in the army camp they were trapped as if in a cage under the scrutiny of uncompromising authority. There have been years when the highest incidence of discharge from the Israeli army for psychiatric reasons was in soldiers both of whose parents were concentration camp survivors.

Reenactment of the survivor parent's past persecutory experiences in the child can occur at periods of stress. A dramatic example of the reenactment of a parent's past persecutory experiences is illustrated in the following case:

A seventeen-year-old girl was admitted for psychiatric hospitalization in a state of severe anorexia. She was the eldest of three daughters. The parents were both concentration camp survivors, the father an active, intellectual, emotionally withdrawn individual involved mainly in activity outside the home, who had left most of the parenting to the mother. The mother presented herself as a self-denigrating, self-apologetic person. She was joyless, lacking in warmth of feeling, but overanxious and systematically devoting herself to bringing up her daughters, whom she contacted via activity rather than feeling. She had lost her parents and two sisters during the war. She had been in a concentration camp at the age of seventeen together with a younger sister whose life she saved by giving her extra food from her own rations, but as a result she herself had become so emaciated that on liberation from the camp she almost died.

When her eldest child was born, she felt that she was a link with her lost mother and two sisters. The girl was very obedient, submissive, and aspired always to maximal achievement in school, thus pleasing her father, but she was cheerless and isolated from her peers. In adolescence she developed increasing interest in the Holocaust and constantly asked her mother to tell her stories of her camp experiences, to which the mother responded freely. This was evident especially during the year preceding the onset of her illness. She began to paint camp subjects—tortured faces full of fear, broken, emaciated bodies, and hands reaching out for salvation. At age sixteen, she developed acne and was advised to diet. Her mother encouraged her in this until she began to refuse all foods and her weight fell drastically. The acne disappeared but she insisted on carrying on with the diet. She demanded to be brought food in her room, isolated from everyone except her mother, who insisted that she alone knew how to care for the girl's needs. Her weight dropped from 50 to 29 kilos (110 to 64 pounds). Eventually, though only after great reluctance and considerable delay, especially by the mother, who had difficulty in recognizing the seriousness of her daughter's state, the parents agreed that she should be hospitalized. Her appearance was that of a camp inmate. When asked why she would not eat, she replied, "My mother also didn't eat when she was my age." When asked why she painted such depressing subjects, she replied, "This is what I am living through." Her only concern was that she was missing school and falling behind in her studies.

The mother refused to leave the hospital and insisted on remaining beside her daughter night and day. She felt that she was back in the concentration camp with her sister and was consumed with guilt feelings and despair, blaming herself for her daughter's state because of her inability to enjoy anything and her preoccupation with death. She dramatically accused herself: "I fed her the poison of the Holocaust as a baby at my breast." She had never discussed these feelings with anyone before, nor her guilt feeling that she had lived while her mother and two of her sisters had died. This endless and overwhelming guilt had at last driven her to some working through of her massively blocked aggression. It was clear that in her relationship with her daughter and in the development of the latter's illness, she had acted out unexpressed feelings about the death of her mother, her two sisters, her own near-death in the camp, and the associated repressed hostility toward her younger sister whose life she had saved almost at the cost of her own. The interactive process between the mother and daughter became intense in adolescence with the mother's induction of acting out via her daughter.

During talks with the mother, it was possible for the first time to create a distance between her and her daughter. As a result, the latter quite dramatically improved, and shortly after her discharge from the hospital she was able to leave home for studies. She later married a volunteer from abroad and left the country with him.

Another group had reached their twenties before presenting themselves for psychiatric help. They suffered from depression, fear of impending catastrophe, feelings of failure and worthlessness. These young people were often successful achievers in their careers and material goals but suffered from a lack of a sense of meaning in their lives. Often well endowed and energetic, they took their parents' ambitions with them from home into their adult lives. Eventually they were confronted by their inability to form satisfactory relationships and to find meaning in their lives because of the lack of genuine warmth and security they had experienced in childhood from their parent survivors. Their parent survivors, themselves often overactive and successful achievers, had always denied their inner emptiness and impaired self-image.

Borderline and Psychotic States. We have found an increased incidence of psychotic states in the children of concentration camp survivors. The diagnoses usually are schizophrenia, schizophreniform state, or schizo-affective psychosis. Frequently, the psychotic behavior shows elements of reenactment of the parents' persecutory experiences.

One eighteen-year-old, when hospitalized after an acute manic psychotic break, announced elatedly, "Now I know what it is like to be put in a concentration camp." Throughout his hospitalization, he was preoccupied with the theme of survival in a camp, boasting to his father, who was an Auschwitz survivor, that he was proving that he too could survive Auschwitz. His psychotic reenactment of his father's experiences showed also an introjection of the father's identification with the aggressor and was manifested in his asking him whether he had been a victim in the camp or an SS guard.

This boy was the eldest of three children. The younger two were girls. The father was a successful professional man who had been extremely elated on the birth of his son, and felt that he had been reborn. The boy had striven throughout his childhood to prove his worth to his "hero survivor" father. The mother was not a survivor, but suffered from an impaired self-image. The boy's psychotic break occurred after he finished high school and failed to be accepted to the elite university where his father had studied.

On witnessing his son's intense, anxious striving to emulate his success in the period preceding the psychotic break, the father realized that he had given his son a distorted picture of his traumatic experiences and had always emphasized his special and heroic qualities in having survived. He had used his son to idealize his traumatic experiences and had never worked through his losses. His decision to enter therapy coincided with his son's psychotic break twenty-eight years after his liberation from the camp.

A series of borderline and psychotic states have been seen in adolescents, mostly girls who had been subjected to intense, clinging, symbiotic-type relationships by their mothers with the collusion of the father. These cases are reminiscent of the "symbiotic survival pattern" described by Slipp in families with a schizophrenic member, in which there is a mutually controlling system of interaction where each individual feels responsible for the self-esteem and survival of the others.[4] With the need to separate from the mother in adolescence, they react with severe depression, schizoid withdrawal, and, often, suicide attempts. Paranoid manifestations may appear and often show close resemblance in their content to the traumatic persecutory experiences that the mother had undergone. The breakdown of the symbiotic relationship is experienced as a loss of identity and releases considerable destructive aggressive tension that is directed against the parents and/or against the self. When a psychotic break occurs, it is often preceded by very strong guilt feelings in the girl that she was saved from all the suffering that the mother had been subjected to in the camp. One girl identified herself with Anne Frank and insisted that the family should change their surname to Frank. In this way she attempted symbolically to include herself in the parents' persecutory experiences. In another case, the symbiotic regression manifested in states of terror when the mother left the daughter, who feared that she would faint and die if her mother was not present. She even had to accompany her mother when the latter went to the toilet and dreamt that her mother was inside her.

The grandchildren of the survivors now are also being referred to our clinics in increasing numbers, suffering from manifestations of anxiety in early childhood, fear of being alone at night, nightmares, fear of journeys, etc. Some of the mothers of these children were in our treatment as adolescents. They are now coming back into therapy as a result of difficulty in coping with maternal nurturing roles, which cause them considerable anxiety. Many of them made unsatisfactory marital object choices, but in contradistinction to their mothers' generation were able to divorce, and some have made better second marriages. However, child rearing is a considerable problem for them, deriving from their exposure to very pathological maternal models.

Family Therapy. At our hospital and clinic, when a child or adolescent in a survivor family is referred, family therapy is always attempted. The problem is to win the cooperation of the parents, especially those who have previously denied their own need for therapy. Resistance to therapy is also related to the fear that it will take the children away from them, and we have seen paranoid outbursts directed against the therapist in very disturbed survivor parents.

When parents were able to cooperate, an attempt was made to work on their need to use the child for projecting their pathological affects and identificatory needs, and on their unresolved separation and mourning problems with regard to the loss of their own parents. When working through these issues was possible, parents became able to tell the child in an appropriate way of their traumatic experiences and losses. When no working through was possible because of the parents' disturbances, and if anxiety and depression were overt, they were offered symptomatic and supportive therapy. Whatever the therapeutic activity involving the parents, the most important component was the establishment of trust in the therapist, especially with the mother. The mothers were encouraged to take on some activity outside the home to relieve the intensity of their investments in the child. With the fathers, it was important to get them to take more direct responsibility and to become more actively involved with the child.

In the treatment of adolescents, the goal was to help the youngster separate from the parents and to modify the parents' resistance to this. However, the therapist must be constantly aware of the powerful forces operating in the family binding the child. The inability of the parent to separate has been seen in depressive reactions, exacerbation of psychosomatic illness, and even suicide attempts of the parent when the adolescent tries to leave the home. Improvement was achieved in about half the cases, in most cases following an acute crisis situation such as the school's refusal to keep or accept a youngster, or acutely aggressive acting out.

With adolescent girls, the intense ambivalence to their mothers and their resultant fear of intimate individual contact made it very difficult to establish a working therapeutic relationship with an individual therapist. Alternatively, group therapy was used very effectively. Most of these girls were able to go on to military service and to marry. Many of them have returned to therapy on the basis of problems that have arisen in rearing their own children. Army service, especially for the boys, who usually serve at distances much further away from home than the girls, has helped toward separation from parents, and every effort is now made to deal with their emotional disorders by ongoing therapy throughout their military service.

Different Styles of Survivor Families

In my clinical practice, I have met with a large range of children of survivors suffering from many manifestations of emotional disturbance. I am well aware, however, of the unrepresentative nature of clinical groups among the large population of survivor families, most of whom have not sought psychotherapeutic or psychiatric treatment. It is therefore vital to make depth investigations at random of children of survivors and their families in the general population in order to avoid the danger of generalizations based on conclusions derived from work with psychiatric patients in clinics and hospitals or in psychotherapy practice.

The problems relating to children of survivors must be seen in the context of their families, the style of the family in its everyday life, and especially in its intrafamilial dynamics. Socialization and individuation problems of children cannot be understood via psychiatric diagnoses and psychological categories. I would go so far as to say that it is absurd to make a priori assumptions that by mere virtue of the fact that the parent had been in the Holocaust the children would inevitably suffer from discernible psychopathology. The complexity of the influence on the children cannot be expressed in traditional psychiatric or psychodynamic terms, but can be discerned in the coloring that the parents give to issues connected with life and death in the family ethos.

Sometimes the influence/impact of the parents' experiences can be seen in the form of "living out" in life situations psychic contents that parents were unable to express or work through. I prefer the term "living out" to the psychoanalytic "acting out" because here we are dealing with real experiences of parents reacted to by children, and not the expression of neurotic conflicts acted out unconsciously. This living out is clearly seen in the prism of the children's lives, however different these are from the circumstances in which their parents had lived in the Holocaust. The concepts of manipulation and utilization of children as scapegoats by their parents have been described in the family therapy literature.[5] Here the children live out their parents' styles. The children repeat their parents' attempted solutions in situations of danger;

fight or flight reactions are unconsciously transmitted from one generation to another. One child who was given an intelligence test was shown a train on tracks that come to an end and was asked what he would do. He answered that he would jump off and escape into the forest.

There are many determining factors in relation to the impact of Holocaust experiences on the survivor and his children: the previous personality, specific Holocaust experiences, and the interplay between them; the psychosocial situation of the family—e.g., living in isolation or in a community of survivors—the influence of the general society (Israel, England, U.S.); the family structure (open versus authoritarian, nuclear versus extended family); the specific phase in the life cycle of the survivor when children were born; the immediate post-Holocaust experience of the parent survivor; and the loss of family in relation to specific age and life phase.

Many survivors were the sole remaining members of large extended families. There were crucial differences in terms of the extent of different survivors' losses and whether there were remaining family members with whom to identify and to serve as models in how to work through losses and separations.

Our repertoire of emotional reactions and processes as human beings is necessarily limited, and therefore the spectrum of behavior patterns seen in survivors is not a unique, sui generis, or new phenomenon that cannot be classified at all in psychopathological terms or psychiatric categories. Nonetheless, the intensity of the quantitative factors of suffering and oppression, depersonalization, derealization, or psychic numbing due to the Holocaust experiences surpasses known human experiences, and these dimensions do give survivors' emotional reactions certain intense colorings and uniqueness. There is also a uniqueness in the kaleidoscopic configurations of each survivor with his children.

Without taking into account all these factors, neither clinical, epidemiological, nor the most penetrating psychoanalytic studies of the children of survivors can encompass the complexity of the effect of the Holocaust on the survivors and on future generations.

Different types of family styles are seen in families of survivors. Some parents bombard the children with their experiences but at the same time hide part of themselves because of guilt and shame. In such a way they develop a kind of emotional and cognitive vacuum in the self-awareness of the children. Who is my mother really, the child asks? Very often there is insufficient congruency between the emotional reaction of the survivor mother, be it an angry outburst or an "attack of love" for the child, and the actual connecting experience in reality. The mother's reactions are connected with some past traumatic associations or thoughts of the past and do not allow the children to have a feeling of congruency with their actual object-relations in their here-and-now reality, which obviously does not not allow for the development of a secure self in the child. An example is the outbursts of a mother against her teenage daughter's use of cosmetics. "What a goyish face you have," the mother screamed at the girl. This mother had escaped from the ghetto in order to get food for her family by making herself up to look like an Aryan, only to come back to the ghetto to find that her family had been taken away. Another example is the outburst of a survivor against her adolescent daughter for smoking. She herself had smoked only when she had been in a work commando to burn corpses!

Some of the survivor parents may see their children as extensions of themselves and assign roles to them that fit their own fantasies and needs rather than the personalities of their children.

The task of individuation and socialization is particularly difficult in the child of survivors because of the lack of historic and emotional continuity within the life of the parent without a generation of grandparents.

Should Survivors Tell the Children the Full Details of Their Experiences? I find that the impact of the telling depends on the quality and on the emotional context in which the parent tells the child. For example, a mother attacks her daughter regarding smoking. "You're destroying your health," she yells at her. When her daughter asks mother why she is smoking, mother says, "I couldn't stand the smell of the corpses. I had to smoke when I worked in the crematorium. But you don't need to smoke because you are not forced to burn bodies." This is an example of talking about the concentration camp experiences in an exploitive and emotionally blackmailing way. There is no relief for the parent in such telling, and no dignity of a story of overcoming and survival. The telling is designed to put the child in a bondage of guilt, if not madness.

The most traumatized children of survivors are those whose parents lost their previous children and cannot speak of their losses and thereby release their present children from being somehow responsible for replacing the dead ghosts they never knew yet cannot equal.

Many survivors who were unable to relate their Holocaust experiences suffer from feelings of shame, degradation, and humiliation about what was done to them.

What a survivor did actively or did not do in order to remain alive often is acted out by his children in their own behavior, such as in overactivity and preoccupation with continuous success, or in a continuous fear that everything will fall apart, which no degree of material success can assuage. As atrocities increased in intensity, the whole structure of self-ideals and values was damaged. Punitive superego guilt feelings pounded at the personality, and often the whole mental apparatus regressed to a robotlike existence. Paradoxically, the punishment and sufferings in the inferno of the Holocaust also permitted the reduction of guilt feelings about surviving, but these guilt feelings often became intensified *after* the Holocaust. Some of survivors' illnesses can be understood as a need for punishment as well as ailments that carry messages to their child(ren): "Take care of me." They have been cheated by the world. They have sacrificed everything for their children. Now their children are required to fulfill lost self-ideals.

Survivors' children often see their parents' experiences as exclusively "belonging" to them. They are possessive and jealous and feel themselves special as scapegoats and victims. They believe that they can fulfill the role of the survivors better than their parents did, and they may even be disdainful of the parents because of the latters' avoidance and shame regarding their experiences.

Other children may fear so strongly feeling like their parents that they shift to denial of any connection with their parents and need to reject them, their values, and their aspirations. Seen in awareness groups, such children express repulsion and rejection of their survivor parent. Sometimes they criticize the survivor parent's passive acceptance of his fate during the Holocaust. Other times they mock their low status as immigrants to whichever country they came after the Holocaust. In one survivor family therapy session, an eighteen-year-old daughter with acting-out symptoms in her sexual behavior screamed at her unhappy mother,

"I have heard enough of your suffering, leave me alone, I can't give you back your youth, your health. I hate the survivor in you. Don't exploit me."

Shame and Overanxiety in Survivor Families. Many problems develop in parent-child interaction in relation to parents "hiding" shameful parts of themselves connected with their experiences in the Holocaust. "Shameful secrets" are a phenomenon well known to psychiatrists and psychotherapists in family life. These "secrets" evoke heightened anxiety and awaken fantasies in the children that become a basis of many transactions between the parents and child, and even lead to expressions in the children's manifest behavior, without either parents or children being aware of the secret information causing it. For example, if father was a "macher" (a leader, a go-getter, or, more usually, "an operator") in the concentration camp, and he hides this from his son but continues this survival pattern style of behavior in a crassly materialistic life in work and in interpersonal relations where he continues to be manipulative and exploitive, he certainly influences the children by his example, and the child himself will also superimpose this knowledge of father on the picture he creates of him in the Holocaust. Some children identify with the parent; some of them even unknowingly accept the inner self-concept of the father; others adopt a distinctly opposite behavior pattern in an effort to reject the manifest parental behavior.

He had survived the Holocaust by his own toughness and highhandedness. Both his children are alternately angry at his brutality but drawn to him. His daughter relates to men as gangsters whom she must castrate in order to save herself; she seduces men and then rejects them on the basis of their not being men. The son is ashamed of his father; he is active in the New Left and other new rebellious social movements and ideologies and makes reparation for father, but he also continues to be dependent on father emotionally and materially.

The parent withholding his shameful secret presents a facade— or false self—accompanied by overanxiety about appearing virtuous. Denying unacceptable parts of one's history becomes a central task, and anyone who threatens to reveal the truth must be crushed. The marital dyad may show excessively strong cohesiveness in sharing the secretiveness, or it may become a fighting relationship because of projective identification of the shameful secrets onto the marital partner, resulting in blaming the partner for one's own deficits, real and fantasied.

Secretiveness is a family pattern that is characteristic of immigrant families in general, who often feel ashamed of aspects of their simple background and fear social ostracism and psychological and social rejection and denigration. However, in survivor families the conception of shameful secrets is of another dimension. In some pathological cases a situation develops in which the survivor's identity as a Jew is rejected absolutely, denied and replaced with a fantasy on the basis of which an attempt is made to start a completely new life and identity unconnected with the Holocaust.

The image presented to the children is often a false self and especially an overethical one. From one point of view, there is a facade of security, hope, planning a "normal life" and normal object relationships. But underneath the normality of life after the Holocaust, there is often overwhelming anxiety. One child of survivors observed, "I felt anxiety in every bone of my body emanating from my parents in spite of their claim that life in the concentration camps was not so bad for them." The anxiety in this case sometimes paralyzed him. Both of his parents had been very active in the camps as well as before the Holocaust in the underground, and again following the Holocaust in rebuilding their social careers and in politics. They tried to avoid admitting to their vulnerability. They were forever careful about avoiding any conflicts with officialdom. Through their identification with fighting for social justice, they made themselves feel potent, and kept carefully hidden from themselves their inner depression and anxiety and their shameful secrets of having been so vulnerable in the Holocaust, and their many losses. Naturally their children *must* also be successful, like them, and justify their parents, who had "sacrificed" themselves for their children. Needless to say, the psychiatric ramifications in the children of survivors are considerable. Many of them suffer anxiety, depression, manic defenses, depression, and character disturbances.

How Were the Survivor Parents Seen by Their Children? Some children of survivors overinvest their parents as heroes and giants. It is forbidden to see them as weak in any way, and the children endow them with superhuman strength. A mutual reinforcing of avoidance of all aspects of the parents' weaknesses or badness takes place. The children do not ask parents any "dangerous" questions because they are afraid to hear their shameful secrets and will not allow real mourning and bereavement in the parents. "I don't want you to mourn, I don't want you to be sad. I don't want to hear terrible stories." The parents place their projective identifications onto the children, and then a kind of mirroring takes place as the children project back onto the parents the mythology of their ideal super selves.

In other cases, the survivor parents are seen as weak, passive, having submitted to the perpetrators, damaged, and in danger of transmitting their faulty or weak heredity to their children. Some of their children are fearful of the burden of their parents. They are not able to have a good talk with the parents, except on very concrete levels. Because they are very concerned about their parents' weakness, they may develop fantasies that they will meet an omnipotent, fantastic parental figure who will embrace them and supply them with the security and strength they have not received from their weak, damaged parents. This fantasy can be projected onto the therapist, so that these children are likely to be constantly dissatisfied with and critical of the therapist when he will not accept a savior role. The children have many feelings that mother didn't give them something that she could have given them (warmth and vitality) had she wanted to do so. This feeling is most prominent in families where the survivor parent had lost a previous spouse and children. The children of the new family feel that the survivor parent(s) can't give them the qualities of caring and love that they gave their pre-Holocaust murdered child(ren) as if, in their hearts, to love the current children would be to be unfaithful to the dead child(ren).

Some children who grew up in the shadow of lost Holocaust siblings, sometimes even bearing their names, experience feelings that their Holocaust siblings are still alive. They may enter into a kind of constant search and fantasy that their siblings can be found. This may manifest in fascination with new relationships in which they "see" their dead siblings.

Some children won't leave their parents because they feel responsible for their continued existence. These are not real symbiotic relationships, but rather the children's responses to parasitic uses of them by the parents as a kind of refueling process for them to replace their own relationships with their own parents, which were so cruelly terminated. Some of the mothers I have seen who are organized in this way came from pre-Holocaust emotionally and economically deprived childhoods, and had run away from their hostility to their parents into early marriage and children who then perished in the Holocaust. They felt that they could never really give their new children love and emotional investment, but they also placed on these children terrible demands to become a source of new life for them.

Influences on the Child's Separation-Individuation Process. Severely traumatized survivor parents could not give a sense of historic continuity with their own past self and relationships with their nuclear family. They could not tell the children about their past family identity, system of values, and the world in which they grew up in a frank, free, unashamed manner because of their inability to work through their losses in that world, and their complex, ambivalent feelings about their families of origin.

There often seem to be in the relationship between the survivor parents and their child(ren) hidden as well as manifest messages transmitted from the parents to the child, at verbal and nonverbal levels, that the child should never separate from them: "You are someone who must stay with us forever, must never leave us; you should never want to be an autonomous, separate individual; you are not a person in your own right; and you have a right to live and develop only if you live for us and our continued existence." In these transactions, the children feel deeply pressured; some succeed in opposing and fighting for their autonomy, but not without the special guilt that a child of survivors must feel, and there are some who have to completely reject their parents and their values in order to survive, obviously at great cost. Many others surrender to their parents' needs and aspirations, obviously at great cost as well.

There is a powerful narcissistic overinvestment of the child, a feeling that the child is special and represents all that is good in them. The child has to satisfy their parents' and their parents' generation's needs and aspirations, if before by not separating from the parent, now by performing for them. "When you marry, you marry for us; when you hate, you express our hates; when you fight, you are fighting our wars that we couldn't fight, and even in defending us, you are carrying out that which we couldn't do for our parents." The child is generally a representative of the good part of themselves. These children are likely to be intelligent, nice, polite, conformist, and successful. Sometimes they are grandiose. Sometimes they are given the job of representing the bad part of the parent's self. The message, on one level, is encouragement to marry, be independent, etc., but on another level there are messages to remain dependent, be fearful of autonomy, with the imperative to remain at all cost in mutual interdependence with the parent.

The parents' Holocaust experiences deeply affect the children. Some children are obsessed with their parents' Holocaust experiences. This is expressed in an awareness that their parents are special, and in overcohesiveness of the family. It can also manifest itself in repeated efforts to get out of the family system by migrating into a different ideology and religion, and opposing the parents and their values as a kind of reaction formation tactic expressing unconscious fears and wishes to run away from their parents' fate as survivors. Not surprisingly, given the overwhelming power of these parents' positions, these escape strategies often are doomed to failure.

Children of Survivors Feel Themselves as Special. Common to most if not all children of survivors whom we have interviewed both in therapy and in nonclinical situations has been an awareness of being in some way *special* as children of survivors. This is expressed in many ways; for example, a young doctor feels special as a doctor, not like other young people who seize on the narcissistic identity rewards of this or another profession, but self-consciously a child of survivors now come to heal and repair the ill.

During the Yom Kippur War, one surgeon survivor/child of survivors with a compulsive need to save lives, operated night and day under heavy fire on the front line without rest. He felt within himself a rearousal of suppressed "death-infested memories" of his childhood in the ghetto, where he saw emaciated bodies falling around him and on top of him. These memories now returned to him during the Yom Kippur War and his pent-up wishes to save lives back in the Holocaust found powerful sublimated expressions in his intensive surgical activity in Israel's war years later.

There are also no few cases where the survivor parents transmitted specialness to their children through their overwhelming efforts to conceal their own and their child's identity as Jews. From the beginning of childhood the parents avoid everything to do with Jewish identity and Holocaust and survival. In one case the child would react with profuse blushing and sweating at every association to war and Jewish persecution. Some survivor parents even refused to circumcise their children in order to fearfully "safeguard" the children from possible persecution as Jews in the future.

Some children who were born in Poland right after the Holocaust whose parents did everything to conceal their Jewish origins and their Holocaust experiences tried to find in Marxist ideology a savior of humanity. On an unconscious level these parents transmitted to their children their nonverbal fears, the unspoken messages of horror and destruction of their Holocaust experiences as well as fears that their Jewish origin would be discovered. Phobic symptoms and nightmares of destruction were manifest in these children. On arrival in Israel in 1967, one such child said, "I feel sweat from anxiety and thus awakening in me my tormented Jewishness."

When this family heard on the radio in Poland in 1967 about the so-called bombardment of Tel Aviv and the victory of the Arabs against Israel at the beginning of the war, the father suddenly began to sweat profusely, and experienced a deep pain; he then remembered in his childhood the bombardment of Warsaw in which he grew up at the beginning of World War II.

Sensitivity to the Wounded Parent. Children of survivors are often aware that their father's or mother's physical discomfort—whether specific symptoms such as migraine attacks, or a general insistence on peace and quiet and consequent isolation in their room —are connected with Holocaust preoccupations, memories, and avoidances. The parents typically avoid telling their children even why they have outbursts of yelling and shrieking. In any case, the children feel the horror affects in their parents' voices.

In therapy we frequently hear different variations of the following words: "We know that father can't play with us as other fathers do, or mother yells at us because of the Nazis, but they, our parents, are not guilty." Very often this attitude changes the children of the survivors into parental figures, or what family therapists call a "parental child." The children have to take on reversed roles of protectors. They may even be the verbalizers for the parent; the child then expresses the anguish and losses that the parents cannot. They are also the family calmers; when the irritable mother has her outbursts, these children take it calmly. They know how to respond calmly and pacify her, bringing her back to reality.

It seems that some of these children convert their parental traumatic experiences even into sources of ego strength for themselves. Very often, their positive management of their parents' distress also becomes a source of sublimation of aggressive drives and tendencies, expressed in their need and unusual ability to pacify and calm, skills that they carry over into their everyday interpersonal relationships as well as into professional choices to be healers—psychologists or surgeons.

Awareness Groups for Children of Survivors. Many of the children identify with their survivor parents' fates as a persecuted minority in other sublimated ways, such as in becoming poets and writers. In identifying with their parents' fates, many of the children have welcomed opportunities to join so-called awareness groups for children of survivors, mainly in the United States but also in other countries. In such a manner they try to achieve an identity, much like other persecuted minority groups. This awareness movement of the children of survivors also seems to represent a sublimated outraged cry of protest from the children of persecutees toward a world that was silent while their parents' generation was being exterminated. This is a kind of primordial cry expressing the need for protest and mourning that the parents could not allow themselves during the Holocaust, and in addition, through this movement, the children leave a legacy for all of mankind.

Children of Survivors Differ According to Where They Have Grown Up. In Israel we have seen various phases with differing waves of awareness of the Holocaust in the generations of children of survivors since the Holocaust. Children of survivors born "near the graves of Europe," immediately after the war, from parents who had just emerged from the Holocaust vortex, were different from those whose parents' puberty and adolescence were shaped some years later after the Holocaust, who grew and developed in new, "good enough" environments, whether in the United States, Britain, or Israel. The parents of the later-born children had better possibilities for role experimentation and for developing their own autonomy and identity with different models available for their identification in the postwar countries where they had settled, in a period of history when the atmosphere was hopeful for the future.

In Israel there was a unique psychohistorical situation with the fight for survival and reestablishment of the Jewish people in its historical homeland that coincided with the rebirth fantasies of the younger survivors. This intense atmosphere with its ethos of pioneering and self-sacrifice and emphasis on the future and playing down of the past and the terrible Holocaust years deeply influenced the survivors who arrived at early adulthood and parenthood during this era. They had to have a self-image of being tough and achievement oriented. They fought actively for survival of the state with which they fully identified with deep pride. Their identity was with their new country of Israel. Looking back with anger on their past homelands made it easier to fully identify with and accept Israel, despite its harsh realities. In this atmosphere they reared their children with conscious ideals of toughness, achievement orientation, and not giving in to emotions and feelings. Afraid of feelings in themselves, they had new and additional reasons not to encourage emotional expression in their children.

The children themselves tried to avoid seeing in their parents the shameful images of the helpless, passive victims going as sheep to the slaughter. Thus, many of the children developed a tough exterior because of the fear of being flooded with emotions and fears. They needed to be heroes defending their parent survivors. "No More Masada" became an expression for a generation of survivors of a fear of return to the status of victims during the Holocaust.

At the same time, many children of survivors also showed ambivalence in their attitudes toward the Arabs. They feared to accept the roles of conquerors, aggressors, and persecutors.

The Need for Research Including Healthy Children of Survivors. It is important to emphasize the danger of making unjustified generalizations that can lead to stigmatization on the basis of clinical findings in survivors' children. Some survivors have been surprisingly successful parents and appear to be unusually well endowed for child rearing. In other families, one of the parents has compensated for the pathological influence of the damaged spouse and thus made for healthy functioning in the children. Those factors that make for healthy family functioning despite traumatization of parents merit deeper study. The parent survivor's ability to share and discuss his Holocaust experiences with his children in an appropriate fashion varies greatly and is related to the degree of working through the parents have achieved in relation to their losses, blocked aggression, guilt, shame, and self-hatred.

In families where parent survivors did everything to avoid and deny and remained silent about their Holocaust experiences, these experiences acquired an aura of secretiveness and shame. The children developed fearful and embarrassed attitudes to these "family secrets" and often weaved horrifying fantasies about what was done to their parents and how they survived. Indirect communications and nonverbal cues from the parents as well as material derived from the media fed these fantasies with associated feelings of shame, guilt, and fear.

These observations relate to our general clinical experience with children of survivors seen in psychiatric outpatient clinics and hospitals in Israel. The parents of most of these children belonged to the age group of concentration camp survivors who married soon after their release from the camps. Many had lost previous spouses and children. Subsequent marriage and the birth of children took place soon after the Holocaust experiences and insufficient time had elapsed for working through and coming to terms with the traumatic experiences and massive losses. The children were thus intensely involved by the parents in their early attempts at recovery. On the other hand, survivors who were late adolescents or young adults during the Holocaust often married some years later, after they had resumed their development and had achieved a greater degree of integration of the massive trauma they had undergone. These survivor parents thus had less need to use the family situation and their children to work through their Holocaust experiences and losses. As a result, the directness of the impact of the Holocaust on the children of these age groups has been less severe and seems to be of a more subtle psychological nature.

Research in the area of the transmission of the effects of parental traumatization to their children is problematic because of the complexity and large number of individual variables involved. These relate to the pretraumatization personality of the survivor, the nature of the traumatization and the age of exposure to it, losses of family members, whether both parents are survivors or only one, the personality of a nonsurvivor parent, additional trauma acting directly on the child in his early years with regard to external conditions (e.g., a D.P. camp), the country in which one grew up, and more. These factors create considerable methodological problems when an attempt is made to measure and compare the specific effects of massive traumatization in groups of parents and in their offspring.

A few studies of interest have been made. In Canada, Sigal and his colleagues, using questionnaires, tests, and interviews on different age groups, reported a greater sense of alienation and anomie as well as problems with impulse control and feelings of depression among adolescent children of survivors than other patient groups of the same age seen in the Jewish General Hospital in Montreal.[6] They related these findings specifically to a nuclear disturbance of maternal preoccupation in survivors, which acts as the traumatic, depriving influence for the children.

In a study in Israel, Aleksandrowicz searched for typical family patterns and symptoms.[7] He excluded from his study parents who were grossly disturbed in order to look for "more subtle changes in personality which may not prevent them from functioning in society and yet impair their ability as parents." Aleksandrowicz described two typical family constellations, which he called "parental disequilibrium" and "affective deficiency syndrome and hyperrepression." In the children there was a relatively high number of cases with phobias, neurotic or reactive behavior disorders, or a combination of both syndromes with no particular diagnostic specificity.

Also in Israel, De Graff studied groups of young soldiers aged eighteen to twenty-one in an army psychiatric clinic, comparing the symptoms of a group of twenty-four youngsters whose parents had been in concentration camps with the symptoms of sixteen youngsters whose parents had suffered the loss of close relatives without themselves having been persecuted.[8] The degree and nature of the disturbances observed in these two groups were then further compared with those found in a control group of twenty Ashkenazi soldiers. The soldiers who were children of survivors were proved to suffer significantly more often from personality disorders and more often showed delinquent behavior in comparison with soldiers of both other groups.

With regard to nonclinical populations, Karr explored seventy-one offspring aged seventeen to twenty-nine in the San Francisco

Bay Area.[9] He compared three groups—thirty-three offspring of parents who had both been in concentration camps, sixteen who had one parent who was a concentration camp survivor, and twenty-two whose parents had escaped from Europe before the Holocaust. His findings, based on interviews and psychological testing, indicated that children of both parent survivors showed significant difficulties in impulse control; males appeared to act out impulsively and tended to be rebellious, while females responded with withdrawal, fear, and passivity. There was also a tendency for children of both parent survivors to be anxious, depressed, and somewhat estranged from society. Hostility feelings toward the parents were associated with considerable ambivalence and guilt. In addition, Karr found that children of both parent survivors sought considerably more psychotherapy than those in the other two groups.

Israel as a Rehabilitative Concept. The psychosocial structure of the society in which traumatized groups settle can have an important influence on the expression of psychopathology in the individual members of the group and especially in their children.

It is my impression and that of other Israeli investigators that the above findings relating to children of survivors who grew up in the U.S. and Canada do not have the same application to the majority of those who grew up in Israel. The psychosocial situation existing in Israel, especially during the early years of the state when the vast majority of the survivors settled in the country, was an important positive influence in making for their successful adaptation and acculturation. In many ways Israel has served as a particularly meaningful rehabilitation project for a traumatized people. Social recognition and validity was given to their traumatic experiences. In the "rebirth" of the Jewish people in a national homeland, Holocaust survivors found hope of their own "rebirth," thus countering their identity impairment. In Israel's fight for survival they found a common theme with their own struggle to survive and constructive channels for expression of their blocked aggression and mourning.

Of course, despite sociotherapeutic influences encouraging a new integration and sense of identity, for many of the survivors the serious psychopathology resulting from their massive traumatization in the Holocaust was only somewhat mitigated. On the other hand, the psychosocial structure of Israeli society was even more valuable for the children of survivors in preventing the alienation, anomie, and identity problems that have been reported in various studies of the second generation in the U.S. and Canada. This is especially evident in the general, nonclinical population. The availability of a healthy identification with Israeli nationality, and its active promulgation by the new state through the educational system and its continuation into army service, have often successfully modified the pathogenic influences of survivor parents' impaired identities on the second generation. In addition, Israeli society's tendency to view society as a virtual extension of the family, which is very different from American society, has reinforced possibilities of acquiring a positive self-image.[10]

Community expressions of mourning and anger that are accompanied by a sense of pride in achievement and hope for the future enable children to continue their parents' effort to work through the Holocaust experiences. Children participate in powerful social ceremonies such as Holocaust Memorial Day. Owing to such "institutionalization" of mourning by the state, "there was less need for the parents to ask from the child to be a sort of living memorial to the tragic fate of the lost families."[11]

These sociotherapeutic influences were especially prominent for those survivors who settled in a kibbutz.[12] The communal structure of the kibbutz provided a readymade community support system for the survivors who chose to live in this framework. In addition, the communal child-rearing practices of the kibbutz, with the sharing of nurturing by multiple mother figures (*metaplot*), relieved the burden of mothering on the overanxious survivor mother, thus reducing her insecurity and mitigating pathogenic effects.

In the U.S. and Canada, immigrant survivors often felt themselves aliens whose ordeal was not recognized as part of the national experience. Under these circumstances, there was much less possibility of working through mourning and aggression than in Israel, and much less openness with children about the parents' concentration camp past. Parents were more frightened, more ashamed, and more denying of their traumatic experiences than in Israel. In America, many survivors hid their concentration camp tattoo numbers and even underwent cosmetic surgery to have them removed. I believe that the attitude of denial and avoidance of the survivors' experiences by U.S. society, one which was also shared by many American psychotherapists, was an important factor in discouraging survivors from entering therapy in the U.S., and a surprisingly small number have had therapy in comparison with Israel.[13]

The Holocaust has been kept alive in the memory and consciousness of the people of Israel in many ways. It was an important motif in the establishment and continued struggle of the state, which in turn has given new meaning to the deaths and suffering of victims of the Holocaust. For the second generation, every one of Israel's wars has carried with it a sense of fighting to prevent another Holocaust. The traumatic memories of the persecutory experiences that still cause so much distress to the survivor parents have been used adaptively by the children in order to activate their determination to continue the fight for the security of their country, thus fostering solidarity and group identity.

As psychiatrists, we deal with the most severely damaged among the large traumatized population of survivors in Israel and our findings are based on our work with these families. Studies of broader, nonclinical populations are of considerable importance. Given its large number and variety of ethnic groups, Israel constitutes a rich laboratory for research into traumatized people.

The study of the reverberating effects of traumatization and the intergenerational transmission of trauma is a vitally important subject for understanding both individual psychiatric disturbances and the intergenerational transmission of pathology in successive generations of a family. Through undermining basic trust and ontological security, massive traumatization can impair the nurturing capacity in prospective parents, and the blocked aggressions and resentments of traumatized parents then create further problems for their children. Binding symbiotic parent-child relationships can result from the effects of massive trauma, with resultant distortion of the separation-individuation process in childhood, manifested in identity and affect disturbances in adolescence. Further understanding of the long-term effects of traumatization and its transmission will carry with it important implications and challenges for community mental health programs.

6.

Group Formation and Human Reciprocity in the Nazi Concentration Camps

We are all brothers, and we are all suffering from the same fate. The same smoke floats over all our heads. Help one another. It is the only way to survive.
— Elie Wiesel, *Night*

Group bonding experiences in the concentration camp mitigated both the individual and collective trauma processes. The group could prevent regression to complete apathetic surrender to death, and help to maintain hope and the motivation to continue the struggle to live. It promoted the psychological survival of the victims by preserving human awareness and a sense of self despite the dehumanization and amorality. We now understand that the supportive relationships experienced by many adolescent survivors protected personality functioning and enabled their growth and development to proceed. The experience of the survivor of the death camps provides an added insight into the meaning of "survival" in extremity, a sense of the possibility of transcendence of evil by the victims acting together in a spirit of solidarity and communion.

Franz Brull was a leader in the development of psychotherapy in Israel. He was deeply concerned about the welfare of Holocaust survivors, and some of his most devoted and instructive psychotherapies were with them. Six of these cases have been described in his book, *Toward a Humanistic Psychotherapy.*[1] In these case descriptions he demonstrated an empathic commitment that is

121

unique in traditional psychotherapy because his availability and his involvement with his young survivor-patient/friends and their families went beyond the limits of what is usually understood as the psychotherapeutic role. He was supportive and sharing in every possible sense and deliberately adopted a parent role as a replacement for the dead parents.

In 1947, Brull had participated in a medical team that spent several months with survivors in the Cyprus detention camps to which the British had shipped "illegal" Jewish immigrants to Palestine. The purpose of the mission was the evaluation of the mental state of survivors in the "youth village" in Cyprus, the majority of whom were aged fourteen to seventeen. Although Brull had only one year of clinical psychiatric experience behind him, he persistently opposed the opinions of the very experienced and authoritative leader of the mission, Dr. Paul Friedman from the United States. Brull was deeply affected by the evidence he encountered in so many survivors of the trauma of the Holocaust, and he was puzzled by the fact that his colleagues—both from the United States and in Israel—seemed to be avoiding the significance of this trauma.

In particular, Brull vehemently criticized Friedman's continued emphasis on the importance of early childhood experiences in the mental state of the survivors and his skepticism about the rehabilitative value of *aliya* (immigration to Israel) for them. Brull was convinced of the central importance of *aliya* in the rehabilitation of the survivors. He understood the basic need of the survivor to create meaning out of the catastrophe, and firmly believed that settlement in Israel would provide the possibility to identify, to belong, to be part of a community. He was closely in tune with the spirit of determination and hope prevailing among the groups of young survivors waiting to go on *aliya*. In the report he wrote summarizing his findings among the survivors in Cyprus, he referred specifically to the "emotional strength deriving from group bonds." That same emotional strength among the youths in Cyprus had previously forged the determination of the groups in the concentration camps to continue the struggle to survive.

Human Reciprocity among the Jewish Prisoners

Cooperation for survival among members of the same species is a basic law of life. Throughout the history of man, sharing relationships have been a central mode of coping with and adapting to the environment. When the conditions of life are particularly harsh and survival is difficult, there is often an increase in reciprocal relationships. This has been demonstrated, for example, in the sociocultural patterns of villages in the Arctic.[2]

The Nazi concentration camp represents the most extreme situation of survival known to man. It was a central component in a system designed for killing many millions of human beings, primarily the Jews of Europe. These tormented people were all condemned to death, but the process took time and was not uniform. The Nazi death machinery addressed the killing of a scattered people in twenty-two different European states and regions. Even in the death camps, there was a technical limit to the numbers that could be killed every day. As the processing for death went on inexorably, there were also delays in the deaths of those selected to work at various "jobs" in the concentration camps. The motivation to continue with the struggle to live in the concentration camps was constantly and deliberately undermined by a ruthless system of unprecedented terrorization and dehumanization. Many died from injuries inflicted, exhaustion, exposure, disease, and starvation.

Interpersonal bonding, reciprocity, and sharing were an essential source of strength for "adaptation" and survival of many of the victims. Apart from the limited opportunities for the starving inmates to share their sparse food rations, it was their interpersonal support that sustained their motivation to carry on with the struggle to live.

There has been little systematic study of the social bonding in concentration camp life. The psychiatric literature, mainly concerned with psychopathology and psychodynamics, and derived extensively from examinations for compensation claims and clinical studies of survivors in therapy, has emphasized the extreme and unprecedented nature of the Holocaust trauma and the destructive after-effects. There has been some study of *individual* "coping" and adaptive patterns of the victims within the concentration camps. These have been described in the psychiatric literature in terms of denial, emotional withdrawal, cognitive constriction, constructive activity, hope, meaning or purpose in living, a belief system, the "will to live," and fantasy.[3] A sustaining fantasy that is particularly relevant is "attachment ideation" or preoccupation with important attachment figures, such as parents, siblings, and children, if believed to be alive, which mobilizes motivation to live in the hope of reunion.

Leo Eitinger, in discussing reasons for survival in the concentration camps, refers to survivors who believed that "their 'being together' had been significant," either because "they were helped by the others who were with them or because they themselves had to think of the others." Eitinger comments,

> Even though this help was often of a minimal and/or symbolic nature it seems to have contributed in a decisive way towards the individual's ability to retain part of his personality and self-respect, and this is given considerable importance in relation to the capacity for survival.[4]

Hillel Klein refers frequently to "cohesive pairing behavior" as a specific psychosocial coping response during the Holocaust. In his study of survivors in the kibbutz, he states, "These individuals attribute their survival to the existence of tightly-knit supportive groups during the Holocaust. Survival is intimately linked with community."[5]

However, little systematic study has been made of interpersonal resources, social bonding, and support among the survivors. This is surprising in view of the clear potential of these protective and buffering resources while in the grip of traumatic processes as well as in the mitigation and prevention of the long-term effects of trauma. Even in the personal accounts of the survivors themselves, there is a surprising lack of emphasis on helping activities, sharing, and mutual support among the inmates of the concentration camps.

Terrence Des Pres, in his literary analysis in *The Survivor* of published eyewitness accounts of survivors describing their experiences, shows a bold sensitivity for understanding the interpersonal relationships in the concentration camps and their significance. In relating to the lack of emphasis on this aspect of behavior in survivors' accounts, he states,

> Primarily survivors stress the negative side of concentration camp existence because their accounts are governed by an obsessive need to "tell the world" of the terrible things they have seen. This determines not only the kind of material they select to record, but also the emphasis they give it. As a witness the survivor aims above all to convey the otherness of the camps, their specific inhumanity, . . . acts of care and decency seem so out of place in the camps that survivors themselves

are perplexed . . . what impressed survivors most indelibly was death, suffering, terror, all on a scale of magnitude and monstrosity not to be faced without lasting trauma. . . . Reports by survivors regularly included small deeds of courage and resistance, of help and mutual care; but in the larger picture the image of viciousness and death grows to such enormous intensity that all else—any sign of elementary humanness—pales to insignificance.[6]

Meir Dworzecki did pioneer work in his studies based on testimonies and interviews of survivors of the destruction of the Jews of Estonia in the ghettos and concentration camps. He comments on the stress laid on the various atrocities and on the "moral degeneration" of the victims in the camps, whereas relatively little mention is made of helping activities in the relations between the victims. In Dworzecki's opinion the "degeneration" among the victims was "an unexpected phenomenon in Jewish life," which left the survivors "utterly perplexed and astonished." On the other hand, the "good deeds" of the anonymous general run of the people in their relations with each other were taken for granted in terms of how they held onto their humanity in their manifestations of solidarity, mutual help, and self-sacrifice. The very acts that have the significance of enabling survival become those that pale into insignificance in everyday life.[7]

Des Pres proceeds to demonstrate that the struggle for life in extremity depends on solidarity, social bonding, and interchange, and that even in Auschwitz and Buchenwald life was intensely social. Scattered among the detailed descriptions of the terrors reported in the eyewitness accounts he quotes are many examples of mutual help, continual sharing, and in some cases an intensely disciplined underground organization based on teamwork and the creation of a social network.

These activities point "to the radically social nature of life in extremity," based on "an awareness of the common predicament and of the need to act collectively," and to the conclusion that "the need *to* help is as basic as the need *for* help."[8] Furthermore, human reciprocity in the group and dyadic relations, by sustaining the morale and the motivation to continue the struggle to live on in the Nazi concentration camps, increased the chances of eventual survival.

Kitty Hart, an Auschwitz survivor, wrote, "I soon realized that alone one could not possibly survive. It was necessary, therefore, to form little families of two or three. In this way we looked after one another."[9]

Richard Glazar, a Treblinka survivor, stated,

Of course there *were* people who survived who were loners. They will tell you now they survived *because* they relied on no one but themselves. But the truth is probably—and they may either not know it, or not be willing to admit to themselves or others—that they survived because they were carried by *someone*, someone who cared for them as much, or almost as much as for themselves.[10]

Women who met Anne Frank in Bergen-Belsen in the month before she died believed that neither the hunger nor the typhus killed her but the death of her sister, Margot. One of these women said, "It was frightening to see how easy it was to die for someone who had been left all alone in a concentration camp."[11]

Eugene Heimler, the ex-Buchenwald inmate and social therapist, put it simply: "None of us who have survived would be here unless there had been others who helped us in our survival."[12]

All were marked for eventual extermination; it was merely a question of time, but meanwhile, from hour to hour and day to day, as Des Pres states, "through innumerable small acts of humanness, most of them covert but everywhere in evidence, survivors were able to maintain societal structures workable enough to keep themselves alive and morally sane."[13]

It would seem that whenever conditions were relatively predictable and routine, no matter how extreme the dehumanization and brutalization, spontaneous bonding occurred between the victims. After the violent shock of induction into the camp system, and within a few days of arrival, pairing and group formations would develop.

Elmer Luchterhand, a sociologist, has made a highly illuminating study of the social behavior of fifty-two concentration camp survivors, based on interviews shortly after their liberation. The survivors originated in the main from Central European countries, and their ages ranged from the teens to the fifties. The majority had been in camps for over two years and "had a sharing relationship of mutuality with one or more prisoners." He discusses the emergence of a prisoner social system, based on pairs and groups, which clearly enhanced survival chances.

"Stable pairing was the most common type of interpersonal relationship pattern." When one partner died or was removed, replacement was swift. Luchterhand states unequivocally,

With all of the raging conflict in the camps, it was in the pairs that the prisoners kept alive the semblance of humanity. The pairs gave relief from the shame of acts of acquiescence and surrender. The pairs produced expertness in the survival skills known as "organizing."[14]

The pair was thus "the basic unit of survival" and, as one of the survivors stated, "One could not exist in the camp without participating somehow in a sharing relationship."

When survival conditions became even more extreme, however, as on the "death marches" after the evacuation of the camps, it became increasingly difficult to maintain interpersonal bonds in the desperate struggle not to fall behind and be shot. One survivor, a researcher of Holocaust literature, Eli Pfefferkorn, states,

> The group ties that I developed in the last camp were of an expedient nature determined by mutual usefulness between the group and myself
> ... these rapidly dissolved in the course of the "death march" as the survival conditions became more extreme.[15]

On the other hand, Luchterhand insists that even in death march conditions, friendship pairs and trios were maintained and actively sustained one another. In a revealing paper, based on interviews with ten survivors, he describes the transport of evacuated Auschwitz prisoners for periods of seven to fourteen days from Gleiwitz, Silesia, to various camp destinations in midwinter, in roofless, low-sided freight cars. The vast majority died on the way, and after the second or third day there were recurrent fights, resulting in the deaths of many, for the coveted corner or side positions. However, even in these unendurable conditions, "some degree of acts of sharing and cooperation was maintained or reemerged" among the handful of survivors in each car.[16]

In my studies of Holocaust experience based on in-depth interviewing of survivors, I became increasingly aware of the extent and significance of interpersonal bonding between the victims in the concentration camps. It seems that survival in a camp involved participation to some degree or other in a sharing relationship, and that to have survived entirely alone without help was rare. Whenever conditions in a concentration camp were relatively predictable and stable, no matter how extreme the dehumanization and brutalization, spontaneous bonding appeared between the victims.

On relating their camp experience, survivors frequently talk in terms of "we" and "us," often without realizing that they are doing so. In a very basic psychobiological sense, life (and death) in the Nazi concentration camp took place in a collective situation. The events of daily life—eating, working, sleeping, excreting, "roll calls" and selections—which were pregnant with suffering, were perforce conducted in group situations. Any "leisure" time was spent in groups huddled together. The capacity "to be" with other persons and share with them was a crucial element in survival. In retrospect, survivors often have difficulty in seeing themselves apart from the collective out of which coalesced friendship pairs and groups, if conditions permitted.

The individual experiences of the victims were heterogeneous and unique. Formulating these experiences in terms of "human reciprocity" and other such concepts involves the use of language from everyday life situations. The words and terminology used cannot encompass the unprecedented and inconceivable events of the man-made extremity of the Nazi concentration camp. The lack of a vocabulary to adequately convey the human experiences of survival and death in that "other planet," together with the agonizingly painful feelings involved in recalling them, makes verbal communication extremely difficult and sometimes impossible. Furthermore, the frequent and unpredictable changes that took place in the camp routine with the constant degradation, anonymity, and meaningless death created an unreal and bewildering atmosphere. The dreamlike quality that many survivors feel in relation to their concentration camp experiences is probably also due to an alteration of consciousness deriving from the numbing cognitive constriction and robotization of the trauma state as well as from the state of starvation. Descriptions of behavior and response among the victims struggling for survival in these conditions and conclusions about the significance of their behavior, especially in relation to acts of humanity versus amoral acts, are often widely divergent and even contradictory. Des Pres writes of this as the "double-vision at the heart of the testimony," and of the "duality of behavior" in the face of "irreconcilable conflicts" resulting from a "choice to live" in extremity.[17] The formulation of concepts that encompass these irreconcilables and that express insights derived from the extreme experiences is an important challenge.

Massive Psychic Trauma—Individual and Collective

Since the 1950s psychiatrists have been studying incarceration in the Nazi concentration camps from the standpoint of massive psychic trauma and its long-term effects. "Massive" or "catastrophic" psychic trauma refers to extreme situations of death and dehumanization that lead to overwhelming injury and paralysis of the adaptive and recuperative mechanisms of the psyche. As a result, long-standing mental impairments of varying severity are liable to occur.[18]

Krystal, an American psychoanalyst who conducted pioneering studies on Holocaust trauma, described the stages of the "catastrophic trauma" process when the psychic defenses are overwhelmed thus: (1) confrontation with death; (2) affective blocking and numbing; (3) construction of cognitive and executive function; and, finally, (4) defeat and surrender (the "Musselman" state, in concentration camp slang) leading frequently to death. Krystal's thorough and in-depth description of the traumatic process relates essentially to *individual* intrapsychic events. The interpersonal dimension, however, was not studied, although Krystal understands and clearly states that "in the acute traumatic state one stands alone and abandoned by all sources of feelings of security" and that this can lead to the "giving up of all hope of satisfactory human contact resulting from the destruction of basic trust."[19]

Survivors of social catastrophes suffer from collective trauma in addition to the individual trauma. When a community is destroyed, it appears that in addition to the individual traumatic process, there occurs a further psychic impairment that enhances the individual traumatic process and makes recovery from the effects of the individual trauma more difficult. Kai T. Erikson has made a study of the psychological after-effects resulting from the scattering and fragmentation of the community after the 1972 Buffalo Creek, West Virginia, flood disaster. He described collective trauma as "a blow to the tissues of social life that damages the bonds linking people together and impairs the prevailing sense of communality." The three main behavioral manifestations of this collective trauma are demoralization, disorientation, and loss of connection.[20]

These observations are especially valid in our studies of Holocaust survivors. In addition to this process of trauma in the individual, the Holocaust catastrophe involved a process of collective trauma resulting from the destruction of the community to which the victim belonged. This collective trauma added a further major dimension of stress to the individual in the grip of the traumatic process. Collective trauma involves "a gradual realization that the community no longer exists as a source of nurturance and that part of the self has disappeared."[21] The psychological after-effects of collective trauma include the collapse of morale and moral standards, a loss of basic trust, and a sense of disconnection and isolation from other people. Individual psychic strength is related to community strength, and with the loss of the significant community, the effects of the individual trauma are enhanced and recovery rendered more difficult.

The survivors of the Holocaust were not only uprooted from their familiar social environment and unable to return to it after liberation, but most of their families and their entire communities were totally destroyed. The extended family and communal bonds were an integral element in Jewish life in Europe, and this collective trauma deeply undermined their basic sense of security and identity. The fact that the Nazi Holocaust was deliberately perpetrated by men who belonged to a highly regarded and advanced culture added another important dimension to the process of collective trauma. This affected, threatened, and undermined the self-image of the victims and their basic trust in their fellow men. Their future adaptation to society suffered from this important aspect of psychosocial trauma in addition to all the direct traumatization they had undergone.

Interpersonal Bonds and Holocaust Trauma

Understanding the role of collective trauma in catastrophic stress situations and their long-term effects leads to two important implications:

1. the establishment of group bonds can mitigate destructive trauma processes while in the grip of the catastrophic stress situation; and
2. the creation of group bonds is essential for recovery from catastrophic stress.

Supportive social bonding has been increasingly recognized in social psychiatry as important in situations of adversity and stress. When absent or deficient, there is reduced resistance to psychiatric illness and medical morbidity.[22] The study of interpersonal and group bonding in the survivors of the Holocaust, both during the actual traumatic experiences and during the process of recovery, enables us to learn about the adaptive strengths as well as the recuperative resources of the psyche in coping with and mastery of major trauma.

There has been an almost exclusive preoccupation with the damaging results of the Holocaust experience in terms of static psychopathology, and not enough study has gone into the process of integration and mastery of the trauma with development throughout the life cycle. Many survivors reported on the value of closely knit group experiences among their adolescent peers in the ghettos. In these groups they learned how to cope with the specific adversities of their situation in the Holocaust and had reinforced values and ideals from their cultural background, which served them well in the concentration camps and in their readaptation after the war.[23]

Interpersonal Bonds in the Concentration Camps

After the violent shock of induction into the camp system, and within a few days of arrival, pairing and group formations would develop. Pairing relationships were the most common and, as indicated earlier, have been termed "the basic unit of survival" by Luchterhand in his seminal sociological study of social systems among concentration camp inmates.[24] The friendships that formed were often intense, with maximal reciprocity and sharing in every possible sense. The friends would do everything they could to protect each other physically in situations of minimal possibility, trying to keep warm together and nursing each other when sick, which often also involved the need for dangerous concealment of illness. Any extra scraps of food that were "acquired," often by mutual efforts, were meticulously shared by the couple. However, the central importance of these relationships was the mutual moral support and encouragement by which hope and the motivation to continue the struggle to survive was sustained.[25]

Groups varied in size but often consisted of three, five, or eight inmates. The groups were well integrated and characterized by a high degree of mutual devotion, mutual aid, and sharing. Group members changed frequently due to the vicissitudes of camp life and death, and would soon be replaced by new members considered compatible with the group, so that cohesion would be maintained. Loyalty, mutual concern, and sharing were usually restricted to one's group, with little or no possibility of concern for those outside it. The intensity and stability of such relationships were related to the length of stay in one camp and the conditions in the camp. Small groups developed in all the camps but especially in the slave labor camps.

Sometimes the group even had to defend its interest selfishly and aggressively against the encroachments of individuals and other groups of inmates in the desperate struggle for survival. Groups were often formed around a nucleus of previous ghetto or childhood relationships, or a common cultural or youth movement background. Various roles and duties were often allocated within the group, as within a family, according to the nature and conditions prevailing in the specific camp. A basic activity of the group was always the acquiring and sharing of food, medicines, and bits of clothing, etc. Sometimes one member of a group got a "good job" that would enable him to help the others. Sharing of news, information, and advice in "organizing" were important. Other activities, such as storytelling, gossiping, reminiscing, playing, singing, "joking," and celebration of birthdays and festivals were important for maintaining group morale. Each group had its own identity and culture, which manifested itself in the style of humor, specific activities, attitudes to others, shared hopes, fantasies, and ideology, according to the sociocultural background of the members.

Mutual aid in the groups often involved direct protection and life saving as occurred when, because of exhaustion or sickness, inmates felt they could not function at roll call or at work and would remain in their bunks. The group would persuade a sick member to appear at roll call and go to work, since to remain behind in the bunk often meant selection for death. At work the sick comrade would be hidden or somehow helped to function. If manifestations of regression to the resigned, apathetic stupor of the "Musselman" state would appear, the group would fight against them, encouraging, cajoling, and coercing the group member into carrying on the struggle to survive. Despite the extreme adversity, everyday human interactions and emotions were manifested with expressions of anger, love, greed, and rivalry, etc., thus helping to preserve the human image.

Larger groups were formed for any special venture such as

resistance activities, although opportunities were minimal. They were more commonly manifested in symbolic morale raising by groups of teenage youths through such acts as collecting the sweet substance distributed as "jam" and inserting it into the petrol tanks of the SS cars as an act of "sabotage." In fact, the maintenance of morale and sustenance of hope were the essential element of human relations in the concentration camp, for they strengthened the motivation to live and nurtured the possibility of resistance.

When hope is verbalized in the group interaction it becomes more powerful through suggestion and mutual validation. The promise and hope of bearing witness, fantasies of wreaking revenge, and visions for the creation of a new future were central themes of group morale. Activities were often closely linked with religious, political, and ideological beliefs, among which dreams of settlement in Palestine were the most widespread among the groups of youths and young adult men and women studied by the author. Many had belonged to youth movements before the war or had been drawn into them in the ghettos; some became involved for the first time in the concentration camps. The groups often had a leader endowed with special qualities. For example, a large group of twin boys selected for "research purposes" by Mengele in Birkenau-Auschwitz were "looked after" by an older twin inmate in his late twenties. Of the many protective activities carried out by this man, of particular significance was the sensitive, gradual way in which he transmitted to the twin children the facts of the deaths of their parents after their tragic and brutal separation from them at the entrance to Auschwitz. The continuing deep attachment of some of these "boys" to their leader was still very much evident when they were interviewed by the author forty years later.

Where a group of religious Jews was formed, religious practices and rituals could be sustained through such group activities as praying together, sharing part of a prayer book or tefillin, collecting combustible material for a Chanukah lamp, etc.[26] In women's groups, feminine interests were discussed, including even the exchange of recipes and cooking in fantasy. What was significant was the hope implied in thinking of a future in which such activities would again be possible, different "from the unbearable present" in which the time perspective was "limitless and totally owned by others."[27]

Intense Group Belonging

Sometimes a group became fused with an exceptional quality of cohesion, as portrayed in the following example.

One of the survivors interviewed who spent the last five months of the war in Buchenwald was a member of a group of six Hungarian Jewish youths aged seventeen to nineteen years. With them was a teacher of literature, aged thirty-five, who was given a special role that was invested with great moral authority. He was nicknamed in Hungarian "the wise brainy elephant." Although they met by chance because of their consecutive numbers and were allocated a group bread ration, they created an unusually cohesive group and laid down rules of conduct that they called their "Ten Commandments." These rules were decided upon only after much group discussion and various suggestions for each "commandment." After group decision the "commandments" became a binding code of rules dogmatically applied as a day-to-day credo by the members of the group. These "commandments" were designed to serve group and individual survival together with the preservation of ethical standards in "resisting" Nazi ideology. The "Ten Commandments" were

1. Thou shalt not barter.
2. Thou shalt not speak of food or invoke the image of food.
3. Thou shalt not speak of family members.
4. Thou shalt not speak of festivals (as celebrated within the family but only in the general and ceremonial sense).
5. Thou shalt not steal.
6. Thou shalt not masturbate.
7. Thou shalt not urinate in the bunk.
8. Thou shalt not be deprived of your human dignity; you are not a number, you are a human being.
9. We must not die, we must survive (which meant that they had to actively think of each other, to help each other by constant conscious efforts and to remind each other of the imperative to survive).

My informant could not remember the tenth "commandment."

Group bonds and mutual interdependence were intense, and they believed almost mystically that as long as they remained together and remained constantly aware and actively helped each other, no harm could come to them and they would survive. The rules were directed to keeping themselves from becoming dehumanized, which meant becoming "Nazis" and harming other inmates. Maintaining their ethical standards was primary in their survival struggle. They looked after each other with devotion, spending every possible moment they could together. They kept themselves aloof from the other inmates, considering themselves somewhat superior because of their ethical code and readiness to occupy themselves in discussion of cultural themes, which would remove them from the pain and horror around them. When there were events such as killing sprees and selections, it was every man for himself and they would run away and hide singly, but always at the end of the day they would seek each other out in great anxiety until all were found. They slept together on the bare wooden bunk with their starved bodies moulded into each other, hugging and squeezing out some warmth and comfort from each other. Careful not to transgress their "Ten Commandments," the food they got was scrupulously shared between them, with the last portion going to the "sharer." They spent many hours together in a game that consisted of detailed imaginary walks in the streets of Budapest, with which they were all familiar, arguing good humoredly about the details of the route. Together they felt a sense of communion in being alive; they were asserting their identity, dignity, and humanity, and rejecting and resisting the concentration camp system and Nazi ideology.

Group belonging of this intensity involved mutual idealization with expansion of self-esteem and self-image into the group image. Jaffe has described two similar groups in Auschwitz accompanied by the fantasy of "creating a holy order."[28]

The Significance of the Group Experience in the Concentration Camp

The spontaneous manifestation of social bonding with the formation of a group enabled mutual support, mutual protection, and sharing, however minimal, in the face of starvation, fear, hopelessness, and death. The group helped to restore something of the lost sense of communality by creating a sense of belonging, restoring a feeling of identity, and preserving some links with the destroyed community and cultural past. In the grip of the SS concentration camp regime of total domination and deprivation of identity, the victim became helpless, hopeless, and dehumanized. The reconstruction of bonds of trust with "significant others" in a group restored individual identity and enabled the victim to be "relocated in a social realm."[29] In the face of helplessness, the preservation of a sense of being able to influence one's fate through maintaining individual activity and decision making, however minimally, was reinforced by the group. A sense of humanizing and transcending the state of dehumanized, numbered anonymity was thus created. The strengthening of life-preserving denial processes was an essential aspect of these group interactions.[30]

Group bonding experiences in the concentration camp thus mitigated both the individual and collective trauma processes. The group could prevent regression to complete apathetic surrender to death, and helped to maintain hope and the motivation to continue the struggle to live. It promoted the psychological survival of the victims by preserving human awareness and a sense of self despite the dehumanization and amorality.

A Study of Teenagers in the Holocaust

From my life-cycle studies I have come to understand that the supportive relationships experienced by many adolescent survivors protected personality functioning and enabled growth and development to proceed. The experience of the solidarity of mutual support in the ghettos and concentration camps during adolescence often became an important source around which the sense of self was rebuilt and the "survivor identity" was created.

In our Holocaust and Psychosocial Trauma Research project, we studied the role of social support in the life cycles of concentration camp survivors in the general population, that is, in "nonclinical" groups, and particularly the possible protective and strengthening role of social support in preventing or modifying the long-term effects of massive psychic trauma. At the time of our study, the survivors were in their fifties; they had been fifteen to twenty-one years old at the end of the war, and came from East European and traditionally Jewish backgrounds. All had spent at least one year—the majority up to two years—in concentration camps, most of the time in slave labor camps, but all had been in concentration camps. We studied these survivors by means of semistructured interviews and questionnaires relating to the role of social support in their lives from the onset of the Holocaust trauma to the present.

Three time phases in the life cycles of the survivors were studied in terms of coping behavior and social support:

1. the first period, while in the grip of the traumatic situation and process in the concentration camp itself;
2. the period after liberation and the reentry into society; and
3. the life cycle of the survivor up to the present day.

It is well-nigh impossible, nearly forty years later, to clearly differentiate between the long-term effects on the psychosocial functioning of supportive bonds during each of the three specific periods: in the concentration camps; the reentry into society; the life cycle up to the present. We have, however, found definite indications in our "nonclinical" group of survivors of a correlation between pairing and group relations in the concentration camps and good psychological, marital, family, and social functioning.

Before their deportation to the concentration camps and separation from the family unit, the majority of the youngsters had spent periods of one to three years in ghettos and other specially designated areas for Jews under the Nazi regime. In this early pre-camp exposure to fear, death, brutality, and hunger, they were to some extent protected by family and other supporting social bonds and went through an important preparatory process in learning "adaptive behavior" to the Nazi persecution and terror together with parents, older siblings, friends, and others in these closely knit communities. Family bonds were often strengthened during this period, manual skills were learned, and guiding precepts and models for dealing with stress acquired, which were utilized later in reality and fantasy in the struggle for survival in the concentration camps, and indeed throughout their lives ever since. This preparatory stress period, undergone within the family unit, served to some degree as a toughening experience for many of them, which helped to mediate the impact of the initial acute, overwhelming trauma and shock upon arrival in the concentration camp, and increased their chances of "adaptation" and survival. This conclusion is supported by the higher incidence of clinical findings with survivors (e.g., from Hungary) who had not gone through an anticipatory period in ghettos and suddenly were torn from homes and families and transported directly to the camps.

On systematic interviewing, all of them revealed that they had experienced helping relationships of one form or another in the camps. The formation of stable social bonds was related directly to the length of stay in one camp. The longer one remained in one place, the stronger the bonds that were formed. Those who were moved from camp to camp had less chance of forming stable reciprocal relationships. Survivors who had experienced constant changes of camp with no continuity of contact suffered more after liberation from withdrawal and inability to communicate, and the process of their rehabilitation took longer. On the other hand, inmates who were moved from camp to camp as part of a stable group or pair were able to maintain helping relationships with each other.

Many different kinds of supportive human relations were reported. There were those who "found" a protector among one of the older inmates or even camp officials. Many of these relationships were reminiscent of father-son, mother-daughter, older-younger sibling bonds, and the person chosen was often a substitute for a lost loved one. Occasionally, actual family members (rarely more than two) found themselves left together in the same camp and would form a very intensely protective dyad. Pairing friendships were the most common bonding relationship and often the most effective. Choice and compatibility in these couples were related to the specific needs of the situation as well as to individual psychological needs, with each member of the dyad contributing reciprocally to the needs of the other. For example, in one couple of friends, one partner would steal food to share between them, whereas the other, a relatively passive youth, would supply a "listening ear." Too frightened to steal himself, all his active, daring friend demanded of him was to listen empathically to his experiences and exploits. In this way food was exchanged for emotional support, each according to his needs and skills.

Halina Birenbaum, who spent three years, from age twelve to fifteen, in the Warsaw Ghetto, Majdanek, Auschwitz, and Ravensbruck, describes simply and vividly the issues I have been talking about.

> The reality of Majdanek weighed me down even more than that pile of bodies under which I almost stifled in the railroad car. . . .
> I was thirteen. The years of persecution in the ghetto, the loss of my

father and my brother, and, most painful of all, the loss of my mother, had impaired my nervous system, and at a time when I should have forced myself to be as resistant as possible, I broke down completely. . . .

    We had to fight for everything in Majdanek: for a scrap of floor space in the hut on which to stretch out at night, for a rusty bowl without which we could not obtain the miserable ration of nettle soup that they fed us, or yellow stinking water to drink. But I was not capable of fighting. Fear and horror overcame me at the sight of women prisoners struggling over a scrap of free space on the floor, or hitting one another over the head at the soup kettles, snatching bowls. Hostile, aggressive women, wanting to live at any price. Stunned, aghast, famished, terrified, I watched from a distance.

    Had it not been for Hela [her sister-in-law], her boundless devotion and constant care, I would have perished after a few days. Hela had vowed inwardly to my mother that she would take her place, and she kept her vow. . . . Hela fought with redoubled strength—for herself and for me. She shared every bite she acquired with me. . . . She gave me all the love she felt for my brother and did everything in her power to make easier my life in the camp. For a long time I could not rouse myself from my state of listlessness. Had it not been for Hela's efforts I would not have roused myself from my apathy and despair. . . . Only here did I recognize the true nature of my sister-in-law, and only here did I come to love her. Later I was ready to make any sacrifice for her. Out of regard for her, and thanks to her help, I too finally joined the fight for life in the camp of death. . . . I aroused myself from the state of apathy and despair that followed my mother's death. . . .[31]

Halina Birenbaum goes on to describe how eventually, with the constant support of her sister-in-law, she acquired the capacity to adapt to camp conditions. Then, tragically, Halina's sister-in-law began to weaken, and gradually they changed roles.

Most of the survivors interviewed reported having been involved both in a close pairing relationship (friendship) and in relationships in a group. Which situation was more important depended on individual needs and prevailing conditions.

The groups varied in size, but usually contained three, five, or eight inmates. The groups were well integrated and characterized by a high degree of mutual devotion, with mutual aid and sharing of everything. Group members changed frequently due to the vicissitudes of camp life and death, and would soon be replaced by new members, who would be accepted only if considered compatible with the group, so that cohesion would always be maintained. Loyalty and mutual concern were usually maintained only within the group, with little concern for those outside it. Sometimes the group had to defend its interests selfishly and aggressively against individuals and other groups of inmates. Groups were often formed on a nucleus of previous ghetto or childhood relationships, or a common cultural or national background. The isolated "helping hand" experience, remembered by many as occurring at critical moments of particular adversity, and which could be life-saving, often occurred between inmates with some common feature of collective identity and language. The communication of a familiar phrase, a reminiscence, a joke, gossip, even a smile, could be sufficient to arouse in an apathetic, despairing inmate the feeling of a touch of solidarity, humanness, the flicker of hope that would enable the "will to live" to reassert itself. Various roles and duties were often allocated within the group, according to camp conditions. Group activity included, apart from the basic collection and sharing of food and provisions, and whenever possible the dangerous activity of stealing food, etc., from the camp stores, also the sharing of information and advice on "organizing."

Further social bonding experiences, dyadic and group, for these young people, who found themselves bereft of families after the war, were crucial for their integration back into society. A nurturing communal setting within which they could belong was essential for the restoration of identity, values, and positive social behavior. The new group relations were often connected with bonds established in the ghettos and the camps, and the capacity for bonding and attachment evident throughout the years of the Holocaust enabled further growth-promoting relationships. The memories of solidarity in extreme adversity and of preservation of the human image in the midst of dehumanization have accompanied many of these young survivors as a sustaining and humanizing influence throughout their life cycles. Thus, what became significant in both the identity and memory of the survivor was not the atrocity witnessed and experienced, but the struggle within a supportive group to maintain the motivation to survive.

Many of the survivors whom we interviewed found themselves entirely alone as teenagers after the liberation. They underwent positive socialization experiences and spent important formative periods of many months in centers specially set up for their rehabilitation in Europe and England. In these centers based on group living, group bonds developed rapidly, and relationships, which sometimes had originated in the camps, deepened. The active encouragement and utilization of these group bonds played an important role in the reintegration of these young people, now aged fifteen to twenty, into society, through the acquisition of values and positive social behavior.

Emerging from the camps as late teenagers, many of them felt that despite the loss of family and their great suffering they had become psychologically stronger and autonomous during the years of living in the camps. The friendships and group relations enabled them to face the deprivation, hunger, hard labor, and perpetual danger of death. Some aspects of personality development continued throughout their adolescent years during the Holocaust despite the destructive traumata. Their bonding capacity continued to be evident during the recovery period and throughout their life cycle. The ability eventually to create well-functioning families was a central manifestation of this phenomenon.

For many of these survivors, the bonds that were created in the concentration camps and during the rehabilitative period after liberation have continued as an important social support system throughout their lives up to the present. In the different countries in which they now live, mainly Israel, England, and North America, many have maintained close contact and affection for each other, often of a sibling-bond nature, with much mutual caring and helping behavior throughout the years.

The Significance of Reciprocal Human Relations in Extremity

The experiences of concentration camp survivors teach us that acts and activities of humanity and mutuality coexisted with the amorality stemming from desperation in the midst of human destruction where the ethical categories of everyday life could not be upheld. The memory of the solidarity of mutual support in the Nazi concentration camps, where death was almost inevitable, accompanies the survivor throughout his life cycle as a sustaining and humanizing influence. Despite the lack of uniformity and the instability of supportive behavior in the concentration camps, the very existence of helping relations—however sporadic—and their spontaneous appearance implies a transcendence of evil and of faceless dehumanization with a preservation of the human image. Halina Birenbaum summed up the transcendental meaning of survival as a human being thus:

The number tattooed on my left arm—personal evidence from Auschwitz ... for me it is a kind of certificate of maturity, from a period in which I experienced life and the world in their naked forms, a desperate struggle for a piece of bread, a breath of air and a little space, from a period in which I learned to distinguish between truth and falsehood, between manifestations of human feeling and animal instincts, between goodness, nobility and evil baseness.[32]

Clearly we must avoid at all cost any "whitewashing" of conditions or idealization of human relations in the most extreme creation of evil known to man: the Nazi concentration camp. On the other hand, ignoring the fact of human reciprocity among the victims in those camps leaves unchallenged the dehumanization deliberately wrought. *The fact that the human image was preserved in such extremity is inspiring.* The experience of the survivor of the death camps provides an added insight into the meaning of "survival" in extremity: a sense of the possibility of the transcendence of evil by the victims acting together in a spirit of solidarity and communion. Thus, however ambiguously, there is a reinstatement of human values in the service of the struggle for survival through the intrinsically social nature of this struggle. In this way the process of supportive social bonding transcends its psychosocial function and adds a further dimension of meaning to "survival."

I would add that the experience of the concentration camp survivor echoes the Jewish psychohistorical theme of survival in the manner in which a negative and destructive experience is transformed into a positive and enduring value.

7.

Reflections on Survival and Some Observations on Survivors in Israel, Germany, and the United States

> Human suffering is the lot of everyone, but the way to the suffering of extremity, like to death itself, is the escape from it;
>
> But what can we do when each attempt to escape always returns us in the end to ourselves, to our childhood, to the camps, and to the ghettoes?
>
> In this circuit of escape and return our self-awareness moves, and until we "work through" it we shall not be free.
>
> —Aharon Appelfeld, *Essays in the First Person*

A large part of my clinical psychiatric practice in Israel has involved the treatment of Nazi concentration camp survivors. The vast majority of these survivors emigrated to Israel during the years following the establishment of the state, but many settled in the United States, Canada, and Europe.

Several years elapsed before the extent of the survivors' psychological damage became apparent. We now know that this damage was life-long; many of the survivors continue to receive treatment. They suffer from chronic anxiety and depression, psychosomatic illnesses, compulsive, photographic, often terrifying flashback memories of the camp experience by day, and nightmares of the persecutions, which disturb their sleep. Thus, they continue to reexperience the persecutory events. These survivors are joyless and preoccupied with memories of relatives who were killed and from whom they were suddenly separated without their ever being able to mourn their loss. These memories are associated with feelings of self-blame for having survived, referred to frequently as "survivor guilt."

The symptoms and personality changes observed in the survivors did not fit into any previously recognized psychiatric category. Hence the diagnostic term "concentration camp survivor syndrome" came into usage. This state was likewise reported among survivors outside of Israel in the different countries of their settlement. Many people have been subjected to intense persecutions and mass murder, and the survivor syndrome is now being widely applied to describe the results of traumatization from many natural and man-made causes. However, the Jews in the Nazi extermination camps experienced particularly intense and destructive forms of traumatization. They were subjected to systematic dehumanization, degradation, humiliation, and sadistic tortures and were exposed to the perpetual danger of death. The destruction of family, community, and their entire familiar world intensified the traumatization. The individual lost his sense of continuity with the past, his sense of identity, and his security. All these factors overwhelmed the individual adaptive capacity and produced irreversible psychic damage.

In the many years that I have been studying the impact of massive trauma on the life cycle of survivors as well as the transgenerational influence within their families, I have become convinced that the degree of recovery and the quality of integration of survivors of trauma are related to an interaction of many forces and resources with a wide range of differing outcomes. Despite the catastrophic dimensions of the trauma and the immense losses, the experiences and their significance were different and unique for each individual survivor.

Many factors determined how the individual was affected, such as age, personality structure and predisposition, quality of family life in childhood, capacity to form relationships, and confidence in one's ability to affect one's fate. However, among the most important factors I find are belonging to a community, group, or ideology; the quality of the marital relationship; and material and professional success. These three factors are perhaps the most important in the struggle to come to terms with the traumatic past in the years since the Holocaust.

It is important to realize that the defenses and coping skills used adaptively and successfully in one age period are not necessarily good for another. For many survivors who had been married and had children before the Holocaust, the multiple losses in relation to their own young families as well as the parental and extended families created colossal burdens of mourning. The memory of the former unmourned spouse and children sometimes cast a shadow over the new marriage and family relationships. Depressions, flashback associations by day, and nightmares have been more evident in this age group, together with other symptoms of the concentration camp survivor syndrome.

A further particularly vulnerable group of survivors were young children during the war. Few survived, and among those who did the deprivation resulting from separation and loss of parental figures in early childhood often had a serious effect on psychological development.

However, a majority of survivors did not become psychiatric patients and have shown remarkable capacities in overcoming the effect of the extreme experiences and multiple losses, creating new lives and healthy and successful, well-integrated families. Unfortunately, generalizations were made from clinical symptoms and psychodynamics that did not do justice to the strength and complexity of the lives of survivors and their families. At the same time, I must also conclude that although psychosocial factors in Israeli society have mitigated psychopathology and have helped to counter deep identity disturbances in many survivors, they still have not been able to obliterate the lasting damage of the concentration camp experience.

More research studies are needed to understand the process of recovery, adaptation, and integration of the survivor into society. My own researches have focused on those who were in their teens and early twenties at the end of the war. This age group seems to have been less affected by the traumatization and made the best recovery despite the fact that their adolescent years were spent in ghettos and concentration camps. Survivor syndrome symptoms were present only to a minor extent and survivor guilt was not as pronounced. The loss of their families came at a time when separation from parents is a stage in the life cycle in the development towards autonomy. Furthermore, this age group was generally able to resume development, education, and occupational training in a way not possible for older survivors. As a result, marriages occurred later on a more solid basis than with many of the older survivors who made hasty liasions and gave birth to children while still in the grip of the Holocaust trauma.

As I reported in the chapter on group formation, an important finding in the studies of survivors in general has been the role of small groups, friendships, and protecting relationships in enhancing the chances of survival in the camps and, through mutual aid, the maintenance of morale and motivation to survive. The shreds of the "human image" were thus preserved, combating the destructiveness of the dehumanization process. In the case of the teenage survivors who have been interviewed, almost all experienced mutually protective relationships, and for many these experiences have remained as valuable memories often cherished as a humanizing and ethical influence throughout their lives. Furthermore, the bonds that were created in the concentration camps and during the rehabilitation period after liberation continued as an important social support system for many of them throughout their lives up to the present. In the different countries in which they now live, mainly Israel, England, and North America, they have maintained close contact and affection for each other, often of a sibling-bond nature, throughout the years with much mutual caring and helping behavior. The intensely supportive quality of the network of relationships of small and large groups, such as the '45 Aid Society, enabled much exchange of reminiscences and mutual support and encouragement. Self-help survivor group formations have been of considerable help for many individuals, allowing for a slow working through of losses and other traumata in solidarity with other survivors who had similar experiences. Some of these groups, especially if families were involved, became substitutes for the lost extended families. This self-help system may well have replaced a need for therapy, which might have arisen without it.

For many survivors who led active and often overactive lives in the successful achievement of social goals and the creation and upbringing of new families, avoidance and silence with regard to their sufferings and losses was the normal mode of coping with the catastrophic past. In this way, they were socially acceptable and even became exemplary citizens in terms of personal, family, and social advancement. Today, years later, many survivors who were adolescents or young adults during the war are showing a willingness and a need to talk about their past—to return to and even to attempt a belated working through of their Holocaust experiences. After reaching middle age and older, they were confronted with a flooding back of repressed Holocaust memories as part of the normal process of reflection on and review of past life at this stage in the life cycle.

The present upsurge of interest by society in looking again at the Holocaust after decades of avoidance, as well as renewed manifestations of neo-Nazism that emerge as the years go by, encourage many survivors to reveal the details of their Holocaust past. However, these memories arouse feelings of anxiety, depression, and shame.

As stated earlier, survivors are often particularly vulnerable to disappointments, separations, and serious illness and death, especially in relation to spouse or children, the loss of activity, and the aging process itself. Some of those survivors who now feel a need to talk see the return of Holocaust memories and their depressive mood as connected with an increasing disillusionment and disappointment with the state of society and the world.

The modes of coming to terms with Holocaust traumata utilized by individual survivors are multiple and complex. Of central importance are the personality resources of the survivor and a nurturing and supportive dyadic relationship. Each phase of the life cycle presented new opportunities for working through the war experiences and losses and possibilities for releasing delayed mourning. Creative artistic expression as well as communal and societal activity have been useful to many survivors for working through their experiences through meaningful communication to society.

Optimism, hopes, and expectation for the creation of a new society and a just world were an important positive force in survivors' adaptation to and reintegration into society. Today, in their sensitive awareness of continuing injustices, inhumanity, the lowering of values and ethical standards in man's relations with his fellow man, recurrent wars and mass deaths, they feel that nothing has changed, that they have been cheated and their survival robbed of its justification and meaning.

At the Study Center for Holocaust and Social Trauma at Bar Ilan University that I direct, our object is to provide a suitable framework for survivors seeking to communicate their Holocaust traumatic experiences and express their hitherto inarticulated feelings of guilt, shame, helplessness, anger, etc. Many of those who have turned to us have been "waiting" for many years to deal with their Holocaust experiences and the associated feelings. They wanted to speak but waited because they did not know how and with whom.

An important area of our research in Israel has been to examine the long-term effects of massive traumatization seen in followup studies of the survivors. Many have shown progressive deterioration with age, loss of activity, and the stresses of the life cycle— disappointments and separations. We now know that the effects of traumatization can be transmitted from one generation to the next through disturbances in the parent-child relationship. Thus, the persecutory traumatization of the Nazi concentration camps can be reexperienced by the survivors' children and can even affect the grandchildren.

The survivors in Israel form a large and integral part of the population. They are our neighbors, friends, and colleagues at work. They are our husbands and wives and their children become our daughters- and sons-in-law.

A specific part of the identity of each Israeli who was not born in Israel itself relates to his country of origin. Thus people are often referred to as "Yotzei Hungary," "Yotzei Lita," "Yotzei Iraq," etc., that is, originating from Hungary, Lithuania, or Iraq. In this way Holocaust survivors are often referred to by the man in the street as "Yotzei Shoa," originating from the Shoa (the Holocaust). "Having been in the Shoa" thus displaces national origins and becomes the central feature identifying the individual and his family origins in the eyes of fellow citizens. Describing survivors in this way demonstrates an important aspect of the Israeli attitude to the survivors. It irrevocably and indelibly defines identity in relation to exposure to the trauma of the Shoa and is used as a stereotype for certain characteristics and reactions.

Nonetheless, Israeli society has taken little recognition of the fact that an individual's Holocaust background is being reacted to as highly sensitized and specific information, for simultaneously the survivors—like all other *olim* (immigrants to Israel)—were expected to forget their origins and become active citizens contributing to the building of the new state and fighting for its survival. The survivors were welcomed by the Yishuv (Jewish community in Palestine). They were looked upon with their European background and skills as potentially valuable pioneers who would participate in the development and building of the country as well as in its defense. Many survivors, however, were sensitive to the fact that little interest was shown; in fact, often there was active avoidance of them in relation to their traumatic experiences and losses. By and large people did not want to know how they had lived through the Holocaust—except for those few survivors who were fortunate enough to have fought as partisans or been involved in active armed resistance, such as the Warsaw Ghetto Uprising, who were sought after, singled out, treated as heroes, and urged to relate their experiences of resistance. The dead and murdered martyrs were even condemned as victims who didn't fight back. Today we know more clearly than ever before that it is a universal human phenomenon to avoid the survivors of any extremity, for what they have to say disturbs our conception of man, and makes us feel uncomfortable and guilty. Worst of all, survivors of a calamity can even arouse a feeling of contamination, as if being in contact with their confrontation with death could be contagious.

The survivors themselves had considerable difficulty in finding words to describe their unutterable experiences. They felt guilty at having survived, and shame at having been forced into experiences of dehumanization and brutalization. On encountering reluctance to listen and avoidance in others they kept quiet, and anyway they longed to forget—although, simultaneously, they also had an inner need to bear witness (for many of them this had been a driving motivation that helped enable them to survive to begin with, and it was also a commitment many of them had made to those who perished). In most cases, they turned to silence, which fit the realities of their new society, which did not want them to speak too much. Although they were unquestionably welcomed as active citizens who would contribute to the building and defense of the new state, they could not expect any special recognition of their traumatic past. Their shadowy past in the Shoa was expected to be played down, and especially for many of the young people of the Yishuv, their Shoa past became a matter of some shame to be kept out of sight.

Nonetheless, there was a powerful relevance and coinciding in the psychohistorical themes of the "rebirth" of the Jewish people in the land of Israel and the "rebirth" of the survivors in the creation of new lives as individuals and families. This process of emergence from the trauma of loss of family and community and break in continuity with their pre-Holocaust lives enabled the reestablishment of links with the values and goals of the past. There is no question that the social environment strongly influences the rehabilitation of traumatized human beings. The psychosocial structure of Israeli society, especially during the early years of the state, helped the majority of the survivors and their children achieve genuine social integration. Especially for survivors who came to Israel in their late teens and early twenties, belonging, identification, and activity became fused into a cohesive whole, creating new meaning in their lives as uprooted, traumatized persons. In these ways Israel became a gigantic rehabilitation project for a traumatized people surviving genocide. At community and national levels in Israel, the Holocaust has always been given central significance and expression in annual memorial meetings for destroyed communities, the annual Holocaust Memorial Day, teaching programs in the schools, and through newspapers, radio, and television. In the rebirth of the Jewish people in a national homeland, survivors found hope of their own rebirth. In Israel's fight for survival, they found an expression of their own struggle to survive and channels for their blocked aggression. Holocaust survivors were welcomed as valued citizens who would contribute to the building and defense of the state. This cooperative attitude encouraged them and helped them overcome feelings of dependency. Furthermore, Israeli society facilitated expressions of mourning in a communal way—by holding Holocaust memorial ceremonies in which the whole nation mourned together, as well as individual memorial days for each destroyed community. The survivors' suffering and the death of the six million were recognized as intimately related to the raison d'être of the state. The memory and significance of the Holocaust were kept alive in the social consciousness of the people.

"Coming to terms with the past" involves processes similar to the well-known concept in psychoanalysis of "working through." The stages that people go through in their grief and mourning after the death of a loved one exemplify in everyday life the process of working through. In Jewish history there are long-standing traditional patterns of dealing with traumatic experiences in the long chain of persecution to which the Jewish people were subjected. Jews are enjoined, in their families and communities, to remember previous persecutions and pogroms: from Amalekh through the Roman destruction of the Temple in Jerusalem, from Chelmnitsky to Auschwitz.

The Jewish people developed in their psychohistorical process a way of working through their recurrent encounters with death and destruction through ritualizations that became incorporated in the religious calendar, from the chanting of eulogies and dirges and lamentations and fast days of remembrance (such as the ninth of Av, in memory of the destruction of both Temples). Even in the course of the Jewish wedding ceremony, there is room set aside for an element of mourning and remembering as an ethnic manifestation of the constant Jewish working through of trauma and persecution.

Relating Holocaust experiences to members of one's family can be an important medium for the reestablishment of a survivor's self-esteem and for releasing pent-up after-effects in legitimate ways. Telling enables the survivor also to master traumatic memories from the past, certainly to come out from isolation as an empathic, sharing person.

As the years pass, there develops a separation between two sets of feelings: the general traumatic experiences of horror, helplessness, anger, and revulsion in relation to the perpetrators gradually subsides; on the other hand, the sense and memories of losses of loved ones, awareness of parents and siblings and friends who will never return, become more prominent in the long-range mourning process. As the years go by, the combination of the reduction of desires for vengeance and the rediscovered affects of love and yearning for one's missing intimates allows new possibilities for renewal of self.

The writing of diaries that are eyewitness accounts was an excellent way of providing for working through. It meant placing on record personal, family, and community experiences, and it enabled the recording of names of specific lost family and friends. Many of the eyewitness accounts were placed formally in the archives of national museums such as Yad Vashem, thus enabling not only working through of memories and reliving of the associative painful feelings, but also giving an extra dimension of meaning and long-range survival to the survivor's record and, in a sense, to the memories of the victims themselves, in an atmosphere of acceptance and sharing. Participating in an oral history project and giving testimony through interviews that are recorded on audio or video tape within the framework of respected community institutions, such as universities and museums, provides for many survivors the opportunity to bear witness and for catharsis of hitherto inarticulate experiences and agonizing associative feelings, with a fantasy of transmission of one's burden to present and future communities. It enables many of the survivors who have done oral history testimonies to accomplish further pieces of the working through process for themselves.

In the meetings of survivors in annual memorials on Yom Ha-Shoah, in special meetings such as a world assembly of survivors in Jerusalem, there are many moving encounters as people find others who were in the same sites in the Shoah, and find others with whom to compare their own history as a victim-inmate-slave and how they have arisen to the achievements of which they can boast today. There is a mutual ratification: "I was saved and you were saved." The confrontation with the almost-death of the past is a triumph of survival connected with the pride of achievement for self, and continuity of meaningfulness to the next generation.

Many young survivors joined kibbutzim and volunteered to fight in Israel's various wars. Many chose occupations connected with the helping professions and became pioneers in many fields of social action directly after liberation or years later when they were successfully established. Although all of these are traditional outlets for Jewish occupation, for the survivors in many cases there was a special expression of a need to be a savior in order to compensate for helplessness in the past and the burden of frustration at not having been an active resister and fighter against the horrible injustices of the Holocaust.

The tendency in Israel to view society as an extension of the family has also been important in combating feelings of alienation, estrangement, and identity problems in the survivors' children. The traumatic memories, still responsible for so much suffering in the parents, activate the children's determination that there will never be another Holocaust.

Nonetheless, I must return to the point that despite all of the above, paradoxically and contradictorally, at the interpersonal level survivors' Shoa past has generally been avoided even in Israel. In our Western culture in general, people are uncomfortable in the presence of survivors of disasters, and I believe this is especially true of survivors of man-made disasters. In personal encounters with them, images arise of victimization and confrontation with death, humiliation, horror, helplessness, abandonment and loss, and the dreadfulness and misery of the struggle to survive in extremity. These images arouse feelings of anger, anxiety, shame, guilt, and blame in us, emotions that we prefer to avoid, even though at the same time we also want to know what really happened.

For most of the survivors, recalling and relating their experiences was excruciatingly painful and humiliating—hence the tendency to avoid and to try to forget. The reluctance that they sensed in others to listen to the details of what they had been through in the Holocaust reinforced their tendency to avoid talking about their dreadful experiences. They justified their silence in the general society in terms of the inability of the others to understand what they had experienced. In this way both the survivors and the surrounding society interacted to maintain, by and large, a shameful silence.

If this was true even in Israel, it was certainly true in other Western countries where survivors settled. Accepted as citizens with more or less full rights and opportunities in most of the societies of the democratic world where they settled in the postwar era, their survivor identities and experiences were avoided and remained shadowy and unexpressed except for those who met with fellow survivors in the special intimacy and solidarity of mutual aid or social groups.

The Survivor in Germany

Here are the graves
Here is your grave.
—Shaul Tchernikowsky, *Baruch from Magenza*

After all that has happened and has been said, after their liberation from the Holocaust, there are still Jewish survivors living in Germany.

Out of the five hundred thousand Jews who were left in Europe at the end of the war, less than about eight thousand remained in Germany—a small number in quantitative terms, but somehow each one is so amazing, and the overall grouping of eight thousand people seems to be straining "to tell us something important."

The majority of these survivor residents in Germany are not rooted in German culture. They are not the inheritors of the old proud communities of Worms, Spayer, and Mainz, which were destroyed for the first time by the Crusaders—see the poem "Baruch from Magenza" by the Hebrew poet Tchernikowsky, in which a survivor of the Crusader persecution goes mad and goes to the cemetery to remain at the graves of his family. They are the remnants of Buchenwald, Auschwitz, and Bergen-Belsen, D.P.s from Poland, Rumania, and Hungary. If you ask them in Frankfurt, Munich, and Hamburg why they rebuilt their personal and family lives in the country where perpetrators of the Holocaust still live, one gets many responses, but in my judgment very few real answers.

Some replies I have heard are these: "Our existence in Germany is an expression of triumph over Hitler." "Our presence is an expression of the humanization of Germany today."

Most frequently one hears, "We are living out of suitcases," by which they mean that their stay in Germany is transient—many times this is their comment despite the passage of scores of years. A few of the survivors living in Germany will say that they are mourning in Germany their beloved, murdered lost ones from whom they cannot separate—literally living in the graveyard like Baruch of Magenza. Many of the survivors also say with brutal frankness, "We are here because the Germans are committed to compensate us for all our suffering and losses." In no few cases they did not have the faith in themselves and others to begin again from scratch, and they stayed where they found themselves after liberation in Germany.

Some survivors put themselves in the place of their murdered German Jewish brethren and believe that they are thus playing an important role in Germany, as the German Jews had in the pre-Hitler era. Thus, tragically, they live in the illusion that they are filling the historical vacuum left by the destruction of the great German Jewish communities. In addition, they stress their autonomous Jewish religious cultural life and their connection with and capacity to develop their emotional ties with Israel. They try to live the Jewish life of Germany of the past in a state of "as if," in ambivalent coexistence with the perpetrators in the vicinity of concentration camps and crematoria.

Psychologically, we can speculate that some of these survivors have an unconscious need to live close to the aggressors of yesterday, to continue to be in the situation of *victims*, just as the German people may have the need for the presence of some Jews to assuage their guilt over the Jews of Germany who were driven out and destroyed in the ghettos and extermination camps in East Europe in the "Final Solution."

Other Jews live in Germany as successful professionals and businessmen triumphal. For them, coexistence with the fantasized *victimizers* in the actual place where the crimes were perpetrated seems to be an important psychological factor in their optimal adaptation. The surprising discovery of the friendly attitude to the survivors on the part of the older non-Nazi population and especially the new postwar generation with the liberal atmosphere prevailing in Germany today "invited" them to participate in the successful national effort to rebuild the German economy. Both sides, survivors and Germans together, avoided the Holocaust for many years and invested all their psychic energy in material achievements.

For the Jews in Germany, Israel became a place identified in their minds with their shtetl past or a ritualized place for their identity as Jews and survivors. They come to Israel for religious ceremonies such as Bar Mitzvah, reunion with other survivors, burial of their dead, and Holocaust memorial days, and for refueling of their impoverished spiritual life. One of the survivors who came for a funeral told us, "I am here for the traditional Jewish 'burial of the fathers' but also to be restored to new spiritual life."

I think that on the German side, the catharsis of aggression onto the dehumanized "Jewish scapegoat" during World War II persecution is now connected with a collective shame and need for the presence of Jews for their own restitution through some resurrection of the Jews. An uneasy equilibrium thus prevails between the Germans and the Jews, as in some chronic marital conflict situations, in which each projects onto the other the undesirable, unacceptable aspects of themselves.

It seems to me that in New Left circles among Jews in Germany this situation is projected into fantasized images of Israel as aggressor in an attempt at self-justification. The intensity of demonstration and pseudo-empathy in these circles towards the new scapegoat—the Palestinians—is an expression of the "return of the repressed," the old intensive self-hatred as Jews, and then projection onto Israelis of the roles of victimizers, so that the victim is no longer deserving of the sympathy he never was given to begin with in the self-hating feelings of Jews who disliked themselves.

Children of Holocaust Survivors in America

During a period of sabbatical leave in the U.S. at Stanford University in California, I had occasion to lecture on my work as an Israeli psychiatrist with Holocaust survivors and their children in Israel. Reports filtered through to the news media of the continuing long-term effect of the Holocaust traumatization in the survivors and of the possible effects on their children. During the following weeks I received many letters and telephone calls from children of Holocaust survivor parents throughout the U.S.—some 150,000 Jewish Holocaust survivors had settled in the U.S.

These letters were written by well-educated young adults, many of whom only recently, in their twenties, had begun to consider the possibility that their parents' persecutory experiences as Jews both inside and outside Nazi concentration camps in Europe during World War II had affected them. There was a tendency to relate emotional difficulties they had to their parents' wartime experiences, but few of the parents had told their children of these experiences. All expressed a need to communicate with someone who had special understanding of their situation. They had not met with anyone with whom they felt they could discuss this element in their background, even when, as some reported, they had been in psychotherapy or psychoanalysis. They requested detailed information in order to understand themselves and their parental background. Many wanted direct guidance on "how to deal with and overcome" any possible effects. Many of them volunteered to be "research subjects," expressing hope that the knowledge obtained would "help others who suffer silently and alone."

Despite their young ages, and their being Americans—most of them actually American-born—the majority did not have a feeling of being "wanted" and being genuinely at home as children of survivors do in Israel.

Out of the people who contacted me, seventeen were selected solely because of their geographical proximity to where I was (San Francisco Bay area), and I invited them to be interviewed by me. All of them accepted. Since the interviewees were all essentially self-selected volunteers, even though they didn't know that I would be using them to participate in a study, they obviously cannot be considered to constitute a random sample. Furthermore, there was no control group. However, their spontaneous responses to the reports in the news media may illuminate for us useful issues and questions for further research. In addition, the interviewees represent essentially a nonclinical population. As I have emphasized at other times, although a number of studies have been made of the offspring of survivors in psychiatric or psychotherapy clinics, little study of a nonclinical group has as yet been published (an outstanding exception is Klein's study of Israeli families in a kibbutz).[1]

The interviews were semistructured, and all were conducted by me; in each case I attempted to explore a schedule or series of specific issues.

The seventeen interviewees consisted of twelve men and five women, all of them in their twenties (fourteen were aged twenty-six to thirty), nine were born in the U.S., and eight came with their families to the U.S. in early childhood (six from Europe, three from Israel). Six of the subjects were only children. They were all academically successful and outwardly socially "well adjusted." The group included four law students, three psychologists, three administrators, two physicians, two journalists, and a mathematician. The majority (fourteen) of the interviewees had parents of Polish or Lithuanian origin. In three cases the parents were from Central Europe. In thirteen cases both parents had been in Nazi concentration camps. In four cases, only one parent had been in Nazi concentration camps, but although their spouses had not been in camps, they also experienced some degree of Nazi persecution, so that all the parents of these interviewees had undergone Nazi persecution. All the parents had lost many close relatives. The majority of the parents had been in their twenties during the Holocaust, they had lost spouses from a previous marriage, and they had lost children.

Almost uniformly, the interviewees described their parents as economically very successful, in most cases in some business. They were extremely hard working. Work was always a priority, with little or no leisure time, and many of the interviewees characterized their parents as "workaholics." All of the interviewees perceived their parents' personalities as having been affected to some extent by their Holocaust experiences, although in only two cases was there a report of a parent being in psychiatric treatment.

Some features of survivor syndrome symptomatology manifesting in anxiety, fears, depression, nightmares, guilt, aggressive outbursts, and fearful, untrusting, suspicious, and hostile attitudes to

others were reported in at least one parent by nearly all the interviewees. Survivor syndrome symptomatology when present in both
parents was never identical in its manifestations. Often one parent
was a stronger, warmer, and more protective and supporting figure for the child. In one case, where the mother was chronically
anxious, clinging, suspicious, and fearful of every knock on the
door, the son felt that although his mother had been psychologically damaged by the Holocaust, he had a strong father with
whom to identify. The father was perceived as coming out of the
concentration camp strengthened by his experience. He was seen
as accepting and not disguising the experiences—"We Jews should
never forget, if we do it will happen again."

In another case, where the father showed marked ambivalence
toward his son and had frequent aggressive outbursts against him,
the father's closest friend supported him throughout childhood
and was perceived by the son as his strongest and warmest relationship—a compensatory surrogate father. Outbursts of rage and
aggression were a dominant theme in the family life of three of the
subjects. In these three families, the parents were constantly quar-
reling, criticizing, and complaining to each other. The father would
have raging temper tantrums against the children. These fathers
were extremely demanding of achievement but impossible to please.

A 29-year-old woman described how her mother would provoke
her father's rage against her by telling him in the evenings on his
return from work "all the wicked things" the child had done
during the day, and he would start hitting and shouting at her,
but the mother would then come to her aid, telling her later, "He
would have killed you if I hadn't been there to save you." Both
parents had lost previous spouses in the Holocaust. The daughter
escaped from the destructive home atmosphere by marrying when
aged eighteen; this marriage was a failure, but later she made a
second, successful marriage within which she has felt herself developing. In the other two families where outbursts of rage and
aggression were a dominant theme, the father had lost a previous
wife and son in the Holocaust, although the father had concealed
the loss, which was "accidentally" discovered by the subjects in
late adolescence.

The sons of these fathers had been chosen as scapegoats; on the
one hand, they were constantly attacked and reviled, but on the
other hand they were also clung to by their extremely controlling
fathers, who feared separation above all else in their aggressive

post-Holocaust world. The mothers were usually passive and self-sacrificing, and would play active "repair" roles with zest, ever ready to swing into action when the father and son fought.

Also interesting, and consistent with what family systems thinkers have been teaching about the differential and often complementary roles of different children in the same family, in each of these cases a younger brother was treated completely differently as the father's favorite, "a symbol of hope and a positive future" in contrast with the older brother who, as indicated, was being utilized for projection of blocked aggression and mourning and impaired self-image deriving from the past Holocaust traumatization, and thus represented a "symbol of the suffering and the evil in the past life."

The scapegoated, and one might even say traumatized, sons feared both success and failure, had negative self-images, felt physically numbed from the repeated constant battering by their father, suffered from recurrent depression, frequently changed their activities and thus avoided continuity, and, overall, could not achieve satisfaction in their lives. They felt that they should hate and rebel against their fathers, but instead pitied them, feeling that they must not bring additional suffering to them, who had suffered so much. Two of these young men were the only ones in the group who felt a strong need for psychotherapy and were searching for a therapist who would understand the special problems of survivor families.

Another typical constellation was seen in the family of an only son whose father had lost a previous wife and son. The father never talked about his previous family, but the boy remembers his father poring over old photographs of his dead son. Throughout his childhood, he felt guilty and sad that he had no right to be alive in lieu of the boy who died. The juxtaposition of his father's two different lives constantly preoccupied him.

8.

Mourning and the Holocaust Survivor: Bereavement in Israel from War, Holocaust, and Terror

Central to the existential plight of the Holocaust survivor has been the theme of loss—loss in a truly global sense, the loss of all or almost all the family and friends, home and possessions, community and country, ultimately of identity and meaning in life. How was it possible to mourn for so many and so much? Was it possible? Was it possible to create a new family and friends, a new home, to find a new community, a new country, a new identity, and to recover the sense of meaning in life? In comparison with deaths in everyday life, in all their tragedy, mourning of such dimensions seems an impossible task. Every survivor of the Holocaust has had to struggle to come to terms with massive losses from the moment of his realization of having survived. Thereafter, throughout the lifespan they enjoy, they also have to contend with the essentially meaningless nature of all the deaths they have suffered and witnessed.

The normal mourning process usually starts with the realization of the death of a loved one. Realizing and comprehending one's loss was for many survivors of the Holocaust a very lengthy process. Even for those who did realize their losses, either during the Holocaust or immediately after liberation, it often was impossible to go into the mourning process.

In the concentration camps, as well as in the other Holocaust situations of constant fear for one's life, the necessity to conserve all one's energies for the survival struggle made it impossible to mourn. This was true even when one knew with certainty of the death of loved ones, either from having been physically present at their deaths or from the reports of others. Furthermore, the hope and belief that loved ones were alive and that reunion with them would occur after liberation was an important source for maintaining motivation to go on living. Fantasies of reunion and future life together with loved ones were indulged in by many of the victims as a coping strategy while in the grip of the genocidal machine.

At the end of the war the struggle to construct a completely new basis for existence took all the energies and resources of the survivor, so again mourning had to be postponed.

Although sometimes the survivor actually witnessed the murder of loved ones, the vast majority were killed without the presence of relatives and friends who survived. Separation in families was usually sudden, with family members being torn away from each other as, for instance, at the selection ramp at Birkenau Auschwitz or "actions" in which families were forcibly removed from each other.

Confrontation and realization of the death of loved ones, with the acceptance of the fact of loss, was seriously hindered by not having seen the body after death. The lack of knowledge of date of death and the absence of a grave aborted the normal process of realization that a loved one had indeed died. With the end of the war most survivors hoped and even expected to find some of their relatives and friends alive. There were survivors who sought confirmation of the deaths of specific family members or friends by scrutinizing photographs of heaps of dead bodies, and there were even those who opened mass graves immediately after the war and examined the corpses in them for the bodies of family members. The refusal to give up hope that a beloved relative or friend had remained alive was manifested in commonly reported phenomena of a compulsion to search among faces of passersby in the streets for a loved one. Day after day survivors visited the information centers that had been set up for all those searching for family members. There were those who were unable to face the magnitude of their losses and who committed suicide immediately or soon after being informed of what had happened.

Eventually the vast majority of the survivors more or less accepted the bitter truths of their losses. However, there were significant numbers for whom the hope (and indeed expectation) of eventually finding lost loved ones continued for many years. This was especially so for children who had been hidden with non-Jewish families or in monasteries and institutions and whose parents had disappeared. In countries like France and Holland where there was no prolonged ghetto experience, as there had been in Poland, in which children could get a sense of the constant losses to death by various actions and selections for transportation, there was no clear idea where the parents had disappeared. The children survivors hoped their parents were still alive, and these hopes would return to them persistently and unrealistically for years.

Since the mourning process could not take place at the appropriate time and place, in almost all cases it had to be postponed to a later stage in the life of the survivor. The enormous struggle to return to adapt to normal living demanded all the energies of the survivor. In the majority, mourning was therefore avoided and suppressed together with the painful, disturbing memories of the lost family and friends. Often there was a refusal to speak about separation from parents, which related to that lingering hope that they would yet return, which they didn't want to give up; to speak about it was to accept the possibility that they were dead.

In terms of intrapsychic processes, although the fact of the losses was perceived sooner or later by the vast majority, the emotional responses of pain and of grief were denied, so that mourning could never be completed.

In everyday life, a stage of denial in which the full meaning of the loss of a loved one is not comprehended is normal, especially when the loss is sudden or unexpected. Sooner or later it gives way to the painful grieving of the mourning process proper, and moves through stages of "hypercathexis" with intense grieving and preoccupation with memories of the relationship with the loved one, through stages of gradual "decathexis" and resolution of the separation, to gradual acceptance of the lost loved one as irrevocably dead and gone but valued in memory (internalization). The bereaved person is then free for new love relationships.

With Holocaust survivors, the dimensions of pain involved in mourning over global losses were so overwhelming that denial processes continued for many years, and mourning was characteristically postponed to later stages in the lifespan. The inability to separate from one's dead through processes of normal mourning was seen in the maintenance of idealized images of parents and other lost family members. Poignantly, many aging survivor children carried photographs for scores of years of their parents, whose ages at the times of their deaths were much younger than their—the survivors'—ages at present, yet looked at their parents in these pictures as revered figures. Unable to go through the stages of the normal mourning processes because of the extreme and immeasurably traumatic nature of their losses, the number of loved ones lost, as well as the atrocious circumstances in which the losses were incurred, many survivors remained truly traumatized, helpless, and numbed about their massive losses.

The defensive denial also enabled survivors to proceed with their immense problems as refugees after the war and then reentry and adaptation to new lands and lives. It seems that with many survivors, only after five to ten years later, with the achievement of initial adaptation in their countries of resettlement, were they able to begin to allow themselves the revival of painful memories of their former lives with their murdered family members and friends, and at last to commence the work of the mourning process. Until then, hope often was still maintained that the lost loved ones were alive, and daydreams and fantasies of reunion continued. With the end of denial and giving up of hope, the realization of death meant the beginning of mourning work, and for many this also meant the onset of clinical survivor syndrome symptomatology, especially the chronic depressive component.

The long-delayed mourning process for so many lost objects had to compete with commitments and relationships in the new life situation of the survivor. Even now mourning could only be partial and was therefore often prolonged throughout the years. The depressions and inner preoccupations with memories often interfered with the survivor's new family roles as spouse and parent. For those survivors who had married nonsurvivors who did not carry a similar burden of unresolved mourning, a warm, empathic, nurturing spouse could be invaluable in listening to the survivor's memories of pre-Holocaust relationships with parents and siblings who were murdered. But too often it was still terribly difficult to tell of Holocaust experiences to the other person. The memories aroused painful affects of shame, guilt, and anger, as well as feelings that in any case the spouse "would not understand," and that the spouse would have less respect for them thereafter. Such feelings, let alone spouses' real difficulties with listening to terrible stories, prevented many survivors from using the marital relationship as a supporting framework for their mourning process.

So they suffered in silence, revealing their mourning only by their occasional inner preoccupation, or by prolonged gazing on old photographs in deep sadness and perhaps weeping, or by dreams of their dead loved ones from which they would awaken in the night crying out in fear or in sorrow.

The personality structure of the survivor and such complications as there had been in the relationships with the lost loved ones could result in pathological, interminable mourning or actual depression. Since ambivalences are essentially common in most if not all human relationships, guilt feelings about anger and other bad feelings toward the dead ones were inevitable.

Not surprisingly, many survivors suffered from survivor syndrome symptomatology of varying intensity and duration with manifestations of persecutory dreams, anxiety, depression, preoccupation with the past, psychic numbing, excessive fatigue, restlessness, irritability, and preoccupation with fears of helplessness.

Two Life Stories of Survivors: Self-Fulfillment versus Breakdown. The following is a vignette of the life story of a survivor who is one of those who have succeeded in being true to themselves and fulfilling their potential, perhaps even transcending themselves because of their creative responses to the losses experienced in the Holocaust. This is a story that illustrates the possibilities of growth and inspiration even after the massive trauma of the Holocaust.

> Mr. A is a 54-year-old Polish-Israeli engineer whose life is characterized by a degree of integration of the Holocaust in his life, both in positive and negative aspects. He has not run away from his experiences nor has he chosen to be a "professional survivor or witness." At age fifteen, at the onset of the Holocaust, he lost his entire nuclear family (parents, older sister, younger brother). He is intelligent, with a strong ideological background of traditional Judaism, Zionism, and Socialism. In the concentration camp he met a young Polish Jewish girl from the same town, who later became his wife. After the liberation in 1946, he was immediately mobilized by the Israeli military mission and given a leadership role in the organization of the rescue and illegal immigration operations from the D.P. camps

of Europe into Palestine, which he was involved in for the next two years until the establishment of the state of Israel. Meanwhile he entered Poland illegally to search for the girl he met in the concentration camp, and found her and married her.

In Israel he helped to set up a new kibbutz where he became a mechanic—work that he had learned to do in the concentration camp—and he fought in the War of Independence. Characteristically, he was constantly searching for friends and families from pre-Holocaust school days and from the concentration camps. He is a man of intense humor who uses anecdotes of the Holocaust for daily living in a humorous fashion to illustrate actual problems of life with moral meanings, but he manages to avoid undue pathos, sentiment, and emotion. He very consciously lives with the Holocaust, remembers vividly the details of his experiences, and derives strength from the memories of how he and his comrades mastered many situations of extreme difficulty, fooling the Germans in many different ways and managing to survive against all odds.

He participates in a wide range of Holocaust educational and memorial activities, keeps in contact with a large number of survivors, and is always eager to meet them and share any family happenings such as weddings, Bar Mitzvahs, as well as the memorial days for their community. He is concerned to be in contact with them. He functions as a supportive, cohesive influence among his group of survivor friends and makes warm, loyal relations with them and their families, always ready to lend support.

In his own family life, he transmitted his message of active mastery and sharing about the Holocaust as the central theme of life to his children. His daughter in high school researched attitudes to the Holocaust among fellow pupils, and in visits to many countries, like her father, sought out survivor families and used her contact with them to discover more of the past of her parents. In his own family he is the integrating factor who continuously takes on the role of the savior. What he was unable to do in the Holocaust, he is doing now.

With regard to work, he accepted an intermediate level of responsibility; he preferred not to take on himself executive roles with more complex responsibility, which he was offered both in the army and in civilian life. His two children are well adjusted and successful. His son became an engineer, researching security problems. His daughter, trying to understand her parents' experiences in the Holocaust, and in order to help them, became a psychologist.

Throughout his life cycle we see this man accepting his role of survivor without shame but also without grandiosity, fulfilling his professional and civil obligations, but having also an extreme sense of responsibility toward his comrades of ghettos and camps. Fully aware of his losses, he rebuilt his life without having to adopt any extreme position in life. Israel is seen by him as a consequence of the Holocaust. He is closely identified with the country and with the feeling that he contributed to its rebuilding, which gives him a sense of historical continuity. He has been concerned to prove in his life that the survivors are ethical human beings.

The following vignette is the story of a survivor who never succeeded in being true to himself and who goes on with his life with a broken spirit and an absence of joy.

A 45-year-old Polish Jewish storeman who had grown up in a shtetl today lives and works in total isolation. At the end of the war he was aged fourteen, the only survivor of a large family of parents and four brothers. He had only two years' study in primary school. He worked as a child slave laborer in different camps between the ages of ten and fourteen years. Sometimes he even forgot the name of his family. After liberation, in trying to escape from loneliness, isolation, and lethargy, he married a Jewish woman from an Arab country. He was very submissive in relation to his wife and three children; in his family he functions virtually as an emasculated slave. Through a submissive, slavelike manner in his family and in relation to authority figures in his life he denies his own validity and worth as a human being. His attitude and mien seem forever to say, "Excuse me that I am alive."

In therapy, evidences of tremendous suppression of aggressive hostile feelings during the Holocaust were encountered, and as they were touched on in therapy occasionally resulted in really dangerous aggressive outbursts. This man had worked as a slave laborer for five years in different camps, including Auschwitz and Mathausen. As long as he was with his cousin, who was more active and with whom he could communicate, he remembered his family and he resisted and confronted his oppressors with great strength and physical fitness. When his cousin (the last remaining link with his family) died beside him, he became apathetic, lethargic, and sometimes forgot his family name. Only liberation soon after saved him from death. He was brought to Israel by a youth-refugee agency (Aliyat Hanoar) at about age fifteen. He was depressed and inactive, and lay in bed for months.

His adaptation and integration into Israeli society was minimal. To this day he has been unable to learn to write and read Hebrew. He manages to hold down a simple job although he constantly fears that his inability to read and write will be discovered and he will be sacked.

At home he has converted his wife and their three children into authoritarian figures who control him and whom he fears. Pitifully, he longs for barely remembered childhood love and warmth. He is unable to express his needs other than by periodic shrieking, angry outbursts, and occasionally also bursts of extravagant gifts above his poor means, by which he tries to compensate and restore the morale of the family.

Bereavement in Israel from War, Holocaust, and Terror

Israel as a Siege Society. Bereavement following violence has always been an integral part of the climate of Israel because of the recurrent wars, border incidents, and terrorist attacks. Every single family in the country has had to face the ongoing possibility of the death of one or more of its adult males in army service. If this possibility has not become an actuality in one's own family, then it has in the families of relatives, friends, colleagues, and neighbors, so that literally everyone in Israel has been personally involved in the tragedy of the bereaved families. Furthermore, the fact that a large number of Israelis were refugees and Holocaust survivors of the Nazi regime in Europe has meant that violent and massive death is, sadly, a familiar theme in the background of many Israeli families.

Death by violence complicates the universal experiences of bereavement and mourning, adding a further dimension of trauma to the already highly stressful life event of loss. Important elements in this additional trauma relate to the untimeliness that is often a feature of death by violence, and to the suddenness and unexpectedness that preclude anticipatory or preparatory grieving and mourning. When violent death is deliberately perpetrated by other persons, it shakes basic trust in human relations. If the death is actually witnessed, helplessness, passivity, and the inability to intervene may result in persisting feelings of shame and guilt. Furthermore, death from other than natural causes challenges the meanings and symbols that are available to us for coping with life and death in their regular and nonviolent modes. As a result of these elements, the mourning process after violent loss is often complicated and more difficult to resolve, with possible consequent disturbance in psychosocial functioning.

Since the establishment of the state in 1948, the wars of Israel have resulted in the deaths of about sixteen thousand, mainly young men and women soldiers, and terrorist attacks have resulted in the deaths of civilians of all age groups, which means a total of about twenty thousand bereaved families.

At one level, every bereavement from war or terror touches the lives of all the citizens and is thus a shared experience. Nonetheless, at the same time, avoidance and denial of the psychosocial and sociocultural implications of such large-scale loss in a small country has been typical of the Israeli context, just as it was also evident in the first years of the state in relation to the traumatic effects and implications of the uprooting and losses of the Nazi period, culminating in the Holocaust experience. The central motifs and preoccupations of Israeli society were from the outset the absorption of mass immigrations, and building of the country and its defense and security. The tremendous activity generated in the population in relation to these urgent priorities reinforced the tendency to avoid confrontation with traumatic experiences and massive losses of the past. The small established population was involved in dealing with mourning the new losses of the young men, wounded or killed in the 1948 war. This social climate, in which the terrible experiences of the Nazi persecution and genocide were dealt with as a matter of course, can be seen as having been sociotherapeutic for the rapid resettlement and rehabilitation of the hundreds of thousands of uprooted and traumatized refugees and survivors who poured into Israel in the early years of the state.[1] Their main concerns were to create new lives and new families, which coincided with the central needs of the building of the new state.

A further important element in the social climate of the new state was the denial and repudiation of vulnerability and passivity that were associated with the overwhelming confrontation with the mass violent death of the Holocaust, both at individual and societal levels. The Israeli newborn generation with its (Sabra) self-image of activity, mastery, and invincibility replaced the stereotype of the vulnerable, persecuted Diaspora Jew, powerless and helpless in the face of persecution and genocide. This image of the Israeli became the idealized model for a new identity for the immigrants and especially for their children.

The Israeli population is made up of people from vastly differing sociocultural backgrounds. The adaptation and integration processes of these heterogeneous ethnic groups within a Western-oriented society, as well as the need to keep up morale and military efficiency, led to the tendency to restraint and suppression of external emotional expressions of grief. This was especially evident among Jews from Central and Eastern Europe, the majority of whom had shed the religious rituals of their childhood home backgrounds and had readily embraced Western behavior patterns. Those from Middle Eastern Arab countries whose ethnic background and rituals encouraged expressions of grief that were intense and uncontrolled did so less readily.

There were thus five major specific factors involved in attitudes and mourning in Israeli society, especially in the early years: (1) the avoidance of involvement with the trauma and mourning of the Holocaust past; (2) the constant stress of the threat and recurrence of war and terrorist acts and the need to create and maintain an effective defense force with high morale; (3) the repudiation of the vulnerability and passivity attributed to the European Jew; (4) the acculturation process of the mass immigration; and (5) the involvement in building the new state and the struggle for economic security. These factors and others resulted in widespread avoidance and denial in relation to the new and ongoing losses from war and terrorist attacks.[2]

Israeli society thus demonstrated features of a "siege mentality," with the nonvulnerable, stoically coping and fighting "Sabra" (native Israeli born) stereotype as the identity model. This enabled the citizens of Israel to continue energetically building and defending the country and absorbing waves of mass immigration despite the continued losses and in the presence of so much accumulating bereavement. The collective image of invincibility and nonvulnerability reached its peak expression in the Six Day War of 1967 and prevailed until the 1973 war.

The nature and the degree of social and interpersonal support provided by the social framework for the bereaved is of central importance in a "survival society" like Israel.

In Israeli society there has always been immediate solidarity of response during the recurrent emergencies of war and terrorism —for as long as the emergency lasted. Similarly, war bereavement was always "shared," with the mobilization of maximal interpersonal and societal support for the bereaved.

However, this personal concern and solidarity with the bereaved individual and his family usually lasted only for the immediate traditional mourning period, especially during the first seven days ("shiva") when there is intensive social support, and to a lesser extent during the first thirty days ("shloshim"). There would then be a rapid lapse back to a matter-of-fact attitude, with the tendency to avoid the bereaved state of the individual and family and to give insufficient attention to the continuing emotional needs of the mourning process, both at the interpersonal and institutional levels of society. The broad tacit social attitude was that it was undesirable to mourn beyond the essential immediate period. As a result, the longer-term emotional needs of bereaved families were not sufficiently expressed. This was not so among the sections of the population (approximately 20 percent) who maintained their religious ritual and traditional forms of mourning during the course of the full year of mourning prescribed in Jewish religious tradition.

This tendency to a lack of acknowledgment and avoidance of the need to mourn was seen very strikingly during the period following the 1967 war, with deaths from the constant Egyptian shelling of Israeli army positions and from Katyusha rockets on the borders (this period was called "The War of Attrition"). In the kibbutz sector of the population, where attitudes were particularly stoic and devoid of religious ritual, bereaved wives and mothers who continued to show excessive emotional distress beyond the "Shiva" week or "Shloshim" month were even sometimes referred for specialized psychological help, as if the need to mourn beyond the immediate period was pathological and thus could be relegated to the experts.

At the institutional and national levels, there has always been central recognition of death from war and terrorism. The deaths by war or terror of soldiers or civilians have always been invested with the heroic quality of sacrifice of life for the survival of people and country, and their families have been accorded special status. The annual Independence Day celebration is preceded by a Day of Remembrance for the fallen of Israel's wars in which the whole nation mourns and there is considerable media participation. Furthermore, memorial monuments, of great variety and form, are seen everywhere throughout the country.

In addition, the memorial division of the Ministry of Defense offers its help and encouragement to the bereaved family for the preparation and publication of a personal commemorative book about the life of each dead soldier. After publication a copy is kept in a special library.

Israel has been a rapidly changing society throughout the thirty-five years of its existence, and each war has brought in its wake a deepening engagement with bereavement by the Israeli people and the social institutions involved.

After the 1967 war, the Ministry of Defense developed a special rehabilitation department to deal with the economic and practical needs of the bereaved families. The emphasis of concern was mainly with the material welfare of the widow and, through her, the children, and was manifest essentially in economic and material terms.

The sudden and unexpected 1973 war, with its large number of deaths, had a profound impact on Israeli society and its attitude to the unexpected losses and the bereaved families. A network of official and informal support systems grew rapidly during the war. A striking example of mutual help was the Notification Team, sent by the local army office to visit bereaved families, both to notify them of the death of the soldier in as human a way as possible, and to provide help at a critical moment. The teams were composed of a soldier from the same unit, the local family doctor, and a mental health professional (usually a social worker) or volunteer. A local rabbi and a representative of the municipal council would often also participate. Subsequently the bereaved family was visited in the period of immediate mourning, during the first "Shiva" week, by a social worker of the Rehabilitation Department of the Ministry of Defense. These social workers were trained in bereavement counseling and were also responsible for supervising the longer-term economic, social, and psychological needs of the bereaved family. The department recruited a large number of additional volunteer mental health professionals and nonprofessional helpers who worked under supervision as bereavement counselors. The importance of the mourning process now became more widely recognized. The bereavement counselors applied the general principles of crisis intervention in the initial mourning period with family sessions. Later, if indicated, self-help groups, etc., were organized.

Although a devastating confrontation for the bereaved family, the notification by an official team as well as the visits by the social workers from the Rehabilitation Department of the Ministry of Defense were also highly significant for them. This was demonstrated by Florian in a followup study of "Yom Kippur War Widows" and seems to indicate "an important psychosocial phenomenon, which may be characteristic" of the war-bereaved in general, and more specifically, of Israel's war-bereaved.[3] "The phenomenon is the strong need to be associated, early in the mourning process, with the representatives of the 'institutions' [Ministry of Defense and the army]" that give concrete form to the *meaning of the loss.* This "emphasized the psychological importance [for the war-bereaved] of identification with values that are strongly approved of by society, such as sacrificing one's life" for the survival of one's country and people. The death is thus invested with heroic quality and arouses expressions of respect, honor, and gratitude for ensuring the continued existence of the state of Israel and its people.

Over the years, with the different wars, the meaning of the loss has changed and affected bereavement reactions. Attitudes have changed particularly since the Yom Kippur War in 1973, and there have been aggressive accusations against the authorities by some bereaved families who felt that the deaths were not justified. The prolonged climate of mourning in Israeli society following the 1973 war was also related to the loss of the collective image of invincibility resulting from the realization of vulnerability. The deaths that followed in the Lebanon War of 1982 have caused particularly severe mourning reactions, with many expressions of bitterness and anger in terms of the relative meaninglessness and lack of justification of this war among certain sections of society, as compared with the "survival wars" of the first twenty-five years.

The Bereaved Individual within the Bereaved Family. In our ongoing therapeutic and research work with the bereaved, it is crucial to relate to the family context as well as the individual mourner. We have to be prepared to be flexible in our interventions and to be able to move when indicated from the family to the individual and back again to the family. This is especially so with bereavement from violent death, which suddenly engulfs a family, disrupting its equilibrium and restructuring previous patterns of interaction. Although family strengths and weaknesses not previously obvious may now appear and play an important part in the outcome, each member of the family is also thrown back on his/her individual resources. The specific individual reaction to the loss depends on many factors such as personality structure, relationship to the dead person, specific individual needs and experiences, and position in the lifespan and the generational span. The recognition of the predicament and specific mourning needs of each member of the family has been growing rapidly in recent years in the social and mental health services of Israel. There is still, however, a lack of systematic studies of how the individual members of families within the specific family context react to the loss of spouse, parents, children, siblings, etc., at different ages and from different causes.

The considerable ethnic and cultural heterogeneity of Israeli families has added to the complexity of the bereavement task, as described by Palgi.[4] Outcome studies since the Yom Kippur War in 1973 have been increasing steadily in number.[5] These, together with the experience derived from the considerable expansion of community services, have provided new insights into the needs and problems of the war-bereaved families.[6]

The Bereaved Wife. As stated previously, the Ministry of Defense's Rehabilitation Department takes full responsibility for the needs of the dead soldier's widow and children. Although for a number of years the main concern was manifested in practical support, since the 1973 war there has been increasing focus also on the social and emotional needs of the widow and her children.

The social workers of the Rehabilitation Department, after establishing initial contact soon after the death, remain available for intervention in a tactful and unobtrusive way to try to meet the widow's needs for releasing emotional tension, to provide advice with regard to problems of daily life and children, and to help with social reorientation and involvement. A professional is thus available who is concerned and interested in the widow and is ready to provide emotional support, reassurance, and advice when these are not available in the personal network of the widow.

Amir and Sharon studied the adjustment of two hundred war widows from two wars (five years after the 1967 war and two years after the 1973 war) in terms of the amount and type of help needed.[7] It was found that those widows who had made a positive adjustment, needing little if any psychological help, were those who were actively able to demand service, rights, and practical help of various kinds for themselves and their children. The largest group were those who needed help to return to normal social living but were unable to demand this help and waited passively for support. If help was not forthcoming they became miserable and isolated. The seriously psychologically disturbed who needed psychotherapy were those who were predisposed and vulnerable but had maintained a tenuous balance of functioning until it was disrupted by their husband's death. The importance of initiating and actively reaching out with support for the passive and vulnerable widow is clear from this study, and a similar conclusion is arrived at by Malkinson.[8] She studied fifty-one Israeli women widowed in the 1973 war or from routine military service, in relation to the association between self-esteem and helpful support from the environment. She found that widows with high self-esteem adjust better, generate and receive more support, and have fewer problems than widows with low self-esteem, who tend to reinforce reduction in social supports.

The challenges faced by widows in a society that both emphasizes productive roles in society and is also couple oriented are complex, since they often involve changing the life patterns, roles, and identity ("being a wife" of married life) to the autonomy of an entirely new status ("being a widow" of widowhood). The cultural and ethnic background of the widow and of the late husband's family may make these adjustments difficult.[9] In Israel widows from a Western cultural background, who have tended to be more educated and to have fewer children and more freedom, have adjusted better than those from a Middle Eastern background, where the traditional role of the widow involves staying close to the parental home and not being very active in building a new life.[10]

It is interesting to note that some young Israeli war widows from traditional male-dominated families reached new levels of emancipation and autonomy as a result of the material help and support of the Rehabilitation Department, which enabled them to feel a new sense of power and self-esteem.[11] Guilt feelings, however, may arise in widows and children whose material conditions improve as a result of the husband's/father's death. Sometimes resentment and hostile criticism may emanate from the bereaved parents toward the bereaved wife in relation to her adjustment to widowhood and single parenthood. These call for sensitive handling by the bereavement counselors.

Bereaved Children. Clinical and research studies throughout the Western world and Israel have shown that a high percentage of bereaved children suffer severe emotional disturbance and impaired functioning for several years following the sudden death of a parent.[12] This is now believed to be at least partially related to the tendency for children to be excluded from the grief and mourning reactions of the adults in the family and social group. The child is usually "helped" to avoid the reality and finality of the death by well-meaning adults seeking to protect him from pain. Many adults, because of the pain they experience in witnessing the emotional distress of anguished crying and longing in children, will try to attenuate the normal grief expressions in ways that often impede and block the healthy mourning process.[13]

In recent years in Israel, and especially in the years following the Yom Kippur War of 1973, there has been increasing awareness of the need of the orphaned child to express grief and experience mourning after the death of a father.[14]

The rehabilitation workers of the Ministry of Defense are now being trained to deal with the specific needs of bereaved children throughout the different stages of the mourning process. Smilansky and Weisman have provided clear guidelines for these bereavement counselors in dealing with the needs of the dead soldier's children.[15]

It is considered essential that the child clearly and unequivocably be informed in an "age appropriate" way of the father's death as soon as possible after the official notification by a person close to and trusted by the child. In accordance with this goal of leading the child to acceptance of the fact of the father's death and to acceptance of the reality—that is, the irreversibility and finality —of the death, the child is encouraged to participate in the funeral, the burial rites, and the mourning rituals of the family and community together with the mother and the other significant adults.

It is now increasingly understood that children are strong enough to cope with the painful reality of death in the family. However, the bereavement counselors often have emotional difficulty in confronting the child with the full truth, and need careful training to develop insight into their own tendencies toward avoidance and denial in the process of helping the child to grasp the reality of the loss and to give vent to the painful feelings.

The child should be present together with the adult during the *Shiva* week of mourning in order to be able to participate in the expression and communication of feelings of grief. The mother in particular should try to share her grief with her child and try to encourage the child to express his pain, anger, and longing.[16]

Social workers are available to help in this process, especially when the widowed mother is so overwhelmed and preoccupied by her own grieving that she is unable to be sufficiently available for her children, or when communication is deficient in the family relationship.[17]

Siblings. The impact on the sibling(s) of the death of a brother or sister has received relatively little attention in the literature.[18] The reactions are varied and related to many factors such as age, developmental level, relationship with the dead sibling, etc. They are further complicated when the death is sudden and violent.

Parents are often totally preoccupied with their own intense grief after the sudden death of an adult son and so the remaining sibling(s) may experience a situation of a double loss of both the dead brother and, emotionally, the parents who are now suddenly not available. Younger children usually receive attention from other family members, but adolescents often do not. Furthermore, the bereaved parents of a fallen soldier in Israel may receive much attention by various official and unofficial institutions and organizations who pay little or no attention to the teenager and elder sibling(s). As a result these siblings do not receive any validation of their experience of loss and may have little opportunity of expressing their often profound and complex grief. Thus, they often feel very angry but have little or no opportunity to express it.

Specific problems may arise from the idealization by the family and society of the dead soldier brother as a hero figure. This attitude may make it difficult for the surviving sibling(s) to relate to him realistically in the mourning process. They may have to struggle with feelings of inferiority in relation to the hero brother.

Furthermore, after a son has been killed, parents in Israel are given the right of refusal to allow the remaining siblings to serve in a front-line fighting unit during their army service. Thus bereaved parents, fearful of a further loss, may protectively prevent the remaining son(s) on reaching the age of conscription for army service from realizing a valued aspiration of many Israeli youths. In addition to blocking the possibility of emulating the idealized dead hero brother, this can result in severe frustration and even depression in the remaining brother(s). Furthermore, they often feel that their life has become limited because of the need to be protective to, and to feel responsible for, the welfare of their suffering parents. Unexpressed feelings of resentment, anger, and guilt often complicate the difficulties experienced in the mourning processes of these adolescents.

The bereavement counselors, with recent increasing awareness of the individual needs of the different members of the bereaved family after the death of a soldier, have been able to play a preventive and supportive role by making contact directly with the sibling(s) in order to help them express their experience of the loss in ways meaningful to them. Peer-group discussions as described by A. Morawetz after the Yom Kippur War have proved of particular value with bereaved adolescent siblings in enabling the ventilation and communication of mutual feelings and problems.[19] In a group situation a wide range of experiences and feelings can be shared about the abovementioned and other issues, such as the need to live up to the dead hero brother and ambivalence about his idealization; angry feelings toward the preoccupied and unavailable parent(s); guilt feelings because of the possible sudden improvement in physical circumstances (e.g., getting a room of one's own, inheriting personal belongings of the brother, etc.); and sensitivity in social situations because of the fear of being avoided and stigmatized. Blaming the authorities, the army, and societal values may result in disillusionment, a crisis of identification and meaning, and this is a further important issue for group discussion.[20]

Bereaved Parents. The death of a grown-up child is considered the most difficult task of mourning. In a study in Jerusalem carried out by Levav in which 125 stressful life events were assessed, the death of a son in military action was found to be the most traumatic experience of all.[21] The emotional plight of bereaved parents has not received nearly as much attention or study as that of the widow and the children, who constitute the dependent economic unit. Some of the most prolonged mourning situations, however, are seen in bereaved parents, as indicated in two Israeli studies by Purisman and Maoz, and Gay.[22] Attenuating factors include a good-quality relationship between the parents, grandchildren, and especially offspring of the dead son, as well as support from other children and an extended family or close friends. A poor outcome is related to unsatisfactory relations between the parents, previous losses (especially of children), the loss of an only son, no grandchildren, the lack of an extended family, and social isolation.

The father in the family often receives less attention than the mother, who is often the most obviously distressed parent. The underlying severity of the father's reaction may be overlooked behind a facade of mastery.[23] This is in accordance with the social expectation of a heroic demeanor of emotional restraint and stoic endurance in Israeli males.[24] It is especially so if, as is often the case, the father himself has been an active soldier, fighting in Israel's previous wars and involved in the defense and survival of the country for many years. The death of a son is a shattering blow for parents who raised their son in a value system of readiness to sacrifice one's life for one's country and is often associated with considerable guilt feelings. Ready to die himself for the survival and security of the next generation, the father did not envisage the fact that he could survive and his son be killed. This opposes his "assumptive world" by implying that he personally has failed and the value system with which he identified has proved to be an illusion.[25] To follow the coffin of his son is a catastrophic trauma, causing him to question the raison d'être of his life, especially when the loss is that of an only son. Suicide has been reported in the press in a significant number of war-bereaved fathers, especially among those who were Holocaust survivors, but has not been researched.[26] The prevalence of depression and alcoholism as well as morbidity and mortality in war-bereaved parents also requires systematic investigation.[27]

When the body has not been actually recovered, the loss may be denied, with the development of beliefs such as that the son is a prisoner in a hostile country, etc. In such cases the wishful thinking is so strong that the parent(s) sometimes believe that they have received communication from their son via the media or by telephone, or otherwise.

Among the religious groups, the loss of a son robs the father of a sense of fulfillment and continuity derived from the knowledge that after his death his son will recite the annual anniversary mourning prayer—the *kaddish*—in his memory.

The traditional expressions of mourning among Israeli families from Middle Eastern ethnic backgrounds are often manifested in considerable and even violent emotional display (head banging, pulling out of hair). Parents from backgrounds who have abandoned traditional modes of mourning may have great difficulty in coping with grief and mourning, having given up their only significant means of expressing their loss.

Some bereaved mothers, after the death of a son, insist on having another child even when in their forties. The motivation to give birth again is often expressed as an attempt to overcome the atmosphere of depression in the home and may represent an escape from mourning through the attempted "undoing" of the loss by replacing the dead son. Sometimes instead of the mother, a sister of the dead soldier may feel impelled to have a child.

Bereaved mothers and fathers often feel lonely and isolated. They may feel that they are avoided by others who feel helpless in their presence, often wanting to help but not knowing how. Even well-meaning friends and neighbors may not understand what is expected of them and fear to make contact in case they hurt the feelings of the vulnerable and sensitive bereaved parent. In this way bereaved parents are often avoided by others and deprived of the social support so essential for their recovery.

Parents with sons serving in the army may feel especially uncomfortable and apprehensive in their presence. If they go to meet bereaved parents, they become confronted with what could still so easily happen to them. Furthermore, the evidence of recent death can arouse a fear of "contamination" in anyone and is thus to be avoided. On the other hand, bereaved parents often feel a particular closeness and common identity with other bereaved parents. Some spend much of their spare time in the cemetery, where they experience a sense of communion with their dead son in a situation of belonging and solidarity with other bereaved parents. Participation in a group of bereaved parents can provide particularly meaningful support.

Bereavement of Holocaust Survivors in Israel

The problem of bereavement has been a central theme in the lifespan of the Holocaust survivors, who constitute a significant section of Israel's population. It was impossible to mourn in the Nazi concentration camps and most of the other situations of persecution and death during the Holocaust. The motivation to continue the struggle to survive was often sustained by the hope that relatives were alive. Many survivors of the camps have said that if they had known that their entire families had been murdered, they would not have been able to maintain the motivation for survival. With the end of the war the efforts required to overcome the physical and psychological effects of the massive trauma and for readaptation took all their energies, leaving little for the overwhelming task of grieving for such massive losses.

The mourning process was further complicated by the absence of the sequence of events that normally enables acceptance of the finality of the death. The lack of witnessing the death or burial, and the lack of a grave or even a date of death continue to haunt the lives of many with an uncertainty that was manifest in an endless search for lost loved ones.[28] In those who suffered from survivor syndrome, a central component manifested itself in depressive preoccupations derived from chronic grief due to a prolonged, unresolved process of mourning. In many others suppressed and postponed mourning had been an accompanying theme throughout the life cycle and has been worked on throughout the years episodically, in varied ways and rhythms according to the personality structure, life events, and circumstances of family and social environment.[29] Many of the child and other refugees of the Nazi period who were sent out of Europe before the war were suddenly separated from parents and family and never saw them again. Mourning for losses that could not be faced at the time has often been carried out later in life. Unresolved feelings of loss and separation have often been reawakened as a result of specific stressful life events such as crises in relationships or further separation, loss, etc.

The child born to survivor parents had a vital significance as an affirmation and justification of the parents' survival as well as validation of the existence of the destroyed pre-Holocaust family.[30] The death of this child constituted an utterly devastating event that sets off all the traumatic memories and images of Ho-

locaust experiences and losses, further injuring the sense of connection with the pre-Holocaust family, and in many cases destroying any sense of meaning in the parents' lives. These parents are
particularly vulnerable, especially as their family is often small
and in some cases perhaps also relatively isolated. They may be
unable to stop grieving for their son, especially if he was an only
son. They may decide to remain in a state of permanent mourning
that they see as a true reflection of the reality of their lives. Working with bereaved Holocaust survivors involves a return to the
unmourned losses and traumas of the past. Although this is an
extremely harrowing and prolonged process, these massively traumatized patients can often be helped to live with the incommen-
surate tragedy in their life situation.[31]

Interminable Mourning. In examining concepts of pathological
mourning in families where the loss is particularly tragic, the use
of the term "pathological" can be questioned and even an extreme
response can be seen as appropriate. The difference between normal and pathological disappears here, and a state of permanent
or "interminable mourning" has to be viewed as part of the reality
situation.[32] There are, however, vastly differing individual reactions, as can be seen in the following juxtaposed vignettes.

Mrs. H., a 51-year-old woman, a Holocaust survivor, was referred because of chronic and recurrent depression since her
only son was killed in army service six years previously. She
has two married daughters, but the son had special significance
for her because all the males in her family (father and his two
brothers) had been killed in Nazi Germany during her childhood. Her mother, who had remained with her, died soon after
the war. Her son, who was talented and very successful, was a
source of constant fulfillment and joy. Since his death she has
been inconsolable, in a state of perpetual grief and depression.
She cannot share her grief with her daughters, who feel rejected
and unloved by her, and she refuses to see her friends. The
family cannot cope with Mrs. H's interminable suffering, which
now repels them. The husband escapes into constant overactivity. The daughters married soon after the death of their brother
and already have children of their own.

She frequently visits the cemetery where her son is buried.
There she has a sense of belonging; it is the one place where she

feels tranquil, doesn't weep, and talks animatedly with other mourners. Neither the husband nor the daughters have been able to come to terms with the death, about which they still feel angry and guilty. The interminable mourning situation of the bereaved mother, clinging possessively to her dead son, has gone on for six years at the expense of the other family members, who are unable to proceed with and resolve their mourning. The mother cannot share her mourning with her family so that it remains separated off from them. The unresolved mourning for the loss of her entire family in the Holocaust between the ages of ten and fourteen created the predisposition to react with interminable mourning to the sudden death of her son.

Mr. B. is a 70-year-old man, an American Israeli living in a collective settlement. In the 1967 war, two of his sons were killed on the same day. He felt he was "going mad," especially when the Ministry of Defense Rehabilitation Officer told him that since he lived in a kibbutz and had no material worries and had a community to help him, his plight was not considered problematic. He felt desperate and unable to find anyone who knew how to help him. Eventually he came to the decision that the only way to help himself was to help other bereaved people by providing information on bereavement. Single-handedly he persuaded the Ministry of Defense into allowing him to set up a "Bereavement Library" in a small room in the Rehabilitation Department of the Ministry of Defense, containing every possible publication on the subject of bereavement that he had managed to collect. He spends all his spare time there, adding constantly to his library, and is always available for helping anyone seeking information on bereavement and mourning. He indefatigably attends any meeting or conference in which the subject of bereavement is discussed in order to offer his services and lists of publications and books to the bereaved and those who work as helpers and researchers. For seventeen years, although living in a situation of perpetual grief, he is constantly active and feels that his life has purpose and significance.[33]

Bereavement Following Terrorism

Among the many incidents of bereavement following terrorist attacks in Israel, I have chosen an incident that demonstrates how helping resources within the community can be mobilized immediately on the occurrence of a disaster, with the possibility of modifying the outcome in the bereaved and traumatized victims.

In March 1978, there was a terrorist attack on two civilian buses on the Haifa-Tel Aviv coastal road. Most of the victims were drivers and other workers of the Egged Bus Cooperative and their families returning home in a holiday mood after an organized Saturday outing.

The sudden unexpected attack caused a catastrophic reaction. Families were decimated and many children were among the dead and wounded. Immediately after the incident the entire membership of the bus cooperative throughout the country was alerted, and all the helping resources of the cooperative were put into action. Many members throughout the country volunteered in a demonstration of solidarity with the wounded and their families and the bereaved. This resulted in the immediate setting up of a social support system, helping in a wide variety of ways, both during the immediate aftermath of the disaster (visiting and supporting the victims, their families, and those in mourning), and later during the long process of rehabilitation and reintegration of the survivors. Guidance was provided throughout by the psychologist of the cooperative and other professionals who volunteered.[34] Our mental health center set up a crisis intervention team that made contact with the casualties and their families in the nearby general hospital, but this was of secondary significance.[35] What was particularly important was not the availability of mental health experts, but the mobilization of the self-help resources that exist within a community.

The close identification with the victims enabled the fellow members of the bus cooperative to respond immediately, efficiently, and devotedly. The network of helping activities set up at all levels constituted a "significant community" within which the survivors and their families could be immediately heard and understood. Feeling social acceptance and innocence of blame, they could freely express the grievances, anger, and guilt feelings that inevitably arose from the events of the tragedy.

The survivors of catastrophe require recognition and "consensual validation" of their suffering through a social process of "bearing witness" within a "significant community."[36] These interactive processes between the survivors of disaster and a significant community constitute the optimal framework for the expression of grief and the work of mourning. The presence of a significant community is essential for the survivors of catastrophe in order to be able to bear witness. The social process of bearing witness enables them to achieve recognition and "consensual validation" of their suffering.

The community of fellow workers in the bus cooperative has accompanied the bereaved families ever since, attending to their material and emotional needs. The network rallied to support them through the prolonged and harrowing court proceedings in the trial of the surviving terrorists. It has set up a monument to the memory of the dead and organizes annual memorial ceremonies. It counteracts cynicism and hopelessness at what happened by repeatedly formulating and promoting as a community issue societal values of fostering pride in the national significance of the cooperative as a pioneer in opening the roads and keeping them open for the public even in dangerous conditions and at the cost of the sacrifice of life by the members.[37]

We see here a sociotherapeutic paradigm for dealing with collective castastrophic events of trauma and loss. Through the medium of a social support structure and a system of values, the bereaved victims are enabled to go through the mourning process as well as to find some sense of meaning in their losses.

Coming to Terms with the Past: Processes of Recovery from the Holocaust Trauma

With the passage of years, the traumatic dreams faded for many Holocaust survivors. As the years have passed, with the normal events of the life cycle bringing new challenges and crises in the lives of the survivors and their families, survivor syndrome symptoms of the early period slowly changed and became absorbed by different modes and styles of functioning. Now, decades later, the traumatic memories, and especially the intensity of feelings associated with them, have faded and the experiences themselves often seem as if they belong to another life, to a "previous existence" reminiscent of a feeling of having lived before.

In some survivors there has apparently taken place, at least in relation to everyday life functioning, a more or less complete overcoming of the traumatic destructive experience. Others continue to show in their psychological makeup and interrelationships styles or modes which originally were of survival and life-saving value but after the Holocaust represent inappropriate responses to daily life events. A typical example of such a behavior pattern is seen in a need always to hoard food products and an inability to throw out food.

The range of styles, modes, and responses involved in this process of recovery is extremely rich and diverse and is related to many different processes of development and unfolding of the self. Some survivors have moved from self-images as victims to that of heroes, or from self-images of damaged and invalid even to those of grandiose supermen. Others have remained broken and "excremental," doomed to life-long shame as victims. Still others have almost miraculously pulled together renewed images of themselves as happy, worthy people, deeply appreciative of their lives and respectful of the life opportunity for others. The achievement of a sense of meaning and purpose in life, and specifically in their survival, was a vital organizing force for the recovery of these survivors from the terrors of the Holocaust. Giving a sense of significance to the present and future reduced preoccupation with the past.

Many of the survivors who suffered from unremitting anxiety and depressive and hypochondriacal symptoms consulted physicians, psychiatrists, and neurologists and were treated essentially with tranquilizers and antidepressant drugs. Some more sensitive and more complex personalities who felt the need to recover the "meaning" of life that was lost in the apocalyptic totality of Holocaust, where the destruction was total and their world came to a sudden halt, were able to turn to psychotherapy. A few of these survivors were in fact able to gain a great deal from therapy that contributed to their real recovery.

There were also others who came to treatment because of their "acceptance," by internalization, of the negative identity given them by the perpetrators of the Holocaust, who had made them subhuman and dangerous and thus deserving of annihilation. Therapy for these survivors, who had come to believe that they were as worthless as the victimizers claimed, and who also often had to contend with continuing survivor guilt over their survival in the face of the deaths of so many others, was not always helpful.

Other survivors rejected psychotherapeutic help because of a refusal to accept themselves as "patients." They insisted on transforming themselves into heroes who overcame death, and invested all their resources in building a secure and predictable world with overinvestment in material achievement, overcathected family ties, and close, supportive friendships with other survivors as a replacement for their lost families and communities. Many of them "succeeded" in this way to be emotionally healthy in the sense of being symptom free, yet in many cases conservatism, conformism, and devotion to law and order and the normative values of their new social frameworks became their guiding precepts. The need to be "super normal," with overpatriotic loyalty ties to their new homeland, replaced past inner psychological structures of security and basic trust. These survivors overidentify with the prevailing values of the society and life style of the various countries in which they settled.

"Coming to terms with the past" involves processes similar to the well-known concept in psychoanalysis termed "working through." In the lives of survivors, working through involves a day-and-night reliving of aspects of the traumatic experiences they underwent during the Holocaust. For many survivors, it is a process that is ongoing for many years, although it varies considerably in intensity according to life events and phases in the life cycle. It may be aroused by a chance and trivial stimulus or a vivid fantasy of a lost relative aroused by a chance encounter in a public place.

Processes of working through are, of course, expressed in memories, dreams, and fantasies, such as memories of a happy childhood family, but also often in memories and dreams of terror-stricken flight from persecutors. The intricacies of working through can be seen in everyday life when survivors unwittingly deal with difficulties and obstacles in their everyday lives by mobilizing traumatic experiences, so that they end up handling the situation they are dealing with in terms of their Holocaust past and not in terms of objective, present reality. Thus, the unlimited, tenacious, energetic devotion and hope that some survivor parents show when one of their children becomes desperately ill. Similarly, anxieties, fears, and overindulgences are often transferred to children, who are related to as persecuted victims when the survivor has not completed working through his own past status as a victim.

The working-through process is also expressed in the well-known phenomenon of survivor guilt. "Why did I survive while so many others perished?" is the eternal human question. *In my opinion, the posing of this oft-expressed question is also the first attempt at humanization and consolidation in the fragmented injured self of the survivor. I believe that in addition to the fact that survivor guilt is, as its name conveys, existential guilt and anxiety over surviving in the face of others' deaths, survivor guilt served several important positive functions.*

For survivors of the Holocaust, survivor guilt represented the first step in leaving the anonymity of the "faceless crowd" of nameless victim-survivors, emerging from the death camps, hiding, and false identities. It was a declaration of a return to a separate individual identity, a return to the old though tormented self. It was an attempt to begin the postponed process of mourning for the many losses of family, friends, and community. It was an expression of a renewed need for psychological-ethical cohesiveness and restoration to the universal family of man. For the victims of a period of collective evil that had never before been seen or imagined possible, survivor guilt represents a restoration of lost human values in the service of the reconstruction of the self through an acceptance of sharing in responsibility for what happened.

Guilt was a manifestation of the process of restoration of the pre-Holocaust psyche, with its old conflicts, clashes, and hopes, which were an integral part of the pre-Holocaust personality development. The internalized world of childhood that was obliterated during the Holocaust was restored through guilt feelings deriving from past relationships with parents and other key childhood figures. The recurring questions about not having saved lost relatives and friends constituted a painful inner dialogue with one's self, God, and with humanity. It drove the survivor to accept his essential individual helplessness in the face of the total catastrophe, but also reconfirmed his humanity as a person who cares and wants to do the best he can for his fellow man.

Remembering and relating Holocaust experiences can be an extremely valuable mode of working through. Unfortunately, this direction was denied a great many survivors because most of the societies to which they arrived after the Holocaust needed to deny the individual survivor's experiences. Many survivors suppressed their memories for years because of fears of being overwhelmed by their own emotions, and because of fears that their memories would be destructive to their new hard-won self-images and self-esteem. They feared to tell their children, believing that such knowledge would be damaging for them and would spoil their relationship with them by impairing their respect for them as human beings.

There were some survivors who were driven to tell their persecutory experiences over and over again to whoever would listen, but with only a limited sense of relief and sense of confirmation of their survival. For these survivors, it was as if the present did not really exist, except as a stage for presenting the past over and over. They remained fixated in the roles of victims in the Holocaust, as if time had stood still. A true confrontation between their past and present reality never occurred in their stereotyped accounts, and thus they remained unable to change their self-image from that of the permanently damaged (ego-depleted) victims to free men once again. This kind of repetitive, insistent relating is not a successful working through, but rather a perseveration that creates in the listener a feeling of meaninglessness and depression. In the long run, perseverative accounts, whether by an individual or by a society that over-ritualizes the telling of the Holocaust, will lead to a banalization of Holocaust experiences without evoking any real echoes or empathy in the hearts of listeners—only apathy.

9.
Recovery and Integration in the Life Cycle
of the Individual and the Collective

Traumatic experiences have always been an integral part of life in Israel, with recurrent wars and the continuous threat of a new war, with border incidents and terrorism, in a population many of whom had been traumatized by the Holocaust as well as by uprooting and mass immigration.

Israeli psychiatry has been much involved in dealing with post-traumatic stress disorders, and notable papers on theoretical concepts of trauma have been written by many of Israel's leading psychiatrists.[1]

Each of these authors, starting from different positions and orientations, abandoned the attempt at exact definitions of trauma and the traumatic event and moved their focus of significance onto an emphasis on the subjective aspects—the traumatic experience that results from the event and the state of traumatization that comes into being. When the trauma reaches severe or catastrophic (massive) dimensions, as experienced in the Holocaust or in some events of battle or serious illness, there is a breakdown of psychic integration, a dislocation in the functioning of the structure of the self. The traumatic experience is seen as changing the individual's inner and outer worlds, resulting in

1. the disruption of the sense of continuity of life;
2. the destruction of the sense of meaning in life; and
3. an undermining of the sense of security and basic trust.

189

Although catastrophic trauma cannot be integrated into the psychic functioning or into the new reality of the present, traumatized individuals show a great variety of adaptive and coping responses, enabling functioning even at high levels despite the fragmentation of the traumatic experience.[2] However, integration remains an ever-present challenge to be faced and taken up in response to events and stages in the lifespan, with great variety in possible extent and outcome.

For many years we have been following up Holocaust survivors in Israel, both in clinical frameworks and in the general population. Avoidance and denial of various degrees, forms, and complexities seems to constitute the psychic mechanism most fundamentally and widely used for dealing with traumatic memories. Different degrees, forms, and complexities of avoidance and denial are manifested in mechanisms such as simple avoidance and conscious suppression and isolation, encapsulation, splitting, and psychic numbing. Survivors have described how they consciously mobilized degrees of psychic numbing in order to cope with stressful life events that aroused traumatic memories.

The new social frameworks that the uprooted and traumatized survivors found themselves in after the war demanded great efforts for adaptation. In fact, surprising quantities of energy seem to have been available to many of the survivors, especially those of the teenage and young adult age groups, in their determination to create new lives. Their capacity for work, associated with tenacity of purpose in their determination to succeed, resulted in considerable productiveness and economic and occupational success. At the same time, the tendency to be constantly and maximally active and self-driving seems to be closely linked with avoidance and denial mechanisms. Denial mechanisms and activity seem to mutually reinforce each other, and as long as the individual can remain active the denial can often be maintained as an efficient defensive system through the lifespan. Limitation or loss of activity can thus seriously undermine the denial defenses, with possible clinical consequences.

The hunger for success and activity in some survivors has also been seen by psychodynamically oriented clinicians to serve omnipotent needs and attitudes that overcompensate for the impotence, helplessness, and abandonment experienced in the situations of catastrophic trauma of the Holocaust.

A further determining factor in the importance of work in the adaptive patterns of survivors is that activity in the concentration camps after selection for various work situations of importance to the Nazis generally enabled postponement of one's death. This sense of the urgent significance of work in warding off the danger of death often continued thereafter into the normal working life and contributed to the anxiety experienced whenever the threat of loss of work arose.

The description of the process of *massive psychic or catastrophic trauma* and the clinical sequelae of the concentration camp survivor syndrome deriving from the most extreme situations of trauma known to man created a new diagnostic paradigm and conceptual modality for psychiatry and the behavioral sciences.[3] These constructs have served ever since as focal concepts for the examination of various catastrophic trauma situations and their long-term effects.

The survivor syndrome became a main vehicle of expression, although varying greatly in severity, of the survivor experience and the survivor's adaptive struggles. Probably a majority of the survivors have suffered from one or more of the traumatogenic anxiety and grief components of the survivor syndrome and their somatopsychic manifestations. In many survivors these seem to me to represent potentially normative responses to the traumatic experiences and losses rather than psychopathology. Many of these "symptoms" often gradually subsided during the course of the years. It appears that *in many of these survivors the recurrent fearful flashback associations and depressive preoccupations represented episodes of grief work and cathartic working through of traumatic memories while at the same time struggling to integrate and to organize new external and internal worlds and to find meaning in life.* Children of survivors frequently report witnessing the distress of parents suffering from flashbacks, experiencing or hearing them awaken, cry out, and weep from a persecutory dream, or seeing their depressive withdrawal while grieving for lost loved ones— lighting candles, gazing at photographs, etc.

These phenomena, which I believe are normal manifestations of fearful experiences and loss, became the symptomatology of the survivor syndrome to be treated mainly by drugs. The syndrome became a somewhat stereotyped diagnostic construct with established, internationally accepted criteria for recommending compensation payments based on percentages of psychiatric disability. A large literature grew out of the examination of tens of thousands of survivors for the purposes of the compensation certificates or from the significantly smaller number of survivors seen in psychiatric clinics and hospitals that by and large confirmed the early descriptions and created a clinically biased view of the sequelae of Holocaust survival.[4] In keeping with the concept of massive psychic trauma causing "irreversible changes," the prognosis of the survivor syndrome was considered poor and psychotherapy of little value. From clinical practice, however, we know that many survivors were in fact helped considerably in the clinics and hospitals throughout Israel by motivated, empathic therapists, although few systematic followup studies have been carried out.

The avoidance of engagement with the traumatic experiences of the survivor was a widespread phenomenon not only among the biologically oriented clinician, but psychotherapists and psychoanalysts also reacted like the rest of society in this regard. The attitude prevailing among many psychotherapists with regard to the treatment prospects with survivors was in my opinion a rationalization of the resistance to become involved with the Holocaust experiences of horror and loss.

What is most significant, in my opinion, is the salient fact that the vast majority of the large survivor population in Israel and elsewhere did not become psychiatric patients. Focusing solely on the pathological consequences of trauma obscures the remarkable potential for new adaptation, recovery, and integration throughout the lifespan. Each survivor is unique in the individual nature and meaning of his experiences and responses to these experiences. This uniqueness may be obscured by the shared events and common behavior patterns, but the fact is that experiencing similar events in the same situation often had entirely different meanings for different survivors.

The Heterogeneity of the Survivor Population. Outcome is related to complex interacting variables. The basic factors relate to age and personality structure. Those who were adolescents and young adults when the trauma was experienced constitute the majority of active survivors today (included here are those who were uprooted refugees from Central Europe in the 1930s). They have lived forty or even fifty years of the lifespan since the traumatic experiences. This has meant a greater possibility of emergence and recovery from, and integration of, the traumatic experiences and more or less uninterrupted developmental sequences. Furthermore, living for forty years after enables the achievement of a psychological perspective that can foster a late working through of trauma and loss. Child survivors whose early development was damaged because of deprivation constitute a special group. Many of the older survivors who were married and had children whom they lost were less able to recover and to develop after the trauma. However, although it was more difficult for them to create new families (and some had had their actual reproductive organs damaged), their adaptive capacity was often preserved and many started new families despite the difficulties and problems. It was among this older group, many of whom died, that we saw the most clinically damaged people presenting with chronic KZ syndromes, severe depressive and hypochrondriacal states, premature aging, and severe psychosomatic disturbances.

With the passage of forty years, the survivor population has changed. The majority of these who are active today forty years after the war are people in their fifties and sixties who were teenagers and young adults on liberation. Many of them, through speaking, writing, and other creative activities, are working on their memories centered on their Holocaust experiences. With recovery processes manifesting slowly throughout the years, personality resources and predispositions became increasingly evident, with considerable interindividual variability as to the degree of inner plasticity.

Emergence from Trauma: The Restoration of Continuity, Meaning, and Security. Recent observations of survivors in Israel among the general population have emphasized again that by studying the nonclinical population we are presented with a unique opportunity to study the adaptability, strengths, and recovery powers of the human psyche. Such studies balance the biased view of the psychic functioning of the survivor as irreversibly damaged and the survivor syndrome as a permanent, static disturbance. Furthermore, we can learn about the factors that make recovery possible. Our concern is with understanding those factors that promoted the recovery process from the massive trauma of social catastrophe.

The struggle to cope with, master, and integrate the traumas of the past into the world of the present is an ongoing dynamic process throughout the lifespan of the survivor and involves interdependent factors in the family structure and the psychosocial environment. The adaptive capacity of survivors has been outstanding in the various societies where they settled. Survivors are experts in coping and adaptation in the service of survival and thus highly sensitive to and aware of the demands of the environment. This meant active acceptance of and conforming with the values and standards of the societies in which they settled in their need to be accepted and in their determination for achievement of material and occupational success and security. Their capacity for *activity* as an adaptive defense reinforcing denial as well as their vigilance, alertness, and capacity for improvisation, which were important survival mechanisms, have proved to be of considerable social value.

The Breakdown of Denial. The large survivor group who were teenagers and young adults during the Holocaust has enabled us to study the struggle throughout the lifespan "to live with" the traumas of the past over the forty years since the Holocaust.

Integration and resolution of catastrophic trauma, although probably impossible to achieve fully, has been an ongoing task throughout the lifespan. For long periods and especially during the years of maximal activity in relation to the demands of occupational and family life, the memories of the traumatic experiences were "held off" and to a greater or lesser degree "walled off" and encapsulated by avoidance and denial mechanisms from the rest of the psychic functioning.

However, this meant that vulnerability was always present, even though it was quiescent for long periods. Denial could break down in the face of stresses and life events. A great variety of life events can have specific significance for individual survivors, according to their unique individual experiences. Generalizations must be avoided that simplify the complexities of survivors' lives, which often demonstrate considerable strengths and resources in facing life's stresses. Toughness and reduced sensitivity may coexist with specific vulnerability, which may only be revealed at particular periods in the life cycle.

The breakdown of denial can result from life events arousing traumatic memories, especially after the midlife period in the lifespan. The emergence of vulnerability manifests itself in a flooding of consciousness with the warded-off traumatic memories and postponed mourning. Clinical decompensation may then manifest itself. This could take the form of acute anxiety associated with flashback traumatic associations and/or depressive states, including preoccupation with memories of Holocaust losses incompletely mourned. The severity of the breakdown was related to the degree of denial involved. The most severe clinical states, often intractable paranoid depressions, were seen in those whose denial defenses were especially strong and rigid. These survivors had claimed to be entirely symptom free and to have emerged unscathed from the traumas of the past. Individuals who had used lesser degrees of denial reacted with milder symptoms of the survivor syndrome.

It is important to stress that the majority of the survivors have not clinically decompensated in the encounter with stressful life events and with the later phases of the lifespan.[5] Furthermore, the threat of the breakdown of denial presents for many survivors new opportunities for further working on the avoided traumatic events of the past. There is thus always this "double-edged" aspect in the lifespan of the individual who went through experiences of extremity. In facing stressful life events there is the danger of decompensation into symptoms, but on the other hand the possibility of reaching a new level of integration. Flexibility in their denial defenses and plasticity in development since the traumatic period have enabled many survivors to embark on a late working through of traumatic experiences and losses, often with major progress towards resolution.

The occurrence of loss in the family has presented particularly significant opportunities for delayed mourning of loved ones murdered during the war. The lives of many survivors, when looked at longitudinally, reveal that there has been a recurrent dynamic interaction in the encounter with and mastery of stressful life events that aroused past traumatic memories and enabled episodes of spontaneous working through. In this way there has often been a progressive reduction of denial and an increasing achievement of integration; long-standing therapeutic relationships with survivors have enabled similar processes.

Recovery and Integration

In our concern and preoccupation with the psychological damage resulting from the catastrophic trauma, we have neglected the study of the processes of recovery and integration that have enabled the majority of the survivors to reestablish their psychological integrity and create new lives, new families, and new psychosocial contexts.

I have had the privilege of treating many massively traumatized survivors. Each is uniquely different and no two have suffered the same. Each demands a special effort of attention, understanding, and empathy. The challenge is to establish a relationship of basic trust in people whose ability to trust and self-image have been shattered. In every survivor there is a universe of inarticulated feeling, of blocked mourning and rage and guilt feelings seeking expression. To succeed in creating an atmosphere of trust in which the survivor can release and work through these destructively pent-up emotions is indeed a great privilege for a therapist.

The therapy of survivors has often required long-standing efforts to maintain the relationship until such a time as the survivor feels himself ready to discharge and relate. Many are doing this now, for the first time, having acquired distance and some degree of integration of the experiences with the passage of the years.

The following themes studied in our lifespan interviews with survivors have emerged as central in the processes of recovery and integration.

1. Reciprocal Human Bonding. The same capacity to form pairing friendships and small groups that was of central importance in protecting, mitigating, and maintaining the motivation for survival during the traumatic experiences was a major source of strength during the arduous period of rehabilitation and reentry into society. Many of the survivors whom we have studied found themselves entirely alone as teenagers after the liberation.[6] They underwent positive socialization experiences and spent formative periods in rehabilitation centers that were set up in Europe and in England after the war.

In these centers based on group living, group bonds developed rapidly and relationships that sometimes had originated in common experiences in the ghettos and the camps deepened. The active encouragement and utilization of these group bonds played an important role in the reintegration of these young people through the reconnection with values and ideals from their destroyed home. The preservation of connection and continuity between self and identity backgrounds and cultures from before and after the war enabled the mobilization of resources for the reconstruction of life and new relationships.[7]

For many, the bonds that were created in the concentration camps and during the rehabilitation period after liberation have continued as an important social support system throughout their lives up to the present. In the different countries in which they now live, they have maintained close contact and affection for each other, often of a sibling-bond nature, throughout the years with much mutual caring and helping behavior. The intensely supportive quality of the network of relationships of small and large groups enabled much exchange of reminiscences and mutual encouragement. This self-help system may well have replaced for some a need for therapy, which might have arisen without it.

For many the group network of relationships had some of the elements of the extended family that had been destroyed. Children of survivors often looked upon their survivor parents' friends as uncles and aunts. The various reunion gatherings that these survivor groups have held throughout the years provided for many survivors a reexperiencing of the solidarity and sense of communion in the face of terrible adversity that was a source of strength and hope for many during the Holocaust experiences within the dyadic and group relationships. The recreation of and participation in communities in the various countries of settlement was of particular specific significance in overcoming the collective trauma experienced by all Holocaust survivors in addition to the individual trauma process.

2. The Past as a Resource. This concept has recently become increasingly recognized in lifespan studies.

The past can be seen as an enduring repository of valuable memories and experiences that can be drawn upon and mobilized as resources to maintain psychological equilibrium and health in the lifespan. This "use of the past" can occur when encountering stressful life events or in response to the demands of adult stages of development or as an instrument of recovery and integration after catastrophic trauma.

In the struggle for adaptation and mastery of the traumatic experiences of the Holocaust, survivors attempt to connect between positive memories, images, and values from the pre-Holocaust past and present-day reality. Integration into the new society often involved finding such points of connection in community,

religious, and ideological frameworks. Sometimes the organization of present-day reality around a specially significant memory
or image from the past can become a central theme in the integration of the survivor, as in the following case:

> A 58–year-old survivor of Auschwitz and Bergen-Belsen was
> thirteen years old when the Nazis confiscated his father's fa-
> mous collection of birds after the German occupation of Carpa-
> tho-Russia. He used to help his father with the birds and tried
> to resist the removal of the birds until his father stopped him
> because of fear of the consequences to him. For him the Holo-
> caust started with the confiscation of his father's bird collec-
> tion, although it was only two years later that he and his family
> were transported to Auschwitz, where everyone in his family
> perished, including both parents and two siblings. Liberated in
> Belsen, eventually, via Cyprus, he got to Israel in 1947, aged
> twenty-one. He immediately started a bird collection, although
> at first he lived in a tent in which he kept his first birds. Today
> he has an exotic aviary containing hundreds of birds in the
> garden of his modest home, open free of charge every afternoon
> to the public and especially to children.
>
> The aviary is in honor and remembrance of his father. He
> personally welcomes the visitors, and is especially interested in
> the children who come. They are welcomed by him with the
> story of what happened to his father, his bird collection, his
> experiences in the camps, and his rehabilitation in Israel. He
> believes that he "survived to help bring people both closer to
> nature through the birds and closer to an understanding of the
> Holocaust."

On the other hand, the reality of the pre-Holocaust past may be
inaccessible because of the destructive traumatic experiences of
horror and loss that invest the past with fear and grief. The past
thus remains split off, containing idealized images that are unavailable as a resource, and it is a therapeutic challenge for the
empathic therapist who is motivated to help construct bridges to
these inaccessible images.

3. Parenting. Parenting and the creation of new families was
central to the recovery of many survivors. The need for the creation of new life was greater than any other creative need after the
genocidal destruction of families. Many survivors report over-

whelming feelings of triumph and elation with the infusion of new motivation and vigor for life after the birth of their first child, which represented for them the defeat of the genocidal design of Hitler and the Nazis. The younger survivors did not usually marry immediately and were not driven by the need to replace the lost family as were many of the older group who had been married and had lost spouses and children. They were able to continue with their development as teenagers and to marry years later after a greater emergence and recovery from the immediate after-effects of the trauma and loss. The children of this younger group of survivors were born at a later stage in the recovery process than children born soon after liberation to parents still in states of psychic numbing and preoccupation with the loss of their families.

The empathic parenting capacities of survivor parents have been questioned by many researchers and although this may be justified in relation to some children born immediately after liberation, one must keep in mind always that parenting is a complex function with its own developmental history related to the way the parents themselves were parented and therefore cannot be viewed as the product of Holocaust experiences alone.

The sense of renewal and continuity experienced by parents through nurturing and rearing a new generation are also the basic ingredients of recovery after catastrophe. Furthermore, psychological reciprocity between parents and children involving the integration of parental expectations with their own ego ideals enhances the parents' self-cohesion and self-esteem.

Failures in parental empathy occur when, because of their own imperative narcissistic needs for affirmation, the parents are unable to respond to the child's legitimate developmental needs. The child then may be "used" to maintain the parents' self-esteem or self-cohesion.

However, the assumption that because of the importance of the creation of a new family and the importance of the next generation in the recovery of survivor parents, they must necessarily show "possessive" narcissistic investment in their children and exploit them emotionally is an unjustified generalization. Some children of survivors feel their parents' needs as an onerous burden, whereas others feel them as a positive commitment and challenge, and in talking with children of survivors one encounters many variations between these two roles.

4. Midlife. From the midlife period there is an increasing return of memories during the day and dreams at night, with an urge towards reviewing one's life. Avoidance and denial defense mechanisms often weaken as work activity loses its significance (with the achievement of success, and the children becoming autonomous). Many survivors seem to be able to avoid anxiety and depression only as long as they can work, and often overwork; when they can no longer work, they can no longer hold off the memories. There is thus an increasing unavoidable confrontation with the past, and then the more so as the aging process proceeds.

5. Aging. The traumatic memories that flood back after having been fought off and avoided for so long can be felt as "retraumatization" or as "being attacked." Traumatogenic flashback associations, nightmares, and dreams of loss may reappear after years. A major task of old age is integration, but how is one to integrate the irreconcilabilities of the utterly different Holocaust world of Holocaust experiences and the world of present-day reality? How is one to effectively mourn and integrate such massive losses?

6. Mourning. The problem of bereavement has been a central theme in the lifespan of Holocaust survivors. It was impossible to mourn in the Nazi concentration camps and most of the other situations of persecution and death during the Holocaust. Energy had to be conserved for the struggle to survive and so grief had to be suppressed. Furthermore, the motivation to continue the struggle to survive was often sustained by the illusionary hope that relatives were alive. With the end of the war the efforts required to overcome the physical and psychological effects of the massive trauma and for readaptation took all their energies, leaving little for the overwhelming task of grieving for massive losses. When confronted with so many losses, mourning as we understand it is an impossible task; it seems that the dimensions of technological mass murder have surpassed man's capacity to mourn. The mourning process was further complicated by the absence of the sequence of events that normally enable acceptance of the finality of death. The lack of witnessing the death or burial, the lack of a grave or even a date of death continued to haunt the lives of many with an uncertainty that was manifest in an endless search for lost loved ones.

Many of the child and other refugees of the Nazi period, who were sent out of Europe before the war, were suddenly separated from parents and family and never saw them again. These child refugees and survivors, many of whom were sent to "safe" countries or were hidden with non-Jewish families in varied conditions in Nazi-occupied Europe (France, Holland, Poland, etc.) often awaited for years the return of parents who had disappeared, with no clear information available about their deaths. The lack of any real separation haunted their lives with a sense of abandonment, and lack of basic trust complicated any possibility of mourning. The disappearance of parents early in life was often associated with life-long uncertainty about identity, origins, and belonging.[8]

Mourning for losses that could not be faced at the time has often been carried out later in life. Suppressed and postponed mourning has been an accompanying theme throughout the life cycle of survivors and has been "worked on" throughout the years episodically and in varied ways and rhythms according to the personality structure, life events, and circumstances of family and social environment.

Lawrence Langer, a professor of English who teaches Holocaust literature, has written a moving description of how a survivor student used a chance situation to begin to express that which she could never articulate.

She was 14 when the Germans invaded Poland. When the roundup of the Jews began a year later, some Christian friends sent their young daughter to "call for her" one day, so that they might hide her. A half hour later, the friends themselves went to pick up her parents, but during that interval, a truck had arrived, loaded aboard the Jewish mother and father—and the daughter never saw them or heard from them again. Their fate we can imagine. The girl herself was eventually arrested, survived several camps, and after the war came to America. She married, had children of her own, and except for occasional reminiscences with fellow survivors, managed to live adequately without diving into her buried personal past. Until one day her instructor in English composition touched a well-insulated nerve, and it began to throb with a painful impulse to express. I present verbatim the result of that impulse, a paper called "People I Have Forgotten":

"Can you forget your own father and mother? If so—how or why? I thought I did. To mention their names, for me is a great emotional struggle. The brutal force of this reality shakes my whole body and mind, wrecking me into ugly splinters; each crying to be mended anew. So the silence I maintain about their memory is only physical and valid as such but not true. I could never forget my parents, nor do I want to do it. True, I seldom talk about them with my husband or my children. How they looked, who they were, why they perished during the war. The love and sacrifices they have made for me during their lifetime, never get told. The cultural heritage to which each generation is entitled to have access to seems to be nonexistent, since I dare not talk about anything relating to my past, my parents. This awful, awesome power of not-remembering, this heart-breaking sensation of the conspiracy of silence is my dilemma. Often, I have tried to break through my imprisoning wall of irrational silence, but failed: now I hope to be able to do it. Until now, I was not able to face up to the loss of my parents, much less talk about them. The smallest reminder of them would set off a chain reaction of results that I could anticipate but never direct. The destructive force of sadness, horror, fright would then become my master. And it was this subconscious knowledge that kept me paralyzed with silence, not a conscious desire to forget my parents. My silent wall, my locked shell existed only of real necessity; I needed time. I needed time to forget the tragic loss of my loved ones, time to heal my emotional wound so that there shall come a time when I can again remember the people I have forgotten."[9]

7. *Creative Activity.* Creative activity is an important mode of expressing and working on traumatic experiences, especially unresolved grief. The emergence of creativity heralded new possibilities for resolution and integration in the lifespan of the survivor. This phenomenon has been observed in many survivors in midlife and later with the return of memories together with the development of a capacity for reflection and fantasy.

The need "to bear witness" is often associated with this creative activity, which manifests through the medium of writing prose or poetry or of painting.

This process of late creative working through may become a family project when a good reciprocal and sharing relationship exists between survivor parents and their children. There have been many striking examples of a creative and artistically talented child taking over "working on" the loss of the parents' family through poetry and painting.

8. *The Societal Context.* The societal context exercises a central influence on the process of adaptation and integration of the sur-

vivors of social catastrophe. The central motives and preoccupations of Israeli society were from the outset absorption of mass immigrations and building of the country and its defense and security. The tremendous activity generated in the population in relation to these urgent priorities reinforced the universal tendency to avoid confrontation with the traumatic experiences and massive losses of the past. The small established population was involved in dealing with mourning the new losses of the young men wounded or killed in the 1948 war. This social climate, in which the terrible experiences of the Nazi persecution and genocide were dealt with in a matter-of-fact way, can be seen as having been sociotherapeutic for the rapid resettlement and rehabilitation of the hundreds of thousands of uprooted and traumatized refugees and survivors who poured into Israel in the harrowing but triumphant early years of the state. Their main concern was to create new lives and new families, which coincided with the central needs of the new state in its struggle for military and economic survival. They were welcomed as valuable citizens and this enabled them to deal with their communal trauma and to quickly feel a sense of belonging.

A further important element in the social climate of the new state was the denial and repudiation of vulnerability and passivity, which were associated with the overwhelming confrontation with the mass violent death of the Holocaust, both at individual and societal levels. The Israeli newborn generation, with its self-image of mastery, activity, and invincibility, replaced the stereotype of the vulnerable, persecuted, disdained Diaspora Jew, powerless and helpless in the face of persecution and genocide. This image of the Israeli became the idealized model for a new identity for the immigrants and especially for their children.

The general difficulty in relating to the survivor's experiences of extremity and their implications and the consequent avoidance and denial resulted in various social attitudes to survivors deriving from split-off aspects of feelings.

Referring to survivors as heroes (ghetto or concentration camp fighters or partisans), or to the dead as holy martyrs represents their glorification by denying and splitting off the shameful vulnerable and helpless aspects of the Holocaust experience. These undesirable aspects were expressed in juxtaposed attitudes of contempt by the Israeli youth in their slang expressions in the 1940s and 1950s for the survivor immigrants—"galuti," "gachaletznik" (disdainful terms relating to the European origins of the survivor), and "sabon" (soap). The denial and repudiation of their own vulnerability were seen in the Sabra self-image of mastery and invincibility.

Blaming the victims as in some way responsible for the Holocaust events (for not getting out before, or escaping, or resisting) implies that "it couldn't happen to us." According to defensive attribution theory, when disaster strikes beyond a certain level, observers insulate themselves from realizing the possibility of a similar danger occurring to them by assigning responsibility to the victims. Blame sometimes angrily directed against the survivors was often derived from guilt feelings at having abandoned their families and friends by Israelis who left Europe as *chalutsim* (Zionist pioneers) before the war. After the survivors began to receive reparations, cynical and vulgar pragmatic attitudes of denial of their experiences were reinforced by contemptuous-jealous references to their receiving these reparations.

The social climate of denial in Israel in which the Holocaust experiences were dealt with in such a matter-of-fact way can, however, be seen also as having been sociotherapeutic for the rapid resettlement and adaptation of the hundreds of thousands of survivors who poured into Israel in the early years of the state. The psychohistorical theme of the reestablishment of the state of Israel after two thousand years and its struggle for survival coincided with the psychosocial theme of struggle for survival and rebirth in the individual lives of the survivors. Active involvement in working to achieve the goals of the new society in Israel—building a new life, a new family, and a new country and fighting for its survival—served for many as constructive substitutes and an escape from the insurmountable task of mourning in a manner appropriate to the prevailing values and needs of the new society.

Collective trauma relates to viewing how a social group or people responds to, emerges from, works through, and attempts to come to terms with a catastrophic experience that shatters the life of a group or a people. As with the individual victims, the traumatic events cannot be forgotten or integrated into present-day reality. A dynamic changing process occurs that is interconnected with similar processes in individuals and groups affected in different ways according to their particular experiences and sociocultural backgrounds. Three phenomena can be discerned:[10]

1. *Denial:* The massive shock is so disorganizing that confusion and numbness result. Individual avoidance and denial processes connect with avoidance and denial on a social scale because of the inability of society to cope.
2. *Institutionalization, Ritualization, and Codification:* This involves establishment of museums, memorials, research centers, and special remembrance days, as well as mourning in prescribed ways with use of language according to accepted codes and patterns (e.g., from religious texts). Archetypes and myths related to the identity and the survival ethos of the people are mobilized for coping.
3. *Reelaboration of the Past by the Group or Society:* When shame about the Holocaust was intense in the 1950s in relation to the ideal image of Israelis of heroism and strength, all aspects of heroism in the Holocaust were given emphasis over the shame of genocide. When the existential climate in Israel changed, a further reelaboration of the meanings of the Holocaust has begun to take place based on much greater empathy for all the victims and the unbearable hardships they endured, as well as the implications for future Jewish life of a need to be strong and self-reliant.

At the entrance to the Yad Vashem Holocaust Memorial in Jerusalem, the inscription quotes Rabbi Nachman of Bratslav, the great Hassidic teacher: "In remembrance is the secret of redemption." The Old Testament (especially in Deuteronomy) warns us repeatedly to "remember" and "not to forget." In his farewell address, Moses enjoins the people, "Remember the days of old; Consider the generations long past; Ask your father and he will tell you; Your elder, and they will explain to you" (Deuteronomy 32:7). This means that one must not only "remember" historical facts but also reflect upon them in order to understand their meaning. Because the Jews are a traumatized people, they have always emphasized the significance of memory. Perhaps more than any other group, most Jewish memories are of traumatic events of persecution and destruction.

In recent years there has been a steady increase in the activities of remembering and bearing witness of survivors:

1. At international and national conferences of survivors and children of survivors. These assemblies strengthen the sense of belonging and identity of Holocaust survivors.

2. Writing, speaking, studying, and teaching the Holocaust.
3. Recording personal testimonies on audio and video tape.

What is noteworthy about most remembering of the Holocaust is that *instead of demanding revenge, the demand is to remember.* It is a demand for consensual validation that the Jewish people in Israel must overcome their past and become a people who can protect their lives. This is the final step in the collective recovery from the Holocaust.

10.

Encounter: The Survivor versus Society

From the beginning of recorded history, we observe the meeting between society and human beings who have experienced disaster and survived. A wide range of interpersonal relations are involved and a variety of intense emotional responses are manifest on both sides.

The theme of survival is seen in such Old Testament stories as that of Noah, the only survivor of the flood, and in the savior-survivor relationship classically presented in the story of Abraham and the "sinful survivors" of Sodom, Lot and his wife—she kept looking back, a metaphor for not staying with the good fortune of her survival, and as a result eventually was transformed into a pillar of salt.

Mankind has always been fascinated by the possibility of life after cataclysm. The survivor is a symbol—a "guilty one" who survived destruction of his world and kin by the graceful mercy of the Lord, and who has the opportunity of rebirth and regaining of new life after the disaster. By staying alive, the survivor is required to accept the price of survival—the existential guilt projected on him by the nonsurvivor, the observer.

There are many indications that society—individuals and groups—are also afraid of the survivor. The survivor awakens guilt and fear. The guilt is an extension of the guilt projected onto the survivor for not having actively intervened to help the victims and derived from fears of the possibility of experiencing the same fate. Hence, there is a combination of fascination and repulsion connected with the Holocaust and survivors. On the broad level of society, two generations of silence and avoidance of the subject have been followed by a flood of popularization and banalization in the media and in salon talk about the Holocaust.

One image of the survivor thus is that he is seen as a toxic object that could contaminate society with the extremity of his horrific experiences. He is a disturber of the peace and security. He represents the possibility of chaos and disintegration of society, which must be denied by every means.

One way of dealing with the survivor in ancient times as a "messenger of evil tidings" was to sacrifice him to the gods, to kill him. Another way was to see him as a lunatic or a "nebich" (helpless, impotent, buffoonlike character) arousing pity without empathy. In this last way, ambivalence was changed into something positive and acceptable to the Judeo-Christian tradition of charity and reparation.

In Jewish families, ambivalent feelings between loyalty to one's murdered family left in Nazi Europe and the desire to get far away from the subject of the Holocaust very often resulted in guilt feelings and desires to make reparations of some sort to the dead, alternating with wishes to completely avoid the issues of the Holocaust.

In Israel, society tried to come to terms with the Holocaust and its survivors in different ways. For many years, Israeli society stressed the heroism of fight and resistance in the ghettos rather than dealing with the concept of survival itself as a positive value. Heroic resistance and the partisans' active fighting was made the honored leitmotif rather than the actual fact of survival, and this minimized the significance of different modes of survival. This focus was clearly seen in the name given to a kibbutz in Israel that was established after the war by survivors—*Kibbutz Lochamei Hageitaot, or "Kibbutz of the Ghetto Fighters."* The emphasis on active fighting and heroism also became the presented ritualized theme on Holocaust Memorial Days. Self-defense, fighting, and heroism are, after all, integral parts of the desired self-image of Israeli society to the present day.

Only after many years of statehood can Israelis begin to relate to the Holocaust without idealizing survival only as representing "fighting and resistance." An important expression of this change of attitude was seen some thirty-five years after the Holocaust in the first systematic preparation of a curriculum for teaching the

Holocaust in Israeli high schools without ritualization of the subject and avoidance of its complexity.

The tendency throughout the years to ritualize and memorialize the Holocaust as an epic historical event has meant that there was often little relating to the survivors themselves as people. The Holocaust was related to as a major fact of history, but without encountering the survivors. In fact, Israeli society at times has characterized the survivors as "bad," "guilt ridden," "envious," "greedy for compensation," "imposters," "overbearing," etc. As individuals, survivors aroused in nonsurvivors a diversity of feelings from shame, pity, and guilt to anger and irritation. This attitude was also connected with the fact that the original European nonsurvivor population who came to Israel before the Holocaust had left their families behind in Europe, and the families they left behind were murdered in the camps while they enjoyed normal lives and felt helpless, passive, and guilty about the fates of their relatives. Moreover, in some situations those who settled in Israel had left their families in the course of some kind of conflict, such as when young persons insisted on going on *aliyah* and their families objected. Confrontation with the survivors awakened in them guilt and ambivalent feelings toward their murdered families. In fact, the motivation to leave Europe and come to Palestine as pioneers was often connected with their conflicting and ambivalent feelings toward their families, if not toward the way of life of the "larger Jewish family" that was their Diaspora community and its traditional ways, which they had rejected as not satisfying their needs. Their wish to create a new pioneering society was a manifestation of this dissatisfaction with and rejection of the way of life of the parents in the shtetls of Central and Eastern Europe.

Confronted with the survivors on their arrival in Israel after the Holocaust, the children of these parents who had left Europe before the Holocaust for Palestine as pioneers often took a stance of *blaming the survivors of the Holocaust.* They saw them as being responsible for their fate by not having come to Palestine before the Holocaust, just as their parents and siblings had not done, and some even went so far as to say that their fate was a *punishment*— again a manifestation of the unresolved guilt they felt toward their murdered families whom they had left behind in Europe.

The leadership of the *yishuv* (Jewish community in Palestine) felt guilt and failure in the face of their ineffective action during the Holocaust. The horror of Jewish suffering in the Holocaust and the terrible losses of the Jewish people led to the shock of having to confront the total and overwhelming defeat the Jewish people had suffered.

In the eyes of their brothers in Palestine who were actively preparing to fight for the survival of the newly reborn Jewish state, the survivors pouring in from the D.P. camps of Europe appeared as unfortunate representatives of a generation that had passively accepted its fate. The image was that of a shameful remnant. They spoke Yiddish, the language of the despised European Diaspora, thus also representing a throwback to the generation of their fathers, whom many of the new Israelis had rejected. Sabra Israelis were often contemptuous of both the Diaspora language and the behavior style of their brothers from the concentration camps. In psychodynamic terms, the survivors were badly disguised objects for projections of internal representations of the Jew as a bad object of self-hatred and self-condemnation. The return of the survivors from the countries of death brought back the long-repressed conflicts and ambivalent feelings of many of the nonsurvivors from similar backgrounds toward their childhood homes and families. This theme is also frequently encountered in the family therapy of survivors when a nonsurvivor spouse projects guilt and anger as well as rescue fantasies onto the survivor spouse.

On the other hand, the *yishuv* also made efforts to be "indifferent" and to overlook the fact that the newcomers were survivors, for now they were simply to be welcomed as equal citizens sharing in the common struggle of the state for survival and upbuilding. The reality of Israel's plight surrounded by enemies served as a justification and rationalization of this paradoxical and ambivalent position with regard to the survivors. Recognition of the Holocaust background of the survivors was often avoided in everyday life. A major structural expression of this avoidance was the lack of official registration of survivor identity on their arrival in Israel.

What was not a subject of doubt was the intense need of the Jewish community in Palestine to bring in the survivors from Europe after the war was over. The deep need of the Jewish people to save and rescue the remnants of the Holocaust was expressed on a social level in the momentous organization of "Escape-Briha." In this epic phenomenon, tens of thousands of survivors were rescued and smuggled from East European countries via D.P. camps to Palestine as a kind of posthumous act of saving that also served as a rehabilitation of the self-image of the guilty nonparticipant nonsurvivors.

On their side, the survivors accepted the idealized *sabra* image of active, tough supermen, "sons of freedom," but this acceptance was not without envy and jealousy of not having had the same experiences of being brought up in freedom.

These mutual false images changed only through a long, painful process in which common achievements, pioneering, joy, fighting together in wars, and common losses and common mourning integrated the two groups. The high point in this process was the Yom Kippur War, in which a new identity was forged for Israeli society, now neither heroes nor victims, no longer cast in a harsh antithesis of being either heroes or victims.

The Capacity to Relate to the Holocaust

In the Passover *Haggada*, it is said that the Jewish people must tell the story of their bondage and deliverance from Egypt: "Relate this to your sons today."

In studying the verbalization of their experiences by survivors, one constantly meets two contrasting extremes of polarization in their modes of expression. In my psychotherapeutic work with survivors, their inability to relate directly to their experiences was often an outstanding feature. They often complained that it was impossible for them to verbalize and articulate their experiences to their families, children, friends, and others. On the other hand, there were some survivors who exhibited a need to relate repetitively their experiences, especially in times of emotional upheaval of a personal and social nature, and this need was felt as oppressive by their children and nonsurvivor spouses.

It was often very painful for survivors, especially women survivors, to experience the changes in their body and self-image that were connected with experiences of illness and starvation. In addition to the terrible personal pain of accepting these changes, to register them in consciousness would also have implied confirming the success of the exterminators in their plan to transform them into dehumanized scapegoats, vermin—the Nazi stereotype of the Jew. In the camps, although fully aware of the skeletal image of their comrades, survivors would deny in themselves that

they were also in such condition. After their liberation, confrontation with their image in a mirror was often a traumatic experience. The encounter with themselves and with the presentation of
themselves to society often aroused great anxiety and feelings of
shame.

Again there can be seen two polarized aspects of the revealed
self and tragic hidden aspects of self that the survivors could not
even reveal to themselves. These they had to deny and avoid, yet
these dimensions of horror would often then return to awareness
in later confrontations with renewed separations, losses, and deaths
in the course of the survivor's life cycle.

Some survivors portrayed their concentration camp experiences in grotesque or even absurd terms in the form of anecdotes
and amusing stories about themselves and their friends, using
ancient folk styles of Jewish wit or mixtures of humor in the midst
of tragedy. Perhaps this is one wise way to convey experiences
that are so tragic that they are made to appear beyond the realm
of the tragic.

To relate to the phantasmagoric experiences of Holocaust events,
and to try to incorporate them into the logical framework of today's realities, in which some semblance of comprehensible order
seems to prevail in society, is an impossible task of language. For
survivors themselves, there seems to be a desire and a need on the
part of many of them to reject any pathetic and dramatic style
when relating experiences to each other because of the fear of
being overwhelmed by feelings of despair.

It is interesting in this context that after the liberation, with the
first experiences of social cohesion in the D.P. camps, the survivors
often created spontaneous amateur vaudevillelike sketches and
plays, songs, and verses of their lives in the concentration camps.
The survivors also expressed in these folk art forms their longing
for love, warmth, and dependency in the lost shtetl life with all its
vitality. At the same time, the dramatic representations included
a good deal of coarse vulgarity, primitive humorous manifestations of sexuality, and open expressions of envy, hostility, aggression, competitiveness, and rivalry. One could see a renewing of
personality consolidation in these wounded people, so long im-
mersed in overwhelming pain, mourning, and loss, pulling themselves together from their previous injured, fragmented selves. It
was as if both the actors and spectators of the drama felt that
recovery from the extreme horror was only possible by emphasiz-

ing the extreme opposite of their surrealistic experiences through earthy, concrete reality rooted in down-to-earth humor. They were creating an antidote and antithesis to the nightmarish psycho-drama of the Holocaust and inferno by reaching back to pre-Holocaust life in all its colorfulness. These were early attempts to "recover" the simple pleasures of life and to disconnect them from the terrible conflicts and struggles for survival they had just endured, so that life could again be enjoyed and free of guilt. The writer Batshevis Singer has described in his comic magic mode these early attempts of the survivors to recover their "lust for life."

Thus, the whole experience of the Holocaust was dealt with in a two-dimensional, polarized way, with constant fluctuation between the two extremes, such as is manifest in the world of Breughels' paintings, with their lively, ribald earthiness, rooted in the simple pleasures of everyday life, and the opposed inner, hor-rifying, uncanny, grotesque world as portrayed in the Hieronimus Bosch paintings. In the folk theaters of the D.P. camps, there was represented a concrete, earthy everyday life that was to stand in opposition to the private, inner, unspeakable Holocaust world, which could never be forgotten and was revealing itself recur-rently in memories, unending private fantasies, unspeakable dreams, and for many in enormous emotional suffering.

The fact that these processes occurred in cohesive group situa-tions in the D.P. camps after the liberation was an integral part of the process of self-recovery. It was a corrective group experience, a continuation of the group experiences that had occurred in the interdependency situations of the ghettos and concentration camps. In the D.P. camps, young survivors in particular went through a kind of collective psychosocial moratorium in which they could experiment in roles that they had been deprived of during adoles-cence, and they applied themselves intensively to studies, friend-ships, and love relationships. In this period of exercising their new roles and regained autonomy, the survivors learned and relearned the rules of community living and interpersonal relationships in freedom.

It is only human that many survivors in their diaries and eye-witness accounts try to humanize their Holocaust experiences. They seek to convey their experiences to the rest of us, which means they must speak in the common language of humanity, although what they have to describe is intrinsically beyond any-thing that we should consider human. Their attempts to give

meaning to their own experiences means a certain degree of less-
ening the impact of the atrocities of the Holocaust, since when the
survivors share with us their own human reactions they succeed
in some measure in modifying and overcoming the unadulterated
evil they experienced. In fact, often *this literary process ends up
attributing a poignant quality to events that in fact do not deserve to
be viewed as poignant.*

The larger question that arises is whether or to what extent we
should all honor the touching descriptions in the literature of the
Holocaust that in truth do not begin to do justice to the overwhelming horrors that really took place? The surprising success
of Gerald Green's television film, "The Holocaust," despite its
popular and even soap-opera style, showed dramatically the vir-
tues and weaknesses of humanizing atrocity and making possible
for millions of viewers a confrontation with the extreme evil of the
Holocaust they had previously avoided. Creative writers on the
Holocaust struggle endlessly with how to express that which goes
beyond the creative limits of artistic imagination. Even survivor
Elie Wiesel has had to try to humanize the Holocaust experience
in order to stand as a witness who can give testimony to the events
he swore could never be described and should not be spoken about
because they were beyond the bounds of the human and of our
humanity.

There is no correct or easy way to resolve the dangers of banalization and kitsch (cheap or trivial literary or artistic productions)
while fulfilling our responsibilities as a human society to remember, recall, and seek to understand the Holocaust, the most horrendous single event of human history.

Notes and References

The following notes and references are taken from Shamai Davidson's manuscripts. As anyone who has written academic works knows, the completion of references generally is left as a last chore after the manuscript text is fully complete, and in this case, of course, the author was no longer with us to finish the task. To make the reader's life easier, some of the more obvious gaps in references have been filled in by the editor, but many of the details that were missing in Shamai Davidson's papers were not completed. It will also be noted that the number of references varies considerably in different sections of the book, in effect depending on the stage of Shamai Davidson's papers on that subject. In these small respects too, we are reminded throughout our reading that the author is very much missing for us.

I wish to express my appreciation to Marc Sherman, M.L.S., Director of the Research Catalogue at Tel Aviv University and a fellow of the Institute on the Holocaust and Genocide in Jerusalem for his assistance with these notes and references.

Chapter 1

The source for the epigraph is from T. Carmi, "Anatomy of a War," *Jerusalem Quarterly* (3): 102 (1977). Reprinted from T. Carmi, *At the Stone of Losses*. Translated by Grace Schulman, Philadelphia: Jewish Publication Society, and Los Angeles: University of California Press, 1983.

1. Lifton, R. J. (1967). *Death in Life.* New York: Random House.
2. Krystal, H. (1978). Trauma and affects. *Psychoanalytic Study of the Child.* Vol. 33. New York: International Universities Press, pp. 81–116.
3. Eitinger, L. (1983). Denial in concentration camps: Some personal observations on the positive and negative functions of denial in extreme

life situations. In Bresnitz, S. (Ed.), *The Denial of Stress*. New York: International Universities Press, pp. 199–212.

4. Eitinger, *ibid.*

5. Winick, M. (Ed.), (1979). *Hunger Disease: Studies by the Jewish Physicians in the Warsaw Ghetto.* New York: Wiley.

6. Zimmels, H. J. (1975). *The Echo of the Nazi Holocaust in Rabbinic Literature.* Marla Publications.

7. Dobroszycki, L. (Ed.), (1984). *The Chronicle of the Lodz Ghetto.* New Haven and London: Yale University Press.

8. Luchterhand, E. (1970). Early and late effects of imprisonment in Nazi concentration camps. *International Journal Social Psychiatry* 5:102–10.

9. Niederland, W. G. (1961). The problem of the survivor: The psychiatric evaluation of emotional disorders in survivors of Nazi persecution. *Journal Hillside Hospital* 10:233–47.

10. Trautman, E. D. (1971). Violence and victims in Nazi concentration camps and the psychopathology of the survivors. In Krystal, H., & Niederland, W. (Eds.), *Psychic Traumatization: After-Effects in Individuals and Communities.* Boston: Little Brown.

11. Rappaport, E. (1968). Beyond traumatic neurosis. *International Journal Psycho-Analysis* 49:719.

12. Shaw, J. I., & Skolnick, P. (1971). Attribution of responsibility for a happy accident. *Journal Personality and Social Psychology* 18:380–83.

Chapter 3

1. Chodoff, P. (1975). Psychiatric aspects of the Nazi persecution. In Hamburg, D. A., & Brodie, K. H. (Eds.), *American Handbook Psychiatry.* Vol. 6., 2d ed. New York: Basic Books, pp. 932–46 (chapter 4).

2. Lifton, R. J. (1968). *Death in Life.* New York: Random House.

3. Des Pres, T. (1976). *The Survivor: An Anatomy of Life in the Death Camps.* New York: Oxford University Press.

4. Sereny, G. (1974). *Into That Darkness: From Mercy Killing to Mass Murder.* London: Andre Deutsch.

5. Klein, H. (1974). Late affects and after-effects of severe traumatisation. *Israel Annals of Psychiatry & Related Disciplines* 12 (4): 293–303.

6. Winnick, H. (1968). Contribution to symposium on psychic traumatization through special catastrophe. *International Journal Psycho-Analysis* 49:298–301.

7. Brull, F. (1974). *Toward A Humanistic Psychotherapy.* Tel Aviv: Lewis-Epstein-Rodan. (Hebrew)

8. *The Eighty-First Blow* is a film produced by Kibbutz Lochamei Hagetaot. The title is taken from the account of a youngster who, after the Holocaust, told of receiving eighty blows from the Nazis and miracu-

lously surviving, and when his audience didn't believe him, that was the eighty-first blow.

9. Niederland, W. G. (1961). The problem of the survivor: The psychiatric evaluation of emotional disorders in survivors of Nazi persecution. *Journal Hillside Hospital* 10:233–47.

Chapter 4

1. Lifton, R. J. (1968). *Death in Life*. New York: Random House.
2. Charny, I. W. (1982) *How Can We Commit the Unthinkable: Genocide, the Human Cancer*. Boulder, Col.: Westview Press.
3. Freud, Anna, & Dann, Sophie (1951). An experiment in group upbringing. *Psychoanalytic Study of the Child*. Vol. 6. New York: International Universities Press, pp. 122–68.
4. Charny, I. W. (1982). Sacrificing others to the death we fear ourselves: The ultimate illusion of self-defense. In *How Can We Commit the Unthinkable: Genocide, the Human Cancer*. Boulder, Col.: Westview Press, pp. 185–212.

Chapter 5

1. Rakoff, V., Sigal, J. J., & Epstein, N. B. (1966). Children and families of concentration camp survivors. *Canada's Mental Health* 14:24–26. Trossman, B. (1968). Adolescent children of concentration camp survivors. *Journal Canadian Psychiatric Association* 13:121–23. Sigal, J. J., & Rakoff, V. (1971). Concentration camp survival: A pilot study of effects on the second generation. *Journal Canadian Psychiatric Association* 16:393–97. Kestenberg, J. (1972). Psychoanalytic contributions to the problem of children survivors from Nazi persecution. *Israel Annals Psychiatry & Related Disciplines* 10:311–25. Sigal, J. J., Silver, D., Rakoff, V., & Ellin, B. (1973). Some second generation effects of survival of the Nazi persecution. *American Journal Orthopsychiatry* 43:320–28. Barocas, H., & Barocas, C. (1973). Manifestations of concentration camp effects on the second generation. *American Journal Psychiatry* 130:821–31. Russell, A. (1974). Late psychosocial consequences in concentration camp survivor families. *American Journal Orthopsychiatry* 44:611–19.
2. Sigal, J. J. (1971), *ibid.*
3. Pseudomutuality is a concept coined by Wynne and his colleagues (1958) and refers to families in which differences and tensions are meshed in pseudotogetherness. Skewed relationships is a term used by Lidz (1957) to refer either to very conflictual or to very symbiotic relationships. Wynne, L. C., Ryckoff, I. M., Day, J., & Hirsch, J. (1958). Pseudomutuality in the family relations of schizophrenics. *Psychiatry* 21:205–20. Lidz, T., Corneilson, A. R., Fleck, S., & Terry, D. (1957). The intrafamilial environment of

schizophrenic patients: II. Marital schism and marital skew. *American Journal Psychiatry* 114:241–48.

4. Slipp, S. (1973). The symbiotic survival pattern: A relational theory of schizophrenia. *Family Process* 12:377–98.

5. Vogel, E. F., & Bell, N. W. (1960). The emotionally disturbed child as the family scapegoat. In Vogel, E. F., & Bell, N. W. (Eds.), *The Family.* Glencoe, Ill.: Free Press, pp. 412–27.

6. Sigal, J. J., Silver, D., Rakoff, V., & Ellin, B. (1973), *ibid.*

7. Aleksandrowicz, D, (1973). Children of concentration camp survivors. In Anthony, E. J., & Koupernik, C. (Eds.), *The Child in His Family.* New York: John Wiley, pp. 385–92.

8. De Graff, T. (1975). Pathological patterns of identification in families of survivors of the Holocaust. *Israel Annals Psychiatry & Related Disciplines* 13 (4): 335–63.

9. Karr, S. D. (1973). Second Generation Effects of the Nazi Holocaust. Ph.D. Dissertation, California School of Professional Psychology.

10. Becker, T. (1976). Other voices—self and social responsibility: A comparative view of American and Israeli youth. *American Journal Psychoanalysis* 36:155–62.

11. Aleksandrowicz (1973), *ibid.*

12. Klein, H. (1971). Families of survivors in the kibbutz: Psychological studies. In Krystal, H., & Niederland, W. G. (Eds.), *Psychic Traumatization: After-Effects in Individuals and Communities.* Boston: Little, Brown, pp. 67–92. Klein, H. (1973). Children of the Holocaust: Mourning and bereavement. In Anthony, E. J., & Koupernik, C. (Eds.), *The Child in His Family.* Vol. 2, *The Impact of Disease and Death.* New York:'John Wiley, pp. 393–410.

13. Tanay, D. (1968). Initiation of psychotherapy with survivors of Nazi persecution. In Krystal, H. (Ed.), *Massive Psychic Trauma.* New York: International Universities Press, pp. 219–21.

Chapter 6

1. Brull, F. (1974). *Toward A Humanistic Psychotherapy.* Tel Aviv: Lewis-Epstein-Modan. (Hebrew)

2. Jensen, B. (1973). Human reciprocity: An Arctic exemplification. *American Journal Orthopsychiatry* 43:447–58.

3. Dimsdale, J. E. (1974). The coping behaviour of Nazi concentration camp survivors. *American Journal Psychiatry* 131:792–97. Eitinger, L. (1964). *Concentration Camp Survivors in Norway and Israel.* Oslo: Universitetsforlaget. Klein, H. (1974). Delayed affects and after-effects of severe traumatisation. *Israel Annals Psychiatry & Related Disciplines* 12:293–303. (See especially the discussion on fantasy and hope). Krystal, H. (1978). Trauma and affects. *Psychoanalytic Study of the Child.* Vol. 33. New York: International Universities Press, pp. 102–3. Lifton, R. J. (1968). *Death in Life:*

Survivors of Hiroshima. New York: Basic Books. Benner, P., Roskies, E., & Lazarus, R. S. (1980). Stress and coping under extreme conditions. In Dimsdale, J. E. (Ed.), *Survivors, Victims, and Perpetrators.* Washington, D.C.: Hemisphere, pp. 219–58 (chapter 9). Frankl, V. E. (1962). *Man's Search for Meaning.* Boston: Beacon. Henderson, S., & Bostock, T. (1977). Coping behaviour after shipwreck. *British Journal Psychiatry* 131:15–20.

4. Eitinger, *ibid.*, p. 79.

5. Klein, H., & Reinharz, S. (1972). Adaptation in the Kibbutz: Holocaust survivors and their families. In Miller, Louis (Ed.), *Mental Health and Social Changes.* Jerusalem: Jerusalem Academic Press. On the significance of relations between pairs of friends, see Klein (1974), *ibid.*

6. Des Pres, T. (1976). *The Survivor: An Anatomy of Life in the Death Camps.* New York: Oxford University Press, pp. 98–99.

7. Dworzecki, M. (1971). The day-to-day stand of the Jews. *Jewish Resistance during the Holocaust: Proceedings of the Conference on Manifestations of Jewish Resistance.* Jerusalem: Yad Vashem, pp. 153–55.

8. Des Pres, *ibid.*, pp. 136, 147.

9. Hart, K. (1962). *I Am Alive.* London, New York: Abelard-Schuman.

10. Sereny, Gitta (1974). *Into That Darkness: From Mercy Killing to Mass Murder.* London: Andre Deutsch, p. 186.

11. Schnable, Ernest (1958). A tragedy revealed. Heroines' last days. Excerpts from Anne Frank: A portrait in courage. *Life,* August 18, pp. 78–80.

12. Heimler, Eugene (1966). *Resistance against Tyranny.* London: Praeger, p. 161.

13. Des Pres, *ibid.*, p. 142.

14. Luchterhand, Elmer (1967). Prisoner behaviour and social system in the Nazi Camp. *International Journal Psychiatry* 13:245–64.

15. Pfefferkorn, Eli. The case of Bruno Bettelheim and Lina Wertmuller's *Seven Beauties.*

16. Luchterhand, Elmer (1966–67). The Gondola-car transports. *International Journal Social Psychiatry* 13:28–32.

17. Des Pres, T., *ibid.*, pp. 98–99.

18. Niederland, William G. (1961). The problem of the survivor: The psychiatric evaluation of emotional disorders in survivors of Nazi persecution. *Journal Hillside Hospital* 10:233.

19. Krystal, Henry (Ed.), (1968). *Massive Psychic Trauma.* New York: International Universities Press, p. 105.

20. Erikson, Kai T. (1976). Loss of communality at Buffalo Creek. *American Journal Psychiatry* 133:302–5.

21. Erikson, *ibid.*

22. Henderson, S. (1977). The social network, support, and neurosis. *British Journal Psychiatry* 131:185–91.

23. Klein, H. (1974). Delayed effects and after-effects of severe traumatisation. *Israel Annals Psychiatry & Related Disciplines* 12:293–303.

220 *Notes and References*

Klein, H., & Reinharz, S. (1972). Adaptation in the kibbutz: Holocaust survivors and their families. In Miller, L. (Ed.), *Mental Health and Social Change*. Jerusalem: Jerusalem Academic Press.

24. Luchterhand, E. (1967). Prisoner behavior and social system in the Nazi camp. *International Journal Psychiatry* 13:245–64.

25. Eitinger, L. (1964). *Concentration Camp Survivors in Norway and Israel*. Oslo: Universitetsforlaget.

26. Eliach, Y. (1984). Jewish religious practices in the concentration camps. In Gutman, Y., & Saf, A. (Eds.), *The Nazi Concentration Camps: Structure and Aims, the Image of the Prisoner, the Jews in the Camps*. Proceedings of the Fourth Yad Vashem International Conference, Jerusalem, January 1990. Jerusalem: Yad Vashem, pp. 195–206.

27. Bravo, A. (1983). Italian women in the Nazi camps. University of Turin.

28. Jaffee, R. (1963). Group activity as a defence method in concentration camps. *Israel Annals Psychiatry & Related Disciplines* 1:235–43.

29. Lustigman, M. (1975). The fifth business: The business of surviving in extremity. *Human Context*, 7:426–44.

30. Eitinger, L. (1983). Denial in concentrations camps: Some personal observations on the positive and negative functions of denial in extreme life situations. In Bresnitz, S. (Ed.), *The Denial of Stress*. New York: International Universities Press, pp. 199–212.

31. Birenbaum, H. (1971). *Hope Is the Last to Die: A Personal Documentation of Nazi Terror*. New York: Twayne Publishers, p. 245.

32. Birenbaum, *ibid.*, p. 245.

Chapter 7

1. Klein, H. (1972). Holocaust survivors in kibbutzim: Readaptation and reintegration. *Israel Annals Psychiatry & Related Disciplines* 10 (1): 78–92.

Chapter 8

1. Palgi, P. (1963). Immigrants, psychiatrists, and culture. *Israel Annals Psychiatry & Related Disciplines* 1:43–59.

2. It is understandable in this social climate that for the first twenty-five years of the state there were no systematic studies of the implications and outcome of the increasing bereavement from war and terror. The first extensive study of death and mourning in Israel was made by the Israeli cultural anthropologist Phyllis Palgi in 1973 under the impact of the Yom Kippur War, and published as a monograph entitled "Socio-Cultural Expressions and Implications of Death, Mourning, and Bereavement in Israel Arising out of the War Situation" (Jerusalem Academic Press, Behavioral Sciences Department, Medical School, Tel-Aviv University). I am

indebted to Prof. Palgi for her valuable psychocultural formulations of the problems of Israeli society and for her advice and comments regarding my work.

3. When the notification teams entered the street, some families, in accordance with their ethnic background, would indulge in "warding off" rituals, and others would act hysterically or aggressively against the team. To serve as a member of these teams was extremely harrowing.

4. Palgi, P., *ibid.*

5. Florian, V. (1982). War widows: Intervention in the first period of mourning. In Lahav, E. (Ed.), *Psycho-Social Research in Rehabilitation.* Jerusalem: Ministry of Defence Publishing House. Amir, Y., & Sharon, I. (1979). Factors in adaptation of war widows. *Megamot* 25 (1): 119–30. (Hebrew). Kaffman, M., & Elizur, E. (1982). Children's bereavement reactions following death of the father. *Journal American Academy Child Psychiatry* 21:474–80. Purisman, R., & Maoz, B. (1977). Adjustment and war bereavement: Some considerations. *British Journal Medical Psychology* 50:1–9. Gay, M. (1982). The adjustment of parents to wartime bereavement. In Milgram, N. A. (Ed.), *Stress and Anxiety.* Vol. 8. New York: Hemisphere.

6. Some of this work was presented at three international conferences in Tel-Aviv (in 1975, 1978, and 1983) on war-related psychological stress in Israel. A selection of the papers presented at the first two conferences was published in Milgram, N. (Ed.), *Stress and Anxiety.* Vol. 8. New York: Hemisphere, 1978.

7. Amir, Y., & Sharon, I., *ibid.*

8. Malkinson, R. (1983). Adaptation to Bereavement of Widows Who Experienced a Sudden Loss of a Spouse. Ph.D. Dissertation, University of Florida.

9. In the Israeli Druze Arab community where there have been relatively many war deaths, there is a taboo against the remarriage of young widows. This is especially strong when there are children for whom remarriage is considered to be detrimental as well as bringing dishonor to the memory of the husband. They receive considerable emotional support from their community, which accords them a special status, and they remain in a state of permanent semimourning. Tzion, Assi (1985). The daughters of Jethro. *Haaretz Supplement,* March 22. (Hebrew)

10. Palgi, P. (1983). Reflections on some creative modes of confrontation with the phenomenon of death. *International Journal Social Psychiatry* 29:29–37.

11. Moses, K., & Moses, R. (1977). A two-step change of role in the emancipation of the war-bereaved widow from the traditional family. In Anthony, E. J., & Chiland, C. (Eds.), *The Child in His Family.* Vol. 5. England: John Wiley.

12. Black, D. (1978). The bereaved child. *Journal Child Psychology & Psychiatry* 21:287–92.

13. Kaffman, M., & Elizur, E., *ibid.*

14. Rappoport, J. (forthcoming). The Concept of Death among Young Children in Israel. A comparative study by Rappoport in Jerusalem demonstrated that Israeli children apparently comprehend death much earlier than their counterparts elsewhere.

15. Smilansky, S., & Weisman, T. (1978). *A Guide for Rehabilitation Workers in Confronting the Needs of Israel Defence Forces Orphans and Their Mothers.* Jerusalem: Henrietta Szold Institute for Research in the Behavioral Sciences.

16. Black, D. Freeman, and Urbanowicz, M. (1983). Family therapy with bereaved children: Process and outcome. Presented at Fourth International Congress of Family Therapy, Israel.

17. Dora Black has described a program in Britain organized by Cruse, the National Organization for Widows, Widowers, and Their Children. Bereavement counselors are available to promote mourning in bereaved children, although at a later stage, three to five months after the death, through brief family-based interventions of three to six sessions designed to open up communication and feelings among family members about the dead parent.

18. Rosen, H., & Cohen, H. L. (1981). Children's reaction to sibling loss. *Clinical Social Work Journal* 9:211.

19. Morawetz, A. (1982). The impact on adolescents of the death in war of an older sibling. *Stress & Anxiety* 8:267–74.

20. In two striking cases of Holocaust families living in nonreligious kibbutzim, after the death of a son, a sibling in each family, both in their early twenties (in one case a brother and the other a sister), became Hare Krishna devotees. This was a devastating event for the families. It was related to the attempt to deal with an unresolved mourning situation through denial of the death and "replacement" through a new belief in reincarnation.

21. Levav, I., Krasnoff, L., & Dohrenwend, B. (1981). Israeli PERI Life Event Scale: Ratings of events by a community sample. *Israel Journal Medical Science* 17:176–83.

22. Purisman, R., & Maoz, B., *ibid.* Gay, M., *ibid.*

23. Gay, M., *ibid.*

24. Palgi, P. (1983), *ibid.*

25. Parkes, C. Murray (1971). Psychosocial transitions: A field for study. *Social Science & Medicine* 5:101–15.

26. Hoz-Peles, Ada (1980). The sacrifice of Abraham. *Monitin*, September. (Hebrew.) Tal-Shir, Rachel (1985). The sacrifice of Abraham. *Haaretz,* Supplement, Janaury 4. (Hebrew)

27. Levav, I. (1982). Mortality and psychopathology following the death of an adult child: An epidemiological review. *Israel Annals Psychiatry & Related Disciplines* 19:23–38.

28. Klein, H. (1973). Children of the Holocaust: Mourning and be-

reavement. In Anthony, E. J., & Koupernik, C. (Eds.), *The Child in His Family.* Vol. 2, *The Impact of Disease and Death.* New York: Wiley, pp. 393–410.

29. Davidson, S. (1983). Psychosocial aspects of Holocaust trauma in the life cycle of survivor-refugees and their families. In Baker, R. (Ed.), *Psychosocial Problems of Refugees.* London: British Refugee Council, pp. 21–31.

30. Davidson, S. (1980). On relating to traumatised/persecuted people. In *The Impact of Persecution.* Vol. 2. Rijswijk, Netherlands: Ministry of Cultural Affairs, pp. 56–63.

31. Davidson, S. (1967). A clinical classification of the psychiatric disturbances of the Holocaust ("Shoa") survivors and their treatment. *Israel Annals Psychiatry & Related Disciplines* 5: 96–98. Palgi, P. (1983), *ibid.*

32. Aleksandrowicz, D. R. (1978). Interminable mourning as a family process. *Israel Annals Psychiatry & Related Disciplines* 16:161–69.

33. I wish to express my gratitude to Yehuda for his outstanding and eager help in making immediately available to me the relevant books and papers in the "Bereavement Library" necessary for my research. [This library is now housed at the Bob Shapell School of Social Work at Tel Aviv University.—Ed.]

34. Zafrir, A. (1982). Community therapeutic intervention in treatment of civilian victims after a major terrorist attack. *Stress & Anxiety* 8:303–15.

35. Davidson, S., Rivlin, D., & Abramovich, I. (1982). Community psychiatric crisis intervention with the victims of terrorist attack. Paper presented at Israel Psychiatric Association Conference.

36. Lowenstein, S. F. (1979). Inner and outer space in social casework. *Social Casework* 69:19–29.

37. Zafrir, A. Verbal Communications.

Chapter 9

1. Winnick, H. Z. (1967). Further comments concerning problems of late psychopathological effects of Nazi persecution and their therapy. *Israel Annals Psychiatry & Related Disciplines* 5:1–16. Winnick, H. Z. (1967). Psychiatric disturbances of Holocaust ("Shoa") survivors. *Israel Annals Psychiatry & Related Disciplines* 15:91–100. Chairman, Symposium of the Israel Psychoanalytic Society. Brull, F. (1969). The trauma: A theoretical consideration. *Israel Annals Psychiatry & Related Disciplines* 12 (4): 293–303. Moses, R. (1978). Adult psychic trauma: The question of early predisposition and some detailed mechanisms. *International Journal Psycho-Analysis* 59:353–64. Weinberg, A. A. (1961). *Migration and Belonging: A Study of Mental Health and Personal Adjustment in Israel.* The Hague: Nijhoff.

2. Saul Friedlander, in referring to his Holocaust experiences, says

that "when memory comes," he experiences "in the very depths of myself, certain disparate, incompatible fragments of existence, cut off from all reality, with no continuity whatsoever." Friedlander, S. (1979). *When Memory Comes.* New York: Farrar, Straus & Giroux.

3. Krystal, H. (1968). *Massive Psychic Trauma.* New York: International Universities Press. Krystal, H. (1978). Trauma and effects. *Psychoanalytic Study of the Child.* Vol. 33. New York: International Universities Press, pp. 81–116.

4. Niederland, W. G. (1961). The problem of the survivor: The psychiatric evaluation of emotional disorders in survivors of Nazi persecution. *Journal Hillside Hospital* 10:233–47. Also in Krystal, H. (1968), (Ed.), *Massive Psychic Trauma.* New York: International Universities Press, pp. 8–22.

5. Davidson, S. (1983). Psychosocial aspects of Holocaust trauma in the life cycle of survivors-refugees and their families. In Baker, N. (Ed.), *The Psychosocial Problems of Refugees.* London: British Refugee Council, pp. 21–31.

6. Davidson, S. (1979). Massive psychic traumatization and social support. *Journal Psychosomatic Research* 23:395–402.

7. Anna Ornstein (1981), using Kohutian concepts has stated, "Only when the ideals of the nuclear self could be relatively well maintained within the camp could the resumption of life with relative vigor and enthusiasm take place after the war was over. The preservation of a relatively intact self made it possible to engage in the lengthy and difficult mourning process that had to occur, and to search out new objects and self objects in the post war environment." Ornstein, A. (1981). The aging survivor of the Holocaust. The effects of the Holocaust on life-cycle experiences; The creation and recreation of families. *Journal General Psychiatry* 14 (2): 135–54.

8. Moskovits, S. (1982). *Love Despite Hate: Child Survivors of the Holocaust and Their Adult Lives.* New York: Schocken.

9. Langer, L. L. (1977). The human use of language. *Chronicle Higher Education,* January 24.

10. Friedlander, S., *ibid.*

Selected Publications of Shamai Davidson
on Holocaust Survivors and Their Families

Davidson, S. (1967). A clinical classification of the psychiatric disturbances of Holocaust ("Shoa") survivors. In Proceedings of the Symposium of the Israel Psychoanalytic Society, Tel Aviv, 1966. *Israel Annals
of Psychiatry and Related Disciplines* 5:96–98.

Davidson, S., Bental, V., Winnick, H. Z. (1967). Psychiatric disturbances
of Holocaust survivors. Symposium of the Israel Psychoanalytic Society. *Israel Annals of Psychiatry and Related Disciplines* 5:91–100.

———. (1973). The treatment of Holocaust survivors. Chapter in S. Davidson, (Ed.), *Spheres of Psychotherapeutic Activity*. Kupat Cholim, pp. 77–
87. (Hebrew)

———. (1979). Long-term psychosocial sequelae in Holocaust survivors
and their families. Chapter in *Israel-Netherlands Symposium on the
Impact of Persecution*, Vol. 1. Rijswijk, The Netherlands: Ministry of
Cultural Affairs, pp. 62–68.

———. (1979). Massive trauma and social support. *Journal of Psychosomatic Research* 23:395–402.

———. (1980). The clinical effects of massive psychic traumatization in
families of Holocaust survivors. *Journal Marital and Family Therapy* 6
(1): 11–21.

———. (1980). Transgenerational transmission in the families of Holocaust survivors. *International Journal of Family Psychiatry* 1:96–113.

225

Davidson, S., Bental, V., Winnick, H. Z. (1980). The survivor syndrome today: An overview. *Group Analysis* (Special Issue): 24–32.

———. (1980). On relating to traumatised persecuted people. Chapter in *Israel-Netherlands Symposium on the Impact of Persecution,* Vol. 2. Rijswijk, The Netherlands: Ministry of Cultural Affairs, pp. 55–63.

———. (1981). Le syndrome des survivants: Revue Generale. [The survivor's syndrome: A general view.] *L'Evolution Psychiatrique* 46 (2): 319–31. (French)

———. (1981). Clinical and psychotherapeutic experience with Holocaust survivors and their families. *The Family Physician* 10 (2): 313–20.

———. (1981). Psychosocial issues in the lives of survivors. *Journal of the '45 Aid Society:* 29–33.

———. (1983). Psychosocial aspects of Holocaust trauma in the life cycle of survivors: Refugees and their families. Chapter in Ron Baker (Ed.), *The Psychosocial Problems of Refugees.* London: British Refugee Council, pp. 21–31.

Charny, I. W., & Davidson, S. (1983), (Eds.). *The Book of the International Conference on the Holocaust and Genocide.* Book 1, *The Conference Program and Crisis.* Tel Aviv: Institute of the International Conference on the Holocaust and Genocide.

———. (1984). Human reciprocity among the Jewish prisoners. Chapter in *The Nazi Concentration Camps.* Proceedings of the Fourth Yad Vashem International Historical Conference, Jerusalem: Yad Vashem Publications, pp. 555–72.

———. (1985). Group formation and its significance in the Nazi concentration camps. *Israel Annals of Psychiatry and Related Sciences* 22 (1–2): 41–50.

———. (1985). *Bereavement in Israel from War, Holocaust, and Terror.* Richmond, Surrey, England: Cruse Academic Papers, No. 3. (Pamphlet, 42 pp.). Cruse is the National Organization for the Widowed and Their Children, Cruse House, 126 Sheen Road, Richmond, Surrey TW9 1VR.

———. (1987). Trauma in the life cycle of the individual and the collective consciousness in relation to war and persecution. In Dasberg, H., Davidson, S., Durlacher, G. L., Filet, B. C., & de Wind, E. (Eds.), *Society and Trauma of War.* Assen: Maastricht, The Netherlands, and Wolfeboro, N.H.: Van Gorcum, pp. 14–32.

———. (1989). Avoidance and denial in the life cycle of Holocaust survivors. In Edelstein, E. L., Nathanson, D. L., and Stone, A. M. *Denial: A Clarification of Concepts and Research.* New York & London: Plenum, pp. 309–20.

A Biographical Note

Shamai Davidson was born on August 13, 1926, in Dublin, as the eldest son of Aaron Davidson and Bunie Cohen (the daughter of Philip and Golda Cohen). His father, born in Slonim (once in Poland and today in White Russia) was educated in Lodz and emigrated to Ireland in 1923. He met Bunie in Glasgow and married her. Bunie's family had come from Lithuania to Scotland, where she was born. After Shamai was born the couple had three more sons, Terry, Julian, and Kenneth. When Shamai was eight years old, the family went from Dublin to Glasgow, where his father became a successful businessman and wool manufacturer.

Shamai grew up in a traditional Jewish atmosphere. He studied in Dublin and Glasgow in Jewish schools and was interested from an early age in Judaism and Zionism. When the Nazis seized power in Germany and started with their anti-Semitic policy and propaganda, young Shamai was troubled by the bad news, and he felt even at an early age a deep concern and involvement.

When Shamai was eleven there appeared in his grandparents' home an alarming book: *The Yellow Spot*. This book contained a detailed account of the persecution, humiliation, torture, and murder of the Jews in Germany. Young Davidson saw the photographs, and the anti-Jewish caricatures of the Nazi *Der Stuermer*, and was shocked. Shamai's father, Aaron, was the only one from his family who had left Poland. He maintained contact by letters with his two sisters, their husbands, and their eight children. Shamai mentions in his written notes that he met and played with some of his relatives when they visited his family in Dublin when he was six or seven years old. In January 1939, Shamai's father traveled to the family in Poland and tried persuading them to leave, but he was unsuccessful.

Finally, when the war broke out, the worry and concern for the family in Poland became more and more oppressing. Shamai's father attempted

227

to trace the whereabouts of his family. The last information was a post-card written from the Lodz Ghetto stamped by the Gestapo censorship. This card said that all was well with the family. Nobody could believe this information. Young Shamai knew that his father was trying continuously to get more information, and that he was preoccupied with thoughts about his lost family and suffered a great deal from insomnia and anxiety.

After the war was over, the Davidson family learned that both Aaron's sisters and their eight children had perished in the ghettos of Warsaw and Lodz and the gas chambers of Treblinka. Shamai's father's suffering at the loss of his family was a heavy burden on Shamai during his early teenage years. The persecution of the Jews by the Nazis and their extermination became an integral part of his consciousness and his Jewish identity. These feelings later became a part of his strong Zionist affinity. He felt that after the Holocaust there was only one place where Jews could and should live. In a 1976 interview he said, "I made *aliyah* because I wanted my children to have a complete Jewish identity, and not a semblance of such as is found in the Jewish way of life in the Western world." In addition, he said, "I saw in Israel a large-scale rehabilitation project of the Jewish people who had undergone vast and massive traumatization, and I felt a need to contribute my own modest share in this rehabilitative process." Shamai's father had visited Israel, bought land there, and hoped to settle there someday, but he could not realize this wish. Shamai decided to fulfill his father's dream and prepared himself for his mission.

At the age of eighteen, Shamai went to study medicine in the medical school of the Glasgow University, from which he graduated in 1950. During his work as a young intern at St. Giles Hospital in London, he met Jenny Silvester, who was a nurse at the same hospital. They fell immediately in love and thus began a wonderful life-long friendship and marriage. Jenny, a non-Jewish young woman, whose maternal grandmother was Kathleen Steel, is from a very old Welsh family, the Bennett Hesketh-Williams family, whose ancestral home is in Bodelwyddan, North Wales. On her father's side, Jenny is descended from the Huguenots. The meeting between Shamai, the young Zionist with his strong Jewish traditional and religious roots, and the gentile open-minded woman was a surprise for Shamai's family. Jenny remembers how dismayed and surprised Shamai was when, at their first meetings, she revealed ignorance regarding the Holocaust of the Jews during World War II. He could not understand how this could not be on the minds of everyone. Shamai and Jenny married, and soon after their two eldest sons, David and Jonathan, were born. Shamai and his wife Jenny, who converted to Judaism, led an open, liberal, nonreligious Jewish home. Shamai had strong Jewish roots but no religious sentiments, though two of his three brothers led an orthodox Jewish way of life. In Shamai's eyes the *aliyah*, which meant living and raising his family in Israel, was much more meaningful than observing the old religious Jewish laws. He felt that staying in the Diaspora was a kind of hypocrisy and bad for Jewish children who, in his opinion, often grew up with a kind of Jewish inferiority complex that they would never have when living in Israel.

Davidson decided to specialize in psychiatry and began his residency training in Warley Psychiatric Hospital in Essex. He continued and finished his psychiatric residency training in the Warneford Psychiatric Hospital of the Oxford University Medical School (1952–1955). The choice of psychiatry and psychotherapy as his specialization seemed a natural choice. Jenny says that Shamai inherited from his mother her love for and interest in people and her warm concern for them. "She was a natural psychotherapist."

In the year 1955, Shamai visited Israel for the first time and secured a position as a psychiatrist at the Talbieh Psychiatric Hospital in Jerusalem.

In the same year Shamai graduated as a psychiatrist and received his diploma in psychological medicine (D.P.M.) from the Royal College of Physicians in London.

In December 1955 Shamai and Jenny, together with their two little sons, emigrated to Israel and settled in Jerusalem. A short while afterwards, their third child, a daughter named Michal, was born.

Shamai knew some Hebrew from his studies in Jewish schools in Dublin and Glasgow. He studied Hebrew intensively for two years and thus mastered the Hebrew language. His adjustment to life in Israel was quick and easy. He identified immediately with the new Jewish state and did not suffer from the absorption difficulties that many other new immigrants to Israel suffered. He loved the country and its people and never regretted his decision to live in Israel.

Dr. Davidson, the new young Israeli psychiatrist, could not understand the silence and the seeming indifference of his Israeli colleagues regarding the fate of many Holocaust survivors who came for treatment. There was a veil of denial around the tragic years 1939–1945. Patients were not asked much about what had happened to them in the Holocaust, and they were not at all eager to tell. The covert message was that all this tragedy should be forgotten. For Israelis it was somehow shameful to remember that Jews were "slaughtered like sheep," without resistance. There was also some kind of covered-over unconscious guilt feeling that while the Jewish people in Europe were annihilated, life within the Jewish community in Israel (then Palestine) had gone on as usual and not too much was done to try to change the terrible fate of the victims in Europe.

Davidson was a pioneer who was one of the first in Israel who lifted the veil of silence. He became obsessed by the subject. He fought against the silence and the denial through investigating, studying, and speaking repeatedly about the Holocaust and its effects on the survivors. Jenny remembers that even when they went for a much-needed vacation, if Sam met someone who was a Holocaust survivor, a conversation and thorough investigation would evolve that could last for hours and put an immediate end to all the vacation plans.

During his first five years as a new *oleh* (immigrant), he worked as a psychiatrist under the tutelage of Professor Winnik, who was a psychoanalyst, and started to teach psychiatry at the Hebrew University Medical School in Jerusalem.

In 1960 Shamai began his studies at the Israel Institute of Psychoanalysis. He was analyzed by two Israeli psychoanalysts, the first in Jerusalem and the second in Haifa. He graduated as an associate member of the Israeli Psychoanalytic Society in 1969.

In 1961, after five years in the Talbieh Hospital, during which he worked as a head of a psychiatric department, Dr. Davidson, now a successful 35–year-old psychiatrist, decided that it was time for him to become independent. He was appointed to head a new psychiatric outpatient clinic at the Linn Clinic of Kupat Holim in Haifa. Now with four children (the youngest son, Ehud, was born in 1959), the Davidson family left Jerusalem and settled down in Haifa, where they lived for twelve years. The psychiatric outpatient clinic that Davidson founded and directed grew and prospered under his guidance.

In 1967, Dr. Davidson went to an advanced study at the Tavistock Clinic in London, where he took training in group and short-term psychotherapy, and in 1968 he was appointed as a senior clinical lecturer in the Haifa University School of Social Work, where he taught psychiatry and psychotherapy.

In 1973, Shamai published in Hebrew a booklet that was a team project of his clinic, entitled *Spheres of Psychotherapeutic Activity*. One of his own articles in the booklet was about "The Treatment of Holocaust Survivors." This was his third publication on this subject. He had published his first article about Holocaust survivors, "A Clinical Classification of Psychiatric Disturbances of Holocaust Survivors," in 1967 in the *Proceedings of the Symposium of the Israeli Psychoanalytic Society*, published in the *Israel Annals of Psychiatry and Related Disciplines*. In the same year he published, together with his analyst, V. Bental, and his teacher, H. Z. Winnick, an article called "Psychiatric Disturbances of Holocaust Survivors" in the *Israel Annals of Psychiatry*.

Some twelve years after they had left Jerusalem for Haifa, in 1973, Davidson was appointed the medical director of Shalvata Psychiatric Hospital in Hod Hasharon, which is affiliated with the Sackler School of Medicine of Tel-Aviv University. In this position he succeeded Prof. Ruth Jaffe, who had retired. Once again the Davidsons packed their belongings to move from Haifa to Hod Hasharon in the center of Israel.

Immediately after they settled down, the Yom Kippur War broke out. The Davidsons' two eldest sons, David and Jonathan, participated in this war. This was a very difficult time for all Israelis. The Davidsons did not hear from their two fighting sons for quite a while, and of course were worried.

The new assignment as medical director of Shalvata Psychiatric Hospital, an open, comprehensive psychiatric hospital in the Sharon plain comprising towns, kibbutzim, and Jewish and Arab villages, was not easy. Together with the inpatient services, there were day-patient, outpatient, and community facilities for all age groups where much psychotherapeutic group and family work was done. Shalvata was also a teaching center with a wide range of postgraduate training activities in the various mental health specialties.

Davidson was full of energy, ambition, and ideas, which he was eager to implement at this very prestigious, highly psychoanalytic, and academic mental health center with an excellent psychoanalytic and academic senior staff. However, many of the staff were devoted to the former director, and only gradually did Shamai Davidson succeed in implementing the changes he planned and become accepted as a creative director. He was a persistent fighter, and in spite of some opposition and criticism of his way of leading and directing, he succeeded in developing, advancing, and expanding Shalvata to a modern mental health center. He learned to appreciate and enhance the special familial atmosphere of the staff, with their warm and human care and devotion for the patients and the friendly collegial relationships among the staff.

Davidson claimed that psychiatry itself was often too restricted and encapsulated within the confines of the psychiatric hospital. He believed psychiatry needed to expand and penetrate all branches of medicine and community services. He strove for psychiatry to become an integral part of the work of physicians at a general hospital, and for more emphasis on the mental components of physical disorders and illnesses. He was aware of the danger involved in developing an overly technological, scientific, and research-oriented medicine that could lead to the abandonment of the traditional holistic model of the doctor-patient relationship and to the dehumanization of medicine.

Along with initiating and developing the community psychiatric services, Davidson devoted a great part of his time and energy to the Holocaust and its traumatic effect on survivors and their families. The subject was always of special interest to him. In one of his interviews he said, "I feel a personal responsibility to work in this field. Unfortunately, it is a problem that has been neglected far too long." He was also especially interested in the mental effects of the Holocaust on children of Holocaust survivors, the "Second Generation." This book is a tribute to his work and thoughts about these problems.

In 1979, he was appointed an associate professor at the Bar-Ilan University School of Social Work. He also held the Elie Wiesel Chair for the Study of the Psychosocial Trauma of the Holocaust at the Institute for Holocaust Studies at Bar-Ilan University. He was on the editorial board of the *Israel Annals of Psychiatry*, and a co-director of the Institute of the International Conference on Holocaust and Genocide in Jerusalem, which he had helped found along with Elie Wiesel and Israel Charny. In 1976, he was a visiting scholar at the Department of Psychiatry and Behavioral Sciences at the Stanford University School of Medicine.

In 1983, he was a visiting scholar at the Oxford Center for Hebrew Studies at Yarnton Manor, where he was able to continue his work on Holocaust survivors. He spent a very fruitful year together with his wife, Jenny, in the beautiful and peaceful atmosphere of the Center.

In the same year (1983), Davidson was appointed as an associate clinical professor in the Sackler School of Medicine of Tel-Aviv University, where he was actively involved until his death. It is worth mentioning that all four children of Shamai and Jenny Davidson have chosen to study and work in various helping professions as their careers. This would undoubtedly have pleased their father very much.

In addition to all of Davidson's activities as a psychiatrist, as director of Shalvata Mental Health Center, and as a researcher, he continued to dedicate much of his time and interest to his psychoanalytic and psychotherapeutic work. He was a gifted, kind, warm, and dedicated therapist, much loved and respected by his many patients, who were mostly Holocaust survivors, their descendants, or victims of other psychological distress.

On Tuesday morning, March 18, 1986, Professor Davidson succumbed to complications following routine bypass surgery. He was fifty-nine years old at the time of his death. His sudden, unexpected, and so untimely death was a terrible shock to all of us who knew him.

Israeli psychiatry lost a leading member. Shalvata Mental Health Center lost the man who had been its director for more than thirteen years, and his patients lost a devoted, warm-hearted, humane, and sensitive therapist.

PROF. MICHA NEUMANN, M.D.
Medical Director, Shalvata Mental Health Center

Name Index

Abramovich, I., 223
Aleksandrowicz, D. R., 117, 218, 223
Amir, Y., 174, 221
Anthony, E. J., 218, 221, 223
Appelfeld, Aharon, 143

Baker, N., 224
Baker, Ron, 223, 226
Barocas, C., 217
Barocas, H., 217
Becker, T., 218
Bell, N. W., 218
Benner, P., 219
Bennett Hesketh-Williams family, 228
Bental, V., 225, 230
Bettelheim, Bruno, 219
Birenbaum, Halina, 138, 139, 220
Black, Dora Freeman, 221, 222
Bostock, T., 219
Bowlby, John, 68
Bravo, A., 220
Bresnitz, S., 216, 220
Brodie, K. H., 216
Brull, Franz, 35, 121, 122, 216, 218, 223

Carmi, T., 7, 215
Charny, Israel W., 79, 217, 226, 232; Editor's Preface, xi–xii; Editor's Introduction, xix–xxvii
Chiland, C., 221

Chodoff, P., 216
Cohen, Bunie, 227
Cohen, Golda, 222
Cohen, H. L., 222
Cohen, Philip, 229
Corneilson, A. R., 217

Dann, Sophie, 68, 217
Dasberg, H., 226
Davidson, Aaron, 227
Davidson, David, 228
Davidson, Ehud, 230
Davidson, Jenny (Mrs. Shamai; née Silvester), xi–xii, 228
Davidson, Jonathan, 228
Davidson, Julian, 227
Davidson, Kenneth, 227
Davidson, Michal, 229
Davidson, Shamai, xv, 1, 215, 223, 224, 233; Acknowledgments, xiii; Editor's Preface, xi–xii; Foreword by Robert Jay Lifton, xv–xviii; Editor's Introduction, xix–xxvii; Self-analysis, 1–5; Selected publications of, 225–26; Biography by Micha Neumann, 227–32
Davidson, Terry, 227
Day, J., 217
De Graff, T., 117, 218
Des Pres, Terrence, 34–35, 124, 125, 126, 128, 216, 219

234 *Name Index*

de Wind, E., 226
Dimsdale, J. E., 218, 219
Dobroszycki, L., 216
Dohrenwend, B., 222
Durlacher, G. L., 226
Dworzecki, Meir, 125, 219

Edelstein, E. L., 226
Eitinger, Leo, 10, 124, 215, 216, 218, 219, 220
Eliach, Y., 220
Elizur, E., 221, 222
Ellin, B., 217, 218
Epstein, N. B., 217
Erikson, Kai T., 129, 219

Father Daniel, 62
Filet, B. C., 226
Fleck, S., 217
Florian, V., 172, 221
Frank, Anne, 65, 126, 219
Frank, Margot, 126
Frankl, V. E., 219
Freud, Anna, 68, 217
Freud, Sigmund, 40–41
Friedlander, Saul, 223, 224
Friedman, Paul, 122

Gay, M., 178, 221, 222
Glazar, Richard, 126
Green, Gerald, 214
Gutman, Y., 220

Hamburg, D. A., 216
Hart, Kitty, 125, 219
Heimler, Eugene, 126, 219
Henderson, S., 219
Hirsch, J., 217
Hitler, Adolf, 69, 73
Hoz-Peles, Ada, 222

Jaffe, Ruth, 135, 220, 230
Jensen, B., 218

Kaffman, M., 221, 222
Karr, S. D., 117, 218
Kestenberg, J., 217
Kierkegaard, S., 9

Klein, Hillel, 35, 124, 157, 216, 218, 219, 220, 222
Kohut, H., 224
Koupernik, C., 218, 223
Krasnoff, L., 222
Krystal, Henry, 10, 129, 215, 216, 218, 219, 224

Lahav, E., 221
Laing, R. D., 55
Langer, Lawrence L., 201, 224
Lazarus, R. S., 219
Levav, I., 177, 222
Lidz, T., 217
Lifton, Robert Jay, 10, 34, 55, 215, 216, 217, 218; Foreword, xv–xviii
Lowenstein, S. F., 223
Luchterhand, Elmer, 126, 131, 216, 219, 220
Lustigman, M., 220

Malkinson, R., 174, 221
Maoz, B., 178, 221, 222
Masaryk, T., 12
Mengele, J., 70, 133
Milgram, N. A., 221
Miller, Louis, 219, 220
Morawetz, A., 177, 222
Moses, K., 221
Moses, R., 221, 223
Moskovits, S., 224

Nachman of Bratslav, Rabbi, 205
Nathanson, D. L., 226
Neumann, Micha, (biography of Shamai Davidson), 227–32
Niederland, William G., 216, 217, 218, 219, 224

Ornstein, Anna, 224

Palgi, Phyllis, xv, 173, 220, 221, 222, 223
Parkes, C. Murray, 222
Pfefferkorn, Eli, 127, 219
Purisman, R., 178, 221, 222

Rakoff, V., 217, 218
Rapaport, Chanan, 233

Subject Index

Aberfan disaster in Wales in 1966, 40
Achievement and activity, need for, xxiii, 13, 33, 43, 80–84, 157, 190
Acting out, 71–75; *See also* "Living out" parents' Holocaust
Adolescent survivor, 50, 70–75, 136–41
Aging, 21–23, 33, 47, 192–93, 200
Aggression: blocking and release of, 32, 41, 44, 150, 166; fear of, to survivors, xix–xxvii; to Nazis, 5; rages of survivors, 69, 158, 166
Aliyat Hanoar, 167
Ambiguity, 82
Anorexia, 99–100
Anxiety, 32, 108–9
Armenian Genocide, 34
Atomic explosions in Japan, 34
Auschwitz, 11, 12, 29, 125, 127, 133, 135, 138, 166, 198
Avoidance and denial. *See* Denial
Awareness groups. *See* Peer support groups

Banalization, 214
Bar-Ilan University, 51, 136, 147, 231
Basic trust. *See* Trust and hope
Bearing witness. *See* Telling the story of the Holocaust
Bereaved family, 172–79; children, 175–76; parents, 177–80; siblings, 176–77; wives, 173–75

Bereavement. *See* Mourning and the survivor
Bereavement counselors, 171–79
Bereavement Library, 182, 223
Bergen-Belsen, 12, 36, 126, 198
Bialystock Ghetto, 70
Birkenau-Auschwitz. *See* Auschwitz
Blaming the victims, 4, 15, 38, 76, 204, 209
Blocking of aggression. *See* Aggression
Borderline conditions in children of survivors, 101–2
Buchenwald, 125, 126, 134
Buffalo Creek flood, 129, 219

Canada, 89, 117, 119
Carpatho-Russia, 198
Catholic countries, 61
Central Europe, 126, 157, 192
Children of survivors, 77, 78, 95–104, 156–59; anxiety, 98, 108–9; borderline and psychotic states, 101–2; family therapy, 102–4; feeling special, 112–13; healthy children, 115–18; "living out" parents' Holocaust, 104–6; perceptions of parents, 109–11; sensitivity to wounded parent, 113–14; separation-individuation, separation anxiety, 68, 93, 98, 111–12
Child survivors, 67–70, 145, 192–93

237

Should survivors tell children? *See* Telling the story of the Holocaust
Shtetl life, 70, 155, 209, 212
Significance of the Holocaust, 58. *See* Meanings of the Holocaust
Silence and suppression of memories, 24, 106–11, 149, 152–53, 164, 187, 211–14. *See also* Telling the story of the Holocaust
Six Day War, 76, 169
Slavery, 34
Slovakia, 64
Staying human. *See* Humanity and human nature
Stop Them Now, 2
Strengths of survivors, xxi–xxvii, 35, 44–45, 50–54, 77, 141, 158, 164, 189–95
Stuermer, Der, 2, 227
Success, need for, 13, 45, 80–84, 190
Suicide, 56, 77, 178
Survival, xxi, 55–87, 121, 124, 134, 142, 143–59, 189–206, 207–14; Ten Commandments of, 134–35
Survivor guilt, 3–4, 32, 36, 51, 185; as working through, 186–87
Survivors: ambivalence toward, 148–49, 155, 207–9; as a guilty one who survived, 207; pre-Holocaust personality, 58–59; projection of bad objects, 73, 101, 210; shame of survivors, 19, 107; survivor versus society, 202–6, 207–14; suspiciousness in survivors, 81–82; symptom-free survivors (*See* vulnerability, latent, emotional)
Survivor syndrome. *See* Concentration camp survivor syndrome

Teaching mental health students about trauma, 29–33
Tel-Aviv University, 223
Telling the story of the Holocaust, xxi, 15, 20, 24, 51, 88, 94, 105–11, 113, 116, 149, 151–53, 187–88, 211–14
Therapists and therapy: avoidance and denial, 16–17, 24, 119, 192, 229; challenge and privilege, 196; confronting trauma, 16–17, 24–27; de-

fenses against involvement, 24–26; projections onto, 25–26; rediscovery of meaning of life, 185–88
Theresienstadt concentration camp, 68
Transgenerational influence, transmission of psychopathology, 88–120, 144
Trauma, 26–27, 177, 189–92; teaching mental health students, 29–33. *See also* Massive psychic trauma
Treblinka, 2, 35, 126, 228
Triumph of survivors, xxiv, 55, 80, 142, 155. *See also* Strengths of survivors
Trust and hope, xxii, 25, 33, 37, 43, 129, 135–36, 189, 196

Ukraine, 64, 65, 66
Uniqueness of each survivor, 58, 196
United States, 76, 87, 89, 105, 114, 118, 119, 120, 122, 143–59, esp. 156–59
UNRRA, 74

Victims, need to continue to be, 154
Vietnamese boat people, 49
Vietnam War, xviii, 40
Vilna Ghetto, 70
Vulnerability, latent, emotional (of survivors), xxvi, 44–45, 48–50, 77, 147, 194–95; breakdown of denial, 194–95. *See also* Israel, defenses against empathy and vulnerability; Psychiatric damage

Wandervogel movement in Germany, 70
War of Attrition, 170
Warsaw Ghetto, 2–3, 10, 36, 60, 64, 70, 138, 228
Western Europe, 65
Will to live. *See* Decision to live
Working through, xxv–xxvii, 23–25, 150, 184–88, 189–206, 211–14
World assembly of survivors, 152

Yad Vashem, 20, 205, 219, 220, 226
Yanowska camp, 64

About the Editor

Israel W. Charny is Executive Director, Institute on the Holocaust and Genocide, Jerusalem; and Associate Professor of Psychology, Bob Shapell School of Social Work, Tel Aviv University. He is the author of *Marital Love and Hate* (New York, 1972), and *Existential/ Dialectical Marital Therapy: Breaking the Secret Code of Marriage* (New York, 1992); and, in collaboration with Chanan Rapaport, of *How Can We Commit the Unthinkable? Genocide, the Human Cancer* (Boulder, Colo., 1982). He is also the editor (with Shamai Davidson) of *The Book of the International Conference on the Holocaust and Genocide: Book One: The Conference Program and Crisis* (Tel Aviv, 1983); *Toward the Understanding and Prevention of Genocide* [*Selected Presentations at the International Conference on the Holocaust and Genocide*] (Boulder, Colo., 1984); *Genocide: A Critical Bibliographic Review*, vol. 1 and 2 (London, 1988 and 1991).

300   Gen 5/16 KK